LAW AND RELIGION

Issues in Law and Society

General Editor: Michael Freeman

Titles in the Series:

Law and Religion

Edited by
REX J. AHDAR
University of Otago

Ashgate

DARTMOUTH

Aldershot • Burlington USA • Singapore • Sydney

Published by
Ashgate Publishing Limited
Gower House
Croft Road
Aldershot
Hants GU11 3HR
England

Ashgate Publishing Company
131 Main Street
Burlington
Vermont 05401
USA

Ashgate website: http://www.ashgate.com

British Library Cataloguing in Publication Data
Law and religion. – (Issues in law and society)
  1. Religion and law
  I. Ahdar, Rex J.
  340.1'1

Library of Congress Cataloging-in-Publication Data
Law and religion / edited by Rex J. Ahdar.
     p. cm. — (Issues in law and society)
  Includes index.
  ISBN 1–84014–745–8 (hb) — ISBN 1-84014-757-1 (pb)
  1. Freedom of religion. 2. Church and state. 3. Religion and law. I. Ahdar, Rex J. II. Series.
K3258 .L38 2000
342'.0852—dc21

                                            00–040613

ISBN 1 84014 745 8 (HBK)
ISBN 1 84014 757 1 (PBK)

Typeset by Manton Typesetters, Louth, Lincolnshire, UK.

Printed and bound by Athenaeum Press, Ltd.,
Gateshead, Tyne & Wear.

Contents

Foreword

The Rt Hon Lord Mackay of Clashfern

This collection of essays under the title 'Law and Religion' contains fascinating insights into one of the most fundamental issues facing our world today. In the heady days of the Enlightenment many thought that religion was doomed gradually to disappear under the searching analysis of human reason. The world view of the Enlightenment, if it had a world view, saw human reason take over from the Divine and in consequence worship of the Divine would gradually disappear as the progress of reason continued.

But this has not happened and I would suggest that there is at least as much interest in religion throughout the world today as there was before the Enlightenment movement came on the scene. However the number of distinct religious views and practices has also grown. The fervency with which adherents of religions embrace and practice their views is, I believe, as high as it ever was. Most who fervently embrace a religion have from that religion not merely a series of private practices of worship but also a world view and attitudes which affect their daily lives far beyond attendance at church or mosque or other religious meeting place.

This also has an effect on the attitude of people to the secular law both civil and criminal. For example, those who believe in a final judgement before a judge with perfect information about the whole of the subject's life are less concerned than others may be about whether or not their wrongdoing is detected by the local police force since the power of conscience looking forward to that final accounting is probably greater than the fear of any merely human retribution might be.

The relevance of these considerations to any system of law is clear. If a legal system allows freedom of religion, how far does that go? and to what extent may actions that appear strange to the majority of people in the state be allowed on the basis that they are performed in satisfaction of a religious obligation? To what extent do appeals to religion arise from a damaged mind? To what extent should the state favour or support any particular religion or religious group?

These are illustrations of lively questions which arise at present in many different legal systems and this collection of essays by distinguished writers, each well qualified, to discuss the issues in his or her essay provide to my mind a challenge to anyone with an intelligent interest in the subject of law and religion but particularly to practitioners in the law and to those responsible for framing legislation.

The range of scholarship called into service in dealing with these questions in this collection is very impressive and therefore the scope of the work as a whole is large. Anyone, and particularly those practically involved in the ways I have mentioned, will find much in these essays to stimulate their own thinking. I believe they will not find in these essays a conclusive answer to the main questions that face us today in the field of law and religion.

For example, the fundamental question which arises in connection with provisions for freedom of religion or for taxation benefits for societies for the advancement of religion are not provided with a clear cut answer to the question 'what is a religion?' but after reading these essays I believe that such people are better qualified to understand the difficulties and hopefully better able to develop practical solutions to the problems that arise from the absence of a clear and universal definition of what is a religion. As is pointed out, when one is considering a question of this kind it is very difficult not to be influenced by one's own understanding and experience of religion and therefore the more one can glean from the experience of others and the analysis of that experience by expert writers, such as we have here, the more effective will the reader's contribution be to resolution of the problems in this area with which he or she is confronted.

In the United Kingdom we have been familiar with questions of the scope of religious freedom and of what is a religion in relation to actions for libel, in relation to taxation, in relation to exemption from military service and within churches when a division has taken place on the destination of property which was previously held for the united church. The incorporation into our domestic law of the principal provisions of the European Convention on Human Rights will certainly widen the areas in which questions relating to religion and law can arise. Indeed there has already been some discussion of the effect in relation to the spiritual jurisdiction of church courts and an attempt is being made in the incorporating statute to deal with this matter. I foresee problems arising in relation to freedom of religion on a wider scale than hitherto in our domestic courts and indeed the possibility of difficult arguments arising from the provision for freedom of religion in relation to other relationships such as marriage and divorce. For readers in the United Kingdom therefore this collection of essays will, I believe, be a valuable source book of discussion of applications of the topic of law and religion to areas of our secular law on which such discussion has not previously impinged. Reading these essays will certainly make the reader better informed and I think the standard of the analysis in the essays is such as to make the reader also wiser in connection with these topics than he would have been without that privilege.

Notes on Contributors

Rex J. Ahdar LL.B. (Hons); LL.M. (Canterbury); Ph.D. (Otago) is Senior Lecturer in the Faculty of Law, University of Otago. He is also Editor of *Competition Law and Policy in New Zealand* (1991) and his recent publications include the co-edited collection, *God and Government: The New Zealand Experience* (2000). His research interests include religious freedom, family law and antitrust law.

Calum Carmichael B.Sc.; LL.D (Glasgow); BD (Edinburgh); B.Litt (Oxford) is Professor of Comparative Literature and Adjunct Professor of Law, at Cornell University. He is a former Guggenheim Fellow and Senior Fellow of the National Endowment for the Humanities. His recent books include *Law, Legend, and Incest in the Bible* (1997); *The Origins of Biblical Law* (1992) and *The Spirit of Biblical Law* (1996). His main research interests are Biblical law, early Jewish law and the New Testament, and law and literature in Antiquity.

Davina Cooper LL.B. (University College, London); Ph. D. (Warwick) is Professor of Law and Dean of Research in the Social Science Faculty at Keele University. Her publications include: *Sexing the City: Lesbian and Gay Politics within the Activist State* (1994); *Power in Struggle: Feminism, Sexuality and the State* (1995); and *Governing out of Order: Space, Law and the Politics of Belonging* (1998). She was a member of the London Borough of Haringey (1986–90). Her primary research areas are normative political theory, feminism, governance, sociolegal studies, cultural geography and sexuality.

Malcolm D. Evans BA; MA; D.Phil. (Oxford) is Professor of Public International Law at the University of Bristol. His principal publications include: *Relevant Circumstances and Maritime Delimitation* (1989); *Religious Liberty and International Law in Europe* (1997); with Professor Rod Morgan, *Preventing Torture* (1998) and *Protecting Prisoners* (1999). His research interests embrace international human rights (especially religious liberty and torture prevention) and the international law of the sea.

Marie A. Failinger JD (Valparaiso); LL.M. (Yale) is Professor of Law, School of Law at Hamline University. She is an Editor of the *Journal of Law and Religion* and a member of the National Equal Justice Library Board. She has published widely in American law reviews and anthologies. Her research interests are in constitutional law, professional ethics, gender, minorities and children.

Michael W. McConnell BA (Michigan State); JD (Chicago) is Presidential Professor at the University of Utah College of Law. He has published widely in law reviews such as the *Harvard Law Review*, the *University of Chicago Law Review* and the *Supreme Court Review*, and is the co-author of an upcoming casebook, *Religion and the Constitution*. His primary research field is constitutional law, particularly religious liberty, constitutional theory and the Fourteenth Amendment.

Reid Mortensen B.Com. (Hons); LL.B. (Hons); Ph. D. (Queensland) is Senior Lecturer in Law at the University of Queensland. He has published extensively on law and religion in Australia and the Commonwealth, and is Australian National Reporter on *le droit religieux* to the International Congress of Comparative Law. His teaching and research interests also extend to the conflict of laws and lawyers' ethics.

James T. Richardson JD (Nevada); Ph. D. (Washington State) is Professor of Sociology and Judicial Studies and Director of the Master of Judicial Studies Programme at the University of Nevada, Reno. He is a former President of the Association for the Sociology of Religion and the current President of the American Association of University Professors. He is the author of around 150 articles and book chapters, plus six books, the latest being, *The Satanism Scare* (1991). His research areas are sociology and psychology of religion, new religions, the social control of minority religions and social science evidence.

Julian Rivers MA; LL.M. (Cambridge); M.Iur (Goettingen) is Lecturer, Faculty of Law at the University of Bristol. His research interests are constitutional law and legal theory.

Sophie C. van Bijsterveld Doct. Law (Utrecht); Doct. Law (Tilburg) is Associate Professor for European and International Law, Faculty of Law at the University of Tilburg. Her recent publications include, *Godsdienstvrijheid* *in Europees Perpectief (Religious Liberty in European Perspective)* (1998). Specific research interests are human rights and the changing role of the state in the development of law.

Dedicated to
Lidwina

1   The Inevitability of Law and Religion: An Introduction

Rex J. Ahdar

In ethics and in law, questions of right and wrong will have some ultimate basis. The curious, if not impertinent, will at some point, when presented with a rule or command, ask 'the grand sez who?', as Arthur Leff put it.[1] At rock bottom, there is someone or something that is 'the unjudged judge, the unruled legislator, the premise maker who rests on no premises, the uncreated creator of values'.[2] Leff continued, 'Now, what would you call such a thing if it existed? You would call it Him.'[3] The ultimate source of law is God or some God analogue. R.J. Rushdoony explains it in these terms:

> Law is in every culture *religious in origin*. Because law governs man and society, because it establishes and declares the meaning of justice and righteousness, law is inescapably religious in that it establishes in practical fashion the ultimate concerns of a culture ... Second, it must be recognized that in any culture *the source of law is the god of that society*. If law has its source in man's reason, then reason is the god of that society. If the source is an oligarchy or in a court, senate, or ruler, then that is the god of that system ... Modern humanism, the religion of the state, locates law in the state and thus makes the state, or the people, as they find expression in the state, the god of that system.[4]

The ultimate source of authority in a legal system (the 'god' of that system) would seem to be either divine and transcendent, on the one hand, or temporal and earthly, on the other. The choice is between God (or Gods) and Man (or mankind). Leff submits, '[p]ut briefly, if the law is "not a brooding omnipresence in the sky", then it can be only one place: in us'.[5] Under that latter view, the answer to the question 'sez who?' is humankind in the form of: each autonomous, rational individual; some outstandingly wise or noble individual or individuals (the king, the highest court); or some abstract collective (the people, the state). Identifying the foundation of the

1

legal system in an abstract principle – the 'rule of recognition' (H.L.A. Hart) or the '*Grundnorm*' (Hans Kelsen), for example – simply begs the question as to *who* promulgated the principle.[6]

Historically, locating the religious root of law was a redundant exercise because law and religion were unified. The secular and the sacred, the legal and the religious, were traditionally coterminous. As Leo Pfeffer recounts:

> The differentiation between the religious and the secular is itself a comparatively modern development in the evolution of human society ... . Every important event in the life of primitive man, from birth to death, was consecrated and solemnized by religious ceremonies.[7]

The unity between law and religion is, of course, present today in many parts of the world – one only has to think of Muslim nations where the *Shari'a* is the divinely ordained guide for law, religion, hygiene and, indeed, all of life.[8]

In contemporary Western thought it is customary to draw a sharp distinction between religion and law, sacred and secular, church and state. The wisdom of such a strategy is not unimpeachable. Lord Denning, for instance, once lamented the severance of religion and law (and morals). The process had 'gone much too far' and, he cautioned, 'without religion, there can be no morality, there can be no law'.[9] Harold Berman, whose writings on the relationship between law and religion are a *sine qua non* to contemporary discourse upon the subject, was adamant that 'the presupposition that law and religion are wholly separate aspects of life – that the way we run our society need have nothing to do with our deepest intuitions and our deepest commitments, and vice-versa'[10] – had led to a crisis in Western society. When our notions of law and religion become too narrow, when the links between these two important dimensions are severed, society becomes 'demoralized'.[11] Law and religion are linked, not fused, by way of a 'dialectical interdependence'.[12] Berman explains:

> In all societies, even the most sophisticated, there are shared beliefs in transcendent values, a shared sense of the holy; and in all societies, even the most rudimentary, there are structures and processes of social ordering, established methods of allocating rights and duties, a shared sense of the just. These two dimensions of social life are in tension: the prophetic and mystical sides of religion challenge, and are challenged by the structural and rational sides of law. Yet each is also a dimension of the other. Every legal system shares with religion certain elements – ritual, tradition, authority, and universality – which are needed to symbolize and educate men's legal emotions. Otherwise law degenerates into legalism. Similarly, every religion has within it legal elements, without which it degenerates into private religiosity.[13]

If religion can provide law with its spirit and *telos* – with the sanctity it needs to function truly effectively – and if law can furnish religion with the structure to express itself, socially and publicly, so much the better. If, as Berman believes, 'law and religion stand or fall together',[14] understanding the interaction between them is hardly an esoteric or unimportant task.

Since religion and law are significant aspects of mankind's social existence a complete compartmentalization of them is hardly practically feasible, even were it desirable in theory (which it is not). Indeed, the worlds of religion and law appear to be increasingly colliding. The reason for this lies in two partly interdependent and conflicting phenomena: the pervasiveness of the modern state (and the reach of the law); and the resurgence of religion at the outset of the new millennium.

For a considerable period historically, religion loomed large in the fabric of society. It played a significant role in family life, education, health, poor relief and other areas of society. The government's role was, by comparison, relatively limited. Over time and driven by the inexorable secularizing logic of the Enlightenment, religion in the West became increasingly 'privatized' – a matter for private concern. Commensurately, its public or social functions came to be taken over by government. If, to quote Berman again, government was once 'the handmaid' of religion, the roles are today reversed.[15] Government is involved in many, perhaps most, areas of citizens' lives and perhaps threatens to swallow up civil society entirely.[16] Short of that, the state is present in, and affects, the activities of religious communities and believers in a fashion not dreamt of a century ago. Can devout parents physically chastize their children? May a church of a certain size and design be erected in a particular locality? Are there restrictions upon whom a Church may ordain as its leaders? These and myriad other concerns are matters on which the state is not indifferent. What religious organizations and adherents do is increasingly an issue of regulatory concern. Religion may seek the solace of the private sphere, but the modern state's writ runs large.

The second phenomenon is at odds with the first, at least to some extent. Modernity and secularization theory foretold the gradual withering of religion, both as a social institution and as a personal comfort. But the closing decades of the twentieth century spoiled the sociologists' predictions. As Peter Berger noted recently in his essay 'Secularism in Retreat':

> The key idea of secularization theory is simple and can be traced to the Enlightenment: Modernization necessarily leads to a decline in religion, both in society and in the minds of individuals. It is precisely this key idea that has turned out to be wrong … . The world today … is massively religious, and it is anything but the secularized world that had been predicted (be it joyfully or despondently) by so many analysts of modernity.[17]

Berger did note two exceptions: Western Europe and the international sub-
culture of persons in the knowledge sector (academics, lawyers, media
people and so on). Even there, however, it may be argued that they follow
less overt surrogate 'religions' (scientistic, humanist) of their own. The very
public resurgence of religion internationally in the last two decades – whether
of the Moral Majority in the United States, Catholic Poles, Iranian Muslims
– has prompted one sociologist to even speak of the 'deprivatization' of
modern religion: namely, 'the process whereby religion abandons its as-
signed place in the private sphere and enters the undifferentiated public
sphere of civil society to take part in the ongoing process of contestation,
discursive legitimation, and redrawing of the boundaries'.[18] The worrying
issue for liberal democrats is that it is the 'reactionary', 'traditionalist'
religions (usually dubbed 'fundamentalist') which are undergoing a revitali-
zation. These religions challenge modernity, and its supposedly invincible
worldview, straining liberalism's renowned tolerance for those who dissent
from its precepts. As enthusiasm for the Enlightenment eschatology of
progress and social, scientific and technological advancement has increasingly waned, man has sought other goals, other 'gods'. Berger puts it well:

> The religious impulse, the quest for meaning that transcends the restricted space
> of empirical existence in this world, has been a perennial feature of humanity.
> (This assertion is not a theological statement but an anthropological one – an
> agnostic or even an atheist philosopher may well agree with it.) It would require
> something close to a mutation of the species to finally extinguish this impulse.[19]

A purely secular social order generates, as Wolfhart Pannenberg argues, 'a
feeling of meaninglessness'. How long the secular state and society has to
run is debatable. Pannenberg drolly prophesies: 'It depends in part on how
long most people will be willing to pay the price of meaningless in exchange for the license to do what they want.'[20] The *anomie* experienced by
postmodern man is a much noted phenomenon.

The resurgence of the major world religions in a conservative, sometimes
militant, form has been, as noted, one response to secularization. Another
has been the flowering of multitudinous new varieties of religion. These
new religious movements (NRMs) – popularly and pejoratively referred to
as 'cults' – capture the public attention and generate sometimes extreme
spasms of antagonism. New Zealand, for example, has attracted attention
for having, on a statistical basis, one of the most densely populated 'cultic
milieux', comprising 'the individualistic, free-floating market of "New Age",
human potential and therapeutic groups'.[21] Groups such as Hare Krishna,
Scientology and the Children of God represent some of the better known
international NRMs, but there are (literally) hundreds of local, small-scale

groups to contend with as well. That last statement may be misleading for many (perhaps most) groups are content to live out their countercultural existence in a peaceful law-abiding fashion. Clearly, however, there are exceptions – Waco's Branch Davidians (1993) and Japan's Aum Supreme Truth (1995) being recent gruesome examples of NRMs producing tragic consequences. As the new millennium opens, a proliferation of, and intensification in, the activities of apocalyptic and other groups seems the surest prophecy of them all. The law will need to call upon all its resources and wisdom to restrain antisocial excesses whilst still preserving religious liberty for these novel and unusual mutations.

The essays in this collection embrace a range of religion and law topics – some philosophical, some practical.

Professor Calum Carmichael has written extensively on biblical law. In his fascinating chapter he analyses the Decalogue, focusing principally on how its promulgator invested it with a divine stamp. The roots of the Decalogue are, argues Carmichael, to be found in the Genesis narratives and the golden calf incident of Exodus 32. The 'first tablet' commandments trace back to Israel's rebellion with the golden idol; the 'second tablet' injunctions hark back to Adam, Eve, Cain and Abel and their 'dysfunctional' family. The central point is that every legal system needs some 'augmentation' of its rules – some supernatural imprimatur to lend authority to its contents. Here, one again finds support from Berman. To work effectively law must rely on more than coercive sanctions (there are simply not enough policemen in the world); it must attract people's trust and commitment.[22] Quite simply, citizens must (in a certain sense) place their faith in it:

> Law itself, in all societies, encourages the belief in its own sanctity. It puts forward its claim to obedience in ways that appeal not only to the material, impersonal, finite, rational interests of the people who are asked to observe it but also to their faith in a truth, a justice, that transcends social utility ... .
>
> Even Joseph Stalin had to reintroduce into Soviet law elements which would make his people believe in its inherent rightness – emotional elements, sacred elements; for otherwise the persuasiveness of Soviet law would have totally vanished, and even Stalin could not rule solely by threat of force.[23]

A divine imprimatur is a 'mask' which can positively contribute to the efficiency of the law. The mythological dimension to law is useful. Investing the law with a supernatural aura is highly expedient and Carmichael (and Weyrauch[24]) suggest that sharing this insight too widely and publicly may not be desirable. The assumption, I suspect, is that there is something deceptive and phoney going on here – the transcendental aura is fake, the divine stamp a fraud. But *if* the Deity really *did* give us His Divine ordinances, exposure is not to be feared. Law would still be based on a myth but, as C.S. Lewis argued, it is a *true* myth.[25] But that is another story.

Professor Malcolm Evans is well qualified to expound upon the protection of religious freedom under international law following the recent publication of his important treatise.[26] Focusing on Article 18 of the International Covenant on Civil and Political Rights 1966 and the work of the Human Rights Committee (whose job it is to oversee its implementation), Evans paints, in Chapter 3, a somewhat sobering and disconcerting picture. Religious persecution is, unfortunately, rife worldwide[27] and thus the *effective* protection of religious liberty is crucial and urgent. In a careful, comprehensive and lucid fashion, Evans analyses the Committee's approach, concentrating on the three key 'pressure points':

1   What counts as a religion for the purposes of protection?
2   What are religious manifestations or actions?
3   When are state restrictions upon religious conduct justified?

The questions are, of course, interdependent, and the interplay between them is critical. For example, a wide interpretation of what is a religion and what is religious practice may be offset by a sympathetic, lenient view of state restriction on the religious conduct. The particular methodology followed by the Committee may not necessarily matter, so long as the approach is coherent, consistent and achieves the 'right' outcome. Obviously, however, (and this is nothing new) there is sufficient malleability in the three steps to produce *any* outcome. From the relatively meagre jurisprudence of the Committee two lessons are learnt. One is that the Committee (unsurprisingly) has struggled as much as national courts have with the perennial conundrums of religious freedom law: that is, 'What is a religion?', 'When is state impingement warranted?' and 'Is religious liberty inherently limited by other rights and freedoms?'. Second, the three pressure points have all been construed fairly narrowly. Cautious and attenuated preservation of religious freedom by the Committee is the verdict. Evans' assessment, and it is not unique,[28] ought to send a wake-up call to the United Nations and to all those who believe that the safeguarding of this fundamental human right merits a brighter future than its beleaguered past.

Coming to grips with the vast American jurisprudence on religion and the First Amendment is no easy task. American scholars on the Religion Clauses concede somewhat sheepishly that the law is chaotic and confused.[29] The next two essays admirably clarify this troubled area. Non-Americans are fortunate that most of the religion and law conflicts that are ever likely to be tested in court have already been so in the United States. The American propensity towards litigation means that the supply of examples is not likely to dry up.

Professor Michael McConnell is one of the United States' foremost legal scholars on the Religion Clauses of the First Amendment. If there were a Cooperstown for Church and state I have no doubt he would be inducted immediately upon becoming eligible.[30] Professor McConnell does not shrink from acknowledging the parlous and tangled state of First Amendment Church–state jurisprudence. The fundamental problem is principally equivocation by successive Supreme Courts on precisely what the primary purpose of the Religion Clauses is. Is the animating object the separation of sacred and secular spheres, neutrality or the protection of religious liberty? What happens when the pursuit of one object conflicts with another?

In Chapter 4 McConnell dissects the voluminous case law by subdividing it into two broad categories: exemptions (or 'accommodations' as Americans quaintly dub them) from the general law of the land for religionists; and government financial assistance to religiously-oriented institutions. The Supreme Court has long wrestled with the question of whether the Free Exercise Clause should allow the first and whether the Establishment Clause can countenance the second. Attempts to maintain an internal consistency between the two Clauses have floundered in the wake of the Court's ambivalence over their very purpose. McConnell, understandably, is impatient with the chaos and incoherence to date. Unlike, for instance, Steven D. Smith whose penetrating, albeit pessimistic book, *Foreordained Failure: The Quest for a Constitutional Principle of Religious Freedom*[31] (the title evidences the thesis), McConnell is more optimistic. Abandoning the quest for a single coherent principle in favour of ad hoc, case-by-case decision-making is rightly rejected. There has been enough 'muddling through' already. Of the alternatives – cutting back the scope of both Clauses or simply cutting back on one but not the other – McConnell favours the latter. Specifically, he advocates retaining the expansive view of the Free Exercise Clause (permitting exemptions for sincere religious conscience) whilst retreating from a strict separationist stance under the Establishment clause. No-aid separation would be replaced with neutrality or evenhandedness when it comes to government largesse. It is a position with which I feel much sympathy but, then, as a non-American, I have never understood how the few simple words constituting the Establishment Clause could be interpreted as a vehicle for thoroughgoing secularization.

In the second of our American Church–state critiques, Professor Marie Failinger, editor of the *Journal of Law and Religion*, provides a penetrating analysis of the First Amendment religion jurisprudence through yet another prism. In Chapter 5 Professor Failinger points out that Supreme Court's treatment of religion can be placed along a spectrum. At each extreme we have prohibitions on direct government discrimination towards, and direct government promotion of, religion. Intermediate positions concentrate on indirect burdens on religion, various forms of religious neutrality (for example, 'formal', 'substantive'), and requirements to accommodate religious difference in governmental or regulatory schemes. Something of a 'doctrinal circle' has been in evidence over the decades: *plus c'est change plus c'est même*. Three concerns are postulated by Failinger as an aid to understanding the complex case law: the problems of power; solicitude for individual freedom; and the contestation of rival ideologies or 'isms'.

The diffusion of power to offset tyranny and corruption is a recurrent American theme. The Founders, especially James Madison, sought to disperse both concentrated governmental and ecclesiastical power. The problem of controlling power in 'an anticultural culture' is acute. In the absence of powerful historical and cultural traditions, power has to be checked by deconcentrating the institutions and by recourse to the law.

Recently, freedom for the individual, the second motif, has also witnessed a transmogrification. From a theological conception of freedom (the freedom to respond to the call of conscience), religious liberty has evolved into a liberal notion (a subspecies of freedom of choice). In the eighteenth century freedom was the freedom to respond to the dictates of conscience, not the right to choose one's religious beliefs. It was a right to exercise a duty, not to make a choice.[32] The modern voluntarist conception (severed from its theological roots) makes it difficult to deny other equally sincere choices. The quandary in defining 'religion' (the product of sincere choice) is one natural consequence. The courts can screen out the most palpably spurious and fraudulent religions – Chief Boo Hoo and his marijuana adherents of the Neo-American Church for instance[33]– but struggle to draw the boundary otherwise.

The problem of ideology is perhaps the key explanatory concept. Is the state under God (the traditionalist, generic Christian view)? Is the state independent of God (the Enlightenment, liberal notion)? Or is the state comfortable with accommodating many gods (a postmodernist, pluralist approach)? Perhaps Steven Smith is correct after all. It would only be possible to agree on a single theory of religious freedom if our foundational beliefs about the 'big' questions –the nature of man, the existence or otherwise of God, the proper role of government and so on – were themselves settled. However:

> The problem, simply put, is that theories of religious freedom seek to reconcile or to mediate among competing religious and secular positions within a society, but those competing positions disagree about the very background beliefs on which a theory of religious freedom must rest.[34]

A theory that is totally 'fair' to everyone of any worldview remains a mirage. Stanley Fish may be right when he characterizes the task of settling the 'just' bounds between Church and state as a 'mission impossible'.[35] That is not, however, as Michael McConnell urges, to resign ourselves to 'muddling along' but to face up to the issue.

Professor James Richardson is eminently equipped to write on so-called 'cults'. Aside from his numerous writings he was recently commended for his testimony in a seminal (but, most unfortunately, unreported) English case concerning 'The Family', *Re ST (A Minor)*.[36] In Chapter 6 Richardson makes a persuasive plea for a cautious and stringent approach to the admissibility of evidence in cases involving unpopular minority religions and NRMs. He analyses the dangers to a fair trial when dubious evidence is allowed in by the exercise of judicial discretion. The defendants' membership of, and participation in, unpopular, countercultural religious sects has commonly played, he argues, a not insignificant role in the decision to countenance 'problematic' and ultimately damning testimony against them. Two notorious Australian decisions – the Hilton bombing and the Ayers Rock dingo homicides – are his illustrations, along with the Satanic ritual abuse scare in Christchurch, New Zealand. There are no doubt more examples. The degree to which a judge is immune from the prejudices and misinformation which permeate a society generally is a moot point. Ward LJ in *Re ST (A Minor)* disavowed that any discharge of his duty would be constrained by 'subjective considerations of personal preference' and quoted Sir Edward Coke that to exercise discretion was 'To discerne by the right line of law, and not by the crooked cord of private opinion'.[37] A more modest charge may be that the 'rules of the [evidential] game' are slanted even if 'the referee' is decidedly not. If the evidential rules do need greater scrutiny, especially concerning expert scientific testimony in cases involving 'unconventional' religious groups, Richardson's concluding recommendations are worth attention. In dealing with such a controversial and, in many ways, mysterious and intractable phenomenon[38] as 'cults', striking the right balance will not be easy. Insistence on solid proof and a healthy scepticism of expert evidence – the common law tradition at its best – will hopefully make the task a little less fraught.

The Human Rights Act 1998 marks a new era in British constitutional law. Its impact on Church–state relations and religious liberty is intriguing. In an erudite essay, Julian Rivers (Chapter 7) provides a most welcome lamp to assist navigation through uncharted waters. In its effort to 'bring rights home' the Blair government received a perhaps unforeseen check from many major UK Churches. Churches' institutional religious autonomy – the freedom to marry whomsoever they saw fit, to ordain candidates of their choosing, to employ or dismiss teachers at denominational schools based on compliance with spiritual standards and so on – was perceived as being threatened by the Act.[39] Lobbying from religious leaders, including the Archbishop of Canterbury, saw the eventual inclusion of a compromise amendment, s.13. Rivers fills in the background to the passage of the Act and its culmination in this, in my opinion, somewhat diluted sop to religious freedom. Will s.13 preserve the existing protections for religious organizations? Rivers steers us through several critical issues: the autonomy of the Church of Scotland and Church of England plus the impact of the Act on religious schooling, marriage, employment and the law on blasphemy. He highlights many important issues that will need sensitive interpretation. I shall simply allude to three which he raises.

First, do international human rights norms have a fixed meaning? The assumption that they do – especially the idea that 'religion' 'religious practice' and so on mean similar things to secular liberals and conservative theists – is surely naïve. A graphic example of a different understanding is the alternative Declaration of Human Rights promulgated by Muslim theorists.[40] Second, it is by no means crystal clear as to what is a 'secular' matter (reserved for civil tribunals) and what is a 'spiritual' one (for ecclesiastical courts alone). Locke in *A Letter Concerning Toleration* may have seen the distinction clearly, but not all of us would be so sure that we could 'distinguish exactly the business of civil government from that of religion'.[41] Differentiation between the two spheres is difficult and leads to the 'sez who?' question again – who, ultimately, decides? Third, and on a positive note, I endorse Rivers' plaudit for the Human Rights Act. The legislation refuses to take a narrow, atomistic view of religion as compromising simply matters of private, individual belief and conduct. (This exemplifies a broader European understanding of religion as our next essayist clarifies.) The institutional nature of religion and its inescapable public and social dimensions are recognized. Britain is seemingly, as Rivers submits, gravitating to a model of public, religious pluralism, from a weak Christian establishment to flotilla of 'mini-establishments'. Such a strategy is not without precedent[42] nor supporters.[43] We await a British corpus of religion law with interest.

In the travail of religious toleration the Netherlands holds a prominent place. It is fitting, then, for leading Dutch Church and state scholar, Dr Sophie van Bijsterveld, to contribute to this collection. In her searching analysis Dr van Bijsterveld plumbs the deeper streams of thought and belief that undergird the contemporary European scene. She depicts a slow, but nonetheless firm, 'mood' change in the mindset of the powers-that-be. The dominant (tacit) assumptions or presuppositions have long been those of the Western Enlightenment. Under the liberal paradigm religion is seen as a personal matter, with the state's principal function being to protect the individual's free exercise of faith in the private domain. That model remains but is being increasingly supplemented by another broader and benign conception of religion. There is a growing European appreciation of the public character of religion and the positive integrative part it can play in building community and revitalizing civil society. Two American scholars, lamenting the strict separationist doctrine in that nation, argue that 'defining religion as purely a private matter and protecting only individual religious rights is insufficient because that denies the public manifestation of faith and devalues the role of religious mediating institutions'.[44] Van Bijsterveld's essay indicates such dangers are both recognized and are (slowly) being addressed. Whether it be the so-called 'Church Clause' of the Treaty of Amsterdam or, even more fascinatingly, the exhortation by the Organization for Security and Cooperation in Europe to participating states for them to 'engage in consultations with religious faiths, institutions and organizations in order to achieve a better understanding of the requirements of religious freedom', the signs are, I believe, encouraging. The area is, of course, complex and the pitfalls of facile and manipulative attempts to use faith in the service of Caesar (and vice versa) are fresh in our memories. Nonetheless, European developments show promise.

Blasphemy law surely occupies an uncomfortable, anomalous place in secular liberal democracies. To treat religion equitably in a pluralist society ought one to abolish the offence of blasphemy or, on the other hand, extend it to protect non-Christian faiths? Is a religious vilification prohibition under human rights legislation an even better response? Each view has its supporters.[45] In Chapter 9 Dr Reid Mortensen traverses some of the intractable issues surrounding blasphemy law in his probing essay. Attempts by offended Christians in Australia and New Zealand in the late 1990s to prosecute public galleries for exhibiting blasphemous artwork came to nothing. These antipodean vignettes – the *Piss Christ* photograph, the *Virgin in a Condom* statuette and the *Wrecked* parody of the Last Supper painting – demonstrate further the strange limbo which prevails. Blasphemy law technically survives, but it is *de facto* a dead letter. One suspects it would be more trouble than it is worth for the government to abolish it. Unfortunately, desuetude finds it difficult to have its way with these recurring attempts to stubbornly invoke the offence. Conservative religionists plainly do not have 'thick skins'. The stance of many secular liberals that religionists ought not to feel offended by degrading depictions of their most sacred symbols is, as Mortensen rightly argues, unrealistic. The resurgence of religion, and of strong 'traditionalist' religion, was noted earlier in this chapter. Artistic sovereignty and literary licence are worthwhile values, but the law cannot ignore genuine expressions of offence that, regrettably, spill over into violence.

If legal constraint is not the solution, and freedom of expression demands that religionists accept jostling in a marketplace of ideas and religions, then what is the answer? If blasphemy law is vanquished as a coercive weapon ('a legal trump card'[46]) in contemporary culture wars, then citizens and institutions will need to demonstrate considerable prudence and self-restraint. The 'ethic of mutual respect', as Mortensen calls it, demands in particular that public institutions be sensitive to *all* sectors of the community. Religious symbols are no less significant than prized icons of ethnic, indigenous or other groups.

Symbols, then, do count. That people feel strongly about them and will pursue expensive litigation to defend them is clear, especially in the United States. The US Supreme Court decisions on Christmas nativity scenes, Jewish menorah and so on are infamous.[47] The American passion for this sort of thing is not unique, for New Zealand recently had a decision on the public display of swastikas erected in support, or so the complainant alleged, of his religious beliefs.[48] Professor Davina Cooper (Chapter 10) has written a fascinating sociolegal analysis of the 'eruv' saga in suburban London in the early 1990s. The very public erection of a Talmudic symbolic perimeter in Barnet aroused much antagonism and exposed all manner of deep and troubling issues about religious tolerance, protection of 'the British way of life' and the challenge of pluralism or multiculturalism. The erection of the Talmudic poles threatened to 'stain' the environment and was symptomatic of a phalanx of horrors – the emergence of ghettos, the public expression of difference, the slippery slope into some form of cultural apartheid, 'balkanization', and so forth. Secular liberal democracy, the so-called 'Enlightenment project', had come too far to regress back to primitive, premodern social structuring of this sort. As Cooper nicely explains, these fears were crystallized in the paralyzing thought (on the part of some residents) of totem poles on Hampstead Heath! The citizen on the Barnet omnibus does not, argues Cooper, need to be scratched too deeply before his or her Christian roots are revealed. The dominant culture is (understandably) sensitive when its most cherished tenets are directly challenged by phenomena such as eruv. In his recent critical, postmodern critique of American church–state relations, Stephen Feldman examines the anti-Semitic strain which he detects running through that polity, despite its claim of strict separation and religious freedom. Faced with pervasive Christian symbolism, 'Any Jew who objects is (take your pick) pushy, odd, a kill-joy, or ridiculous'.[49] Americans, no less than Englishmen (or Australians or New Zealanders) struggle to understand and accommodate, the 'Other'.[50] As the world becomes more crowded, and peoples more intermingled, the challenge will surely intensify.

Notes

1 Arthur A. Leff (1979), 'Unspeakable Ethics, Unnatural Law', *Duke Law Journal* **1979**, p. 1229, at p. 1230.
2 Ibid., p. 1230.
3 Ibid.
4 Rousas John Rushdoony (1973), *The Institutes of Biblical Law*, (Presbyterian & Reformed Publishing), pp. 4–5 (emphasis in original).
5 Leff, 'Unspeakable Ethics,' *op. cit.*, p. 1233. The phrase 'brooding omnipresence in the sky' is that of Oliver Wendell Holmes. See ibid., p. 1233, fn. 5.
6 See, further, Phillip E. Johnson (1993), 'Nihilism and the End of Law', *First Things*, June–July, pp. 19–25.
7 Leo Pfeffer (1967), *Church, State and Freedom*, rev. edn, (Boston: Beacon Press), p. 3.
8 See, for example, Abdullahi An-Na'im (1996), 'Islamic Foundations of Religious Human Rights' in J. Witte jr and J. van der Vyver (eds), *Religious Human Rights in Global Perspective: Religious perspectives*, (The Hague: Kluwer), p. 337.
9 Rt. Hon. Lord Denning (1989), *The Influence of Religion on Law*, Lawyers' Christian Fellowship booklet, p. 10.
10 Harold J. Berman (1974), *The Interaction of Law and Religion*, (Nashville: Abingdon Press), p. 16.
11 Ibid., p. 12.
12 Ibid., p. 78.
13 Ibid., p. 49.
14 Ibid., p. 37.
15 Harold Berman (1990), 'Religious Freedom and the Challenge of the Modern State', *Emory Law Journal*, **39**, pp. 149, 152. The text draws on Berman's analysis in this article.
16 Ibid., p. 160, quoting Polish poet Czeslaw Milosz: 'The basic issue of the twentieth century is that the state has eaten up all the substance of society.'
17 Peter L. Berger, (Winter 1996–97), 'Secularism in Retreat', *The National Interest*, p. 3, at pp. 4 and 7.
18 José Casanova (1994), *Public Religions in the Modern World*, (Chicago: University of Chicago Press), pp. 65–66.
19 Berger, 'Secularism in Retreat', *op. cit.*, p. 10.
20 W. Pannenberg (1996), 'How to Think About Secularism', *First Things*, June–July, p. 27, at p. 30.
21 Michael Hill (1994), 'Religion', in P. Spoonley, D. Preston and I. Shirley (eds), *New Zealand Society: A Sociological Introduction*, (Palmerston North: Dunmore), ch. 18, p. 304.
22 See Francis Lyall (1980), *Of Presbyters and Kings: Church and State in the Law of Scotland*, (Aberdeen: Aberdeen University Press), p. 146: 'Unless the ethos of the community, the common belief as to what is right, underpins the dictates of the law, the law will degenerate into oppression. Obedience to law ought to be almost accidental, and for society to be healthy people must do things because they are right rather than because of a fear of punishment.'
23 Berman, *Interaction*, *op. cit.*, p. 29.
24 Walter Weyrauch (1978), 'Law as Mask – Legal Ritual and Relevance', *California Law Review*, **66**, p. 699, at p. 726.
25 See C.S. Lewis (1979), 'Myth Became Fact' in W. Hooper (ed.), *God in The Dock*, (Glasgow: Collins), p. 7.

26   Malcolm D. Evans (1997), *Religious Liberty and International Law in Europe*, (Cambridge: Cambridge University Press).
27   See, for example, Paul Marshall (1997), *Their Blood Cries Out*, (Dallas: Word Publishing).
28   See also, for instance, Brice Dickson (1995), 'The United Nations and Freedom of Religion', *International and Comparative Law Quarterly*, **44**, p. 327.
29   See, for example, Phillip Johnson (1984), 'Concepts and Compromise in First Amendment Religious Doctrine', *California Law Review*, **72**, p. 817, at p. 839; Rebecca Redwood French (1999), 'From *Yoder* to Yoda: Models of Traditional, Modern, and Postmodern Religion in US Constitutional Law', *Arizona Law Review*, **41**, p. 49.
30   For the uninitiated I should point out Cooperstown is the location of the baseball Hall of Fame.
31   Steven D. Smith (1995), *Foreordained Failure: The Quest for a Constitutional Principle of Religious Freedom*, (New York: Oxford University Press).
32   See Michael Sandel (1989), 'Religious Liberty – Freedom of Conscience or Freedom of Choice?', *Utah Law Review*, **1989**, p. 597.
33   The US District Court rejected a Free Exercise claim by Judith Kuch, 'ordained minister of the Neo-American Church'. Chief Boo Hoo was the head of this 'Church', whose principal 'sacrament' was the partaking of marijuana and LSD. Each member carried a 'martyrdom' record to reflect his or her arrests for narcotic taking. This was simply a mockery of religion in the Court's view: *United States* v. *Kuch* 288 F Supp 439 (1968). The official songs ('Puff, the Magic Dragon') and the Church motto ('Victory over Horseshit!') obviously did not assist Kuch's claim.
34   Smith, *Foreordained Failure, op. cit.*, p. 68.
35   Stanley Fish (1997), 'Mission Impossible: Settling the Just Bounds Between Church and State', *Columbia Law Review*, **97**, p. 2255.
36   Unreported, Family Division, High Court, 19 October 1995, p. 153 (on file with author). Fortunately, the case is analysed in depth (with many extracts from the judgment quoted) in a valuable article by Ian Freckleton (1998), '"Cults", Calamities and Psychological Consequences', *Psychiatry, Psychology and Law*, **5**, pp. 1–46.
37   Ibid., p. 194.
38   As Freckleton, ibid., p. 33 observes: 'there are still major differences of opinion about almost all issues relating to groups popularly known as "cults"'.
39   See, for instance, Helen Saxbee (1998), 'Rights Bill Passes with Safeguards', *Church Times*, 6 November, p. 3.
40   The Islamic Council for Europe on 19 September 1981 promulgated its own Islamic Declaration on Human Rights in Paris (L'Islamic et les droits de l'homme). See Michael King (ed.) (1995), *God's Law versus State Law: The Construction of an Islamic Identity in Western Europe*, (London: Grey Seal), pp. 3–5.
41   John Locke, *A Letter Concerning Toleration* (1689), reproduced in J. Horton and Susan Mendus (eds) (1991), *John Locke, A Letter Concerning Toleration, in Focus*, (London: Routledge), pp. 12–56, at p. 17. Edmund Burke, for one, queried the ability to distinguish between the proper business of each: see Michael W. McConnell's (1995) excellent essay 'Establishment and Toleration in Edmund Burke's "Constitution of Freedom"', *Supreme Court Review*, **1995**, p. 393, pp. 443–444. See also Lyall, *Of Presbyters and Kings, op. cit.*, p. 8.
42   The Dutch experience of 'principled pluralism' comes to mind. For a comprehensive, lucid overview of this see Stephen V. Monsma and J. Christopher Soper (1997), 'The Netherlands: Principled Pluralism', in *The Challenge of Pluralism: Church and State in Five Democracies*, (Lanham, Maryland: Rowman & Littlefield), pp. 51–86.

43 See, for example, Michael McConnell (1998), 'Equal Treatment and Religious Discrimination', in Stephen V. Monsma and J. Christopher Soper (eds), *Equal Treatment of Religion in a Pluralist Society*, (Grand Rapids, Mich: Eerdmans), pp. 30–54 and James Skillen (1998), 'The Theoretical Roots of Equal Treatment', ibid., pp. 55–74.

44 Monsma and Soper, *Equal Treatment, op. cit.*, p. 202.

45 See generally A. Bradney (1993), *Religions, Rights and Laws*, (Leicester, Leicester University Press), ch. 5.

46 Clive Unsworth (1995), 'Blasphemy, Cultural Divergence and Legal Relativism', *Modern Law Review*, **58**, p. 658, at p. 674.

47 See, for instance, *Lynch* v. *Donnelly* 465 US 668 (1984); *County of Allegheny* v. *ACLU* 109 S Ct 3086 (1989). For a comprehensive account see Steven B. Epstein (1996), 'Rethinking the Constitutionality of Ceremonial Deism', *Columbia Law Review*, **96**, pp. 2083–2174.

48 *Zdrahal* v. *Wellington City Council* [1995] 1 NZLR 700.

49 Stephen M. Feldman (1997), *Please Don't Wish Me a Merry Christmas: A Critical History of the Separation of Church and State*, (New York: New York University Press), p. 260.

50 Ibid., p. 258 (Feldman acknowledges his debt to 'Derridean deconstruction' here).

2   The Ten Commandments: In What Sense Religious?

Calum Carmichael

The greatest contribution one can make to religion is to do away with it. (John MacMurray)

In examining legal systems, critics commonly distinguish between law as a branch of religion and law as a secular product independent of religious ideas. They place, for example, biblical and Talmudic law under the former rubric and Roman law and the common law under the latter. Lately, I have been working on the papers of my teacher, David Daube,[1] and recalled that he began his seminal work, *Studies in Biblical Law*, by referring to a widely accepted view that law was not always distinguished from religion, 'that originally, all precepts were deemed to be of a religious character'.[2] According to this view (of which Henry Maine was a principal proponent), only at a more advanced stage of civilization did the separation of law and religion come about. While somewhat sceptical at the time, Daube did not wish to express an opinion on whether or not this scheme was tenable, but he pointed out that it owed a great deal to the influence of the Bible where the emphasis decidedly encourages the belief that law is a branch of religion. I will devote a significant proportion of this chapter to an analysis of what this view actually means when we assess the surprising way in which biblical laws came to be written down. In particular, I will discuss the injunction to honour parents and the prohibitions against murder and adultery in the Ten Commandments, to show how we can arrive at an understanding of their underlying ideas, and how the compiler of the Ten Commandments associates the deity with these ideas. The religious character of the material might appear too obvious to need discussion. The way, however, in which religion attempts to establish authority for its claims differs little from comparable attempts on the part of law.

17

In later years Daube was much more frank about his ideas on the relationship between law and religion. He was not overly impressed with the standard judgement as expressed by R. David and J.E.C. Brierley in their *Major Legal Systems in the World Today: An Introduction to Comparative Law*.[3] For them, there are three great families of law: Romano-Germanic, common and socialist. Set against them, the authors claim, are systems that are religious or philosophical rather than juridical in nature and which possibly are not 'law' at all – namely, the Muslim, Hindu, and Jewish systems. While wishing to see some value in the distinction, Daube considered that David and Brierley exaggerate and take too narrow a perspective. For example, they are blind to religion in their own, apparently non-religious, legal systems, whereas, in fact, religious creeds and comparable 'isms' determine much of the law in apparently secular systems in regard to marriage, incest, children, Sunday observance, treatment of old age, notions of sanity, valuation of ownership, status, freedom, and life itself whether human, animal or plant. On the other hand, they fail to see the rather obvious role of the juridical in the religious and philosophical systems. The Code of Hammurabi is ascribed to the Babylonian god Shamash, but its contents are law of the kind we would readily associate with any secular system. The three tractates of the Mishnah (the earliest codification, about 200 CE, of Jewish Law), *Mishnah Baba Qamma, Mishnah Baba Metzia*, and *Mishnah Baba Bathra* constitute civil law rules familiar to us from private law collections in other non-religious systems of law. Certainly, as I shall shortly note, we do occasionally find the influence of religion on a private law (in the area of torts), but such examples are exceptional.

With regard to the two systems with which he was most familiar, Jewish and Roman, Daube had no doubt that the Jewish was more religious than the Roman. However, as to the contents or the quality of the law, he was sure that the difference means, not nothing, but less than might be expected. For example, either can be open or hostile to aliens and to children, and for or against wars. Although immutability is expected to be a chief characteristic of a religious system, the two principal parties in early Judaism did nevertheless effect changes – the Pharisees cautiously by means of interpretation, the Sadducees, who were no less religious than the Pharisees, rather freely. The Romans, in turn, could scarcely be described as change-seekers. They often proceeded very slowly, Justinian prohibiting even commentaries on his legislation in order to keep it fixed. For Daube the possible value of a religious-oriented system lies not in detail but in a constant general consciousness of a realm beyond the momentary and the petty.

That religion influences law, in ways not just along the lines that Daube claimed David and Brierley failed to appreciate, is obvious, but nevertheless often startling. In the nineteenth century Anton Büchler documented evidence from Talmudic sources to show that, in deference to the doctrine of bodily resurrection, Rabbinic methods of execution were radically modified by the wish to keep the skeleton intact.[4] In Jewish and early Christian law, converts to Judaism and Christianity were regarded as new-born in such a realistic way that relatives – brothers and sisters, for example – became no longer related and consequently could enter marital unions.[5] Such striking instances of religion's influence on areas of law that are not, in the usual sense, religious in character are typically confined to matters outside of private law (counting marriage as public). Now and again, however, one chances on an example – more amusing than startling – from the sphere of private law. In Mishnah *Baba Qamma* 6:6 a camel laden with flax passes a shop in the public domain, some flax gets inside where an open light burns, and a fire breaks out. The camel driver owes reparation. The same case is presented but, this time, the light is kept outside the shop and a fire breaks out. In this instance, the shopkeeper owes reparation. However, if the latter scenario occurs during the religious Feast of Maccabees, when it is incumbent on the shopkeeper to kindle a light in the open, the shopkeeper is not liable.[6]

Law's influence on religion, to turn to the contrary development, is legion. Indeed, so great is it that religion's powerful normative component probably owes a great deal to law. The transfer to the deity of human thinking about creditors, depositors (the soul as a deposit in the body), fathers, judges, masters (with servants), sovereigns, stewards, to cite but a few examples, is at the heart of religious thinking. Sometimes the result can be quite startling, at least for certain religious parties. If J.N.L. Myres is correct, one such example is the fourth-century Pelagian heresy. The use of *gratia*, in the negative sense of 'favour' or 'favouritism', often secured salvation in legal cases. The recognition of such corruption in earthly justice influenced Pelagius' religious view that grace (*gratia*) was not necessary for salvation, because God judged people strictly according to their merits.[7]

Turning to an assessment of what it means to link law in the Bible with religion, there is no doubt that readily accepted views about such a link have played a momentous role in both scholarly (for example, as already mentioned, the views of Henry Maine) and popular thinking. The material that inevitably first comes to mind is the body of rules, the Ten Commandments. These are, in fact, miscalled: in the original Hebrew texts they are correctly designated as the Ten Words, in the sense of divine pronouncements, and the first of these, 'I am the Lord thy God that brought thee out of the land of Egypt', is not a rule at all. They constitute a curious mixture of religious rules and moral injunctions which are, strictly speaking, not legal in that they lack sanctions and useful formulations to make them into manageable law. Thus, for example, we find prohibitions against murder and stealing that relate to ordinary day-to-day life, mixed in with 'religious' rules about observing a special day in honour of the deity and avoiding the dishonouring of his name. The contents are curious, too, in that they share with the injunctions about taking the lives of humans and animals issued to Noah after the Flood the unique feature that they are the only rules in the Bible that come directly from the deity. Ordinarily, biblical rules come from Moses who is depicted as receiving them from God.

It is difficult to say exactly why the Ten Commandments have such a compelling quality. Partly it may be attributable to a notion – not in fact accurate – that they are so inclusive,[8] partly that they are compact enough to be easily remembered, but mostly, I suspect, because of the 'hype' surrounding their alleged origin. God descended upon a mountain that is given a precise geographical location and, having prepared his audience for the experience of hearing a divine voice utter sounds, delivered them – to whom, it turns out, is not clear.[9]

What is the point of such a supernatural presentation of injunctions, some of which are banal in the sense that no one at any time in the history of humankind has needed be told that they should not steal, murder or commit adultery? It would be a great error to assume that the ancients possessed an uncanny sense of the numinous such that they functioned as if they were in communication with a deity. In reality, the compiling and giving of the Decalogue – to use a better term than the Ten Commandments – represents a profound and sophisticated exercise on the part of an unknown ancient thinker. The Decalogue is a myth about the origin of law (in the broadest sense). Indeed, all biblical law is of a mythical kind.[10]

To formulate their laws biblical law-givers focus primarily on their national epics and legends. To these narratives of the past they bring, from their contemporary world – in some shape or form not available to our scrutiny – a variety of legal and ethical rules and reformulate them in light of the epics and legends. Thus, only after contemplating the ethical and legal problems that they encounter in mythical narratives about the origin of the world, the origin of the nation's ancestors and the origin of the nation itself, do they proceed to commit laws to writing. An ancient and a modern parallel – they are no more than that – present themselves when we contemplate the biblical procedure.

The famous Greek tragedies of the fifth century BCE furnish themes that explore profound ethical and legal issues in Greek mythology – that is, in ancient stories about Greek origins. These tragedians are familiar with the rise of forensic science, the new craft of rhetoric for dealing with crimes that are far from straightforward and often have a considerable measure of indirectness attaching to them. This new way of exploring wrongdoing in which circumstantial evidence begins to play a major role – for example, pleading that a wrong was committed but mitigating circumstances existed – is a product of the enormously complicated problems thrown up by the political turmoil in Sicily around 500 BCE.[11] Instead of applying the new way of handling crimes to their contemporary world, the tragedians apply them to the mythical world of their ancestors. Clytemnestra assassinates her husband Agamemnon who has just returned from the Trojan War. While he was away, she had an adulterous relationship. Among other defences she reminds her accusers that Agamemnon had sacrificed their daughter Iphigeneia and had a mistress in Cassandra. Oedipus slaughters his father and marries his mother but is he to be held guilty for monstrous deeds when he acted innocently? His son dies in a rebellion and the ruler Creon denies him burial. His sister Antigone, however, feels compelled by a higher law to grant him it. Her sister Ismene demurs on the ground that women should not take it upon themselves to defy public authority. Sophocles explores the claims of the two competing authorities. Matters of great ethical and legal import are filtered through the doings of mythical personages. The items that make up the Decalogue prove to be similarly mediated: the offences taken up derive from a searching inquiry of the epics of the past.

A modern parallel is the way in which students in an American law school acquire rules – for example, about contracts or criminal intent. They are not told the rules directly but have to search for them by immersing themselves in cases, the equivalent of narratives. They have some sense of what the rules might be – possibly from general awareness, education to date and so on[12] – but only through a series of readings will they eventually emerge with formulations of rules that are more complete than the ones they worked with initially. When scrutinizing biblical rules, we will see that their formulations owe everything to the case, or cases, under review – that is, to the narratives that constitute the history of disputes and problems in the nation's life.

Consider the rule against murder in the Decalogue. A characteristic of the law-giver is to seek out the first ever occurrence of such a crime, and this he finds in the myth about the history of the first human family. Cain kills his brother Abel. The law-giver and the myth-maker share in common a desire to ponder such a matter and each does so in terms of the deity's response to the murder. Cain, a tiller of the soil, is denied the capacity to produce crops because his brother's blood cries out from the ground. As a consequence he becomes a fugitive and a wanderer on the earth. In such an unprotected state Cain faces the prospect of being murdered himself. The deity regards the punishment of banishment from the soil as sufficient and he puts a protective mark on him to prevent his murder. The presentation of the prohibition against murder in the Decalogue has this sophisticated review of Cain's deed in the background. This review is worth further consideration because it represents what we would regard as the religious dimension of the rule against homicide.

One feature of the story's attitude to murder is that the punishment should match the misdeed. In this regard, because Cain has defiled the very earth by spilling Abel's blood upon it, Cain's punishment is to be denied access to that earth for the purpose of growing food.[13] At all times and places, in both secular or religious societies, there has been a notion that, when a fearful crime has been committed, the punishment should reflect some aspect of it.[14] Again, when the deity moves to protect Cain from a violent end his use of a protective mark reflects an ancient practice that corresponds to our notion of the due process of law which guarantees that a defendant be heard in an orderly proceeding.[15] Someone who is implicated in a misdeed seeks shelter at a sanctuary because there may be factors to be taken into account that merit such protection. In Cain's situation there is a judgement that his banishment from the soil is sufficient punishment. There is also the judgement that a stranger, however suspicious his presence in a place, deserves protection from gratuitous attack. In the absence of institutionalized law enforcement agencies the role of a sanctuary, depending as it does on reverence deriving from a consciousness of higher powers, serves an important judicial function. Time and place have to be factored into any assessment of law and religion but, having done so, we are left with similar ideas and methods of dealing with the crime – in this instance, murder.

The law-giver's method of exploring an epic with a view to setting down norms explains the puzzling sequence in the Decalogue: the honour of parents, murder and adultery. The puzzle exercised writers as far back as Philo, the translators of the Septuagint, the authors of the New Testament and the scribe of the Nash Papyrus, all of whom chose to dispose of it by rearranging the rules so that the rule about adultery followed the one about parents. A better solution might be to note that each of the commandments reaches into the life of Cain. With his brother Abel, Cain is the product of sexual union between his parents, Adam and Eve. The author of the Genesis myth links to the deity's prior creation of all life these unions for the purpose of producing children. Human procreation perpetuates the initial process of creation. To destroy a life is a deed that dishonours parents in a most fundamental way. It is Cain's action against his parents' child that prompts the law-giver to promote the positive injunction to honour them. One honours them precisely because, in line with the original creation, they gave one life.

Evidence that this line of reasoning underlies the formulation of the injunction in the Decalogue comes from noting the curious motivation that the law-giver attaches to it. Honouring parents is, the addressed son in the Decalogue is told, to continue long 'upon the ground [in the original Hebrew, not 'land']' that God has given to him. In focus is the situation that Cain finds himself in: he could not continue tilling the ground because he destroyed what his parents had produced.[16] If he had held his parents in honour he would have held back from murdering his brother. This strange juxtaposition of a rule about murder with one about honouring parents is rendered more explicable by a reflection on Cain's biography.

The prohibition against adultery likewise comes from the same biography, and again, the key is the shared attempt by the law-giver and the storyteller to speculate about human origins. Following his offence and its consequences, Cain imitates his father and takes a wife. That the narration is mythical in nature is shown by the unconcern of the author to take account of the impossibility of the situation: no wife can possibly be available to Cain. The author, however, is not dwelling on historical realities but is intent on probing origins. When he states in language identical to that used for Cain's parents before him, 'Cain knew his wife, and she conceived and bore Enoch' (Genesis 4:17, cp. 1), the author links Cain's life cycle to Adam's – one generation to the previous one. In this way, the way of mythical storytelling, focus falls not on a real-life human relationship from a particular time and place, but on maleness and femaleness and the origin of the institution of marriage.

To express the mystery of sexual union the Genesis author traces it to Eve's origination from Adam's body. When a man and a woman unite they recreate the original union of male and female at Eve's creation. That is why the text states that 'a man leaves his father and mother and cleaves to his wife and they become one flesh' (Genesis 2:24). The first man ever to do so is not Adam but his son Cain. Reflecting on the origin of marriage, the law-giver notes that the cleaving to a wife and becoming one flesh with her carries with it, as the Talmudic sages saw (*Babylonian Sanhedrin* 58a), the implicit norm against interference with such a union, the prohibition of adultery. Cain's marriage serves as the impetus for the law-giver to impart his rule against adultery. A religious perspective enters into the presentation in the sense that the law-giver ponders the mystery of the origin of life.

Cain's killing of Abel also, in fact, invites the narrator to puzzle over a conundrum: why can human beings kill animals but not fellow human beings? It is fine, even meritorious, for Abel to kill an animal (by way of giving a gift to the deity), but it is not acceptable for Cain (frustrated in his wish to offer vegetables to the deity) to kill a fellow being. The presence of this puzzle in the myth shows up in Cain's reply to God's question as to Abel's whereabouts after he has been killed. Cain claims that he is not his brother's keeper. The analogy he uses is that of a shepherd with his animals. In using it, he is touching on the wrongful nature of his deed and thereby made to address the puzzle. Cain recognizes that it is permissible for a

shepherd to slaughter an animal but denies that he has that kind of relationship with his brother. It follows that if there is no such distinction in
category of being between himself and his brother, as there is between a
man and an animal, then he is not permitted to kill his fellow human being.
Cain's comment about not being his brother's keeper amounts to a self-
accusation. We can discern the author's method of thinking about such
distinctions by the way in which he sets out the story.

In light of my thesis that the original Decalogue relates back to the
Genesis narratives, I find it suggestive that both in regard to murder and
adultery some of the substance of Jesus' teaching may hark back to these
same narratives.[17] In his time the Hebrew Bible, like the *Odyssey* and the
Iliad, had come to be regarded as possessing all truth and all wisdom. To
obtain guidance and to interpret any part of it, the whole of the work had to
be taken into account. Because in other parts of the Scriptures anger is
associated with murder and lust with adultery, Jesus and others could formulate injunctions that highlight inner feelings. As it happens, in the story
of Cain and Abel the link between murder and anger is made especially
clear and is actually expressed by God himself. It would therefore not be
surprising if that particular narrative is under scrutiny by Jesus.

After God accepts Abel's gift of an animal sacrifice but not Cain's, God
counsels Cain about his anger and the untoward consequences to which it
might lead (Genesis 4:6).[18] The potential evil consequences of anger find
expression in other parts of the Hebrew Bible, but what suggests that Jesus
may, in fact, be thinking back to the episode about Cain and Abel is the
reference he makes to the altar and the presentation of an offering at it. Thus
he counsels that if one is angry with a brother and is offering a gift at the
altar, the correct thing to do is to leave the gift there, go to the brother, seek
reconciliation with him, and then return to offer the sacrifice. As Davies and
Allison point out, the counsel has its curious aspect: 'Could one, without
causing offence or disturbance, really leave a sacrifice in the hands of the
priest or on the altar and go (perhaps to Galilee) and make search for a
brother and then, some time later, return to the temple and pick up where
one left off, with everything in order and the priest waiting?' They also ask
whether the Cain story is being alluded to.[19] The Jesuanic formulation may
owe more to reflection on that story than to a focus on how a moral person
should actually proceed in real life. Certainly, the two situations are not
comparable in that Abel offers his gift on the altar and then Cain, finding his
unwanted, takes out his anger on his brother. The Genesis incident, however, is understandably of a narrowly idiosyncratic nature. Consequently,
any attempt to extract counsel from it but still include an illustration from a
life setting about the relationship between anger and gifts at an altar has to
change the circumstances of the latter gift-giving with a view to setting out

the general teaching. The peculiarity that is still present in the Matthean formulation may betray the link to the incident in Genesis. Matthew elsewhere has Jesus express aspects of the story of Cain and Abel (Matthew 18:22, 23:35).

The teaching about adultery is even more interesting and may well confirm that the interpretations showing up in the Sermon on the Mount reveal the same focus on beginnings that characterizes the original Decalogue. It cannot be claimed that Jesus' prohibition on adultery comes directly from reflection on the Genesis account of how marriage originated. What is telling, however, is that adultery in Matthew 5:27–32 is brought immediately into connection with the topic of divorce, and that topic *does* base its teaching on Genesis. Jesus does not recognize divorce and states that a man who proceeds to divorce his wife causes her to commit adultery. The sense seems to be that because she is still married to him (divorce not being recognized) the husband 'causes the woman to commit adultery (because she, it is assumed, will remarry)'.[20] The man himself, Jesus adds, commits adultery if he marries a divorcee (because she is still another man's wife).

To understand Jesus' position we have to look at his discussion in another part of Matthew. There he quite explicitly links his rejection of divorce to the Genesis accounts of creation. He cites how, to quote the New Testament Greek text literally, 'the one [God] creating from the beginning male and female made them' (Matthew 19:4). In focus is the view found already in Philo (prior to Jesus) that the first being was androgynous, both male and female. When a man marries he reunites with his original female part and restores what the original created order intended. Jesus also quotes from the statement in the Adam and Eve story about the original institution of marriage, how a man leaves his father and his mother, cleaves to a wife and becomes one flesh with her. The quotation also contains the notion of androgyny and clearly links marriage with the ideal order of creation. The act of cleaving to the woman and becoming one flesh with her restores, so to speak, Eve (standing for any woman) to Adam's body (standing for any man).[21]

There are two parts to the Decalogue. From a myth about the beginnings of life the compiler of the Decalogue derives the second part of it (the second tablet): from the command to honour parents to the prohibition against coveting. The first part (the first tablet), from the affirmation about God's bringing the Israelites out of enslavement in Egypt to the command to observe a Sabbath day in his honour, he derives from a legend in Exodus 32 – namely, the incident of the golden calf when, for the first time in the history of the nation, its members commit idolatry.[22] The compiler of the Decalogue views the fracturing of the relationship between the Israelites and their god as a fundamental matter, and the event attracts his attention precisely because, like the story of Adam, Eve and Cain and Abel, it is about beginnings – in this instance, national beginnings. The mythical character of the Decalogue is highlighted by the fact that God knows, in advance, the detailed wrongdoing that occurs in the incident (taking place, as it does, some days after the giving of the Decalogue). It is also revealed by the fact that, in the incident itself, the people, quite astonishingly, make a graven image, use God's name for it, and set aside a special day to honour this man-made god, thereby breaking the very prohibitions that had supposedly just been imparted to them in such awesome circumstances.[23]

The compiler of the Decalogue sets out laws fundamental to the nation's well-being, initially by responding to the first-ever occurrence of rebellion against divine authority in the nation's history (the making of the golden calf). He then turns his attention to the occasion when human beings first encountered this higher authority (in the garden of Eden).[24] In writing up the event at Sinai the compiler suggests that the voice that utters the Decalogue is not the usual voice that gives the nation's laws – that of Moses, or, in the quite specific context of Exodus 19, Moses' father-in-law, Jethro. At Sinai it is the voice of the deity that speaks, representing the same voice that spoke at the beginning of time. Any story contains within it implicit rules. The story of Adam, Eve and Cain and Abel is that of the deity's first ever interaction with human beings and it presupposes the existence of his moral and legal code for them. The Decalogue articulates this code and the voice that enunciates it echoes the 'voice' that is behind the moral and legal rules implicit in the story.

I turn to the major issue of how to evaluate the extraordinary presentation of the Decalogue in Exodus 19, a supernatural event breaking into the history of Israel. I submit that it reveals features characteristic of law and law-making at all times. In his influential book, *The Ancient Constitution and the Feudal Law*, J.G.A. Pocock focuses on conflicting views in European nations of the sixteenth and seventeenth centuries about the origin of their laws.[25] The anti-monarchist Sir Edward Coke, for example, took the position that English laws were without origin, not just ancient but immemorial and unmade. Affirming the royal prerogative, others opposed this stance with the claim that English laws, like those of other European nations, had a more recent history, going back to the Middle Ages and to national origins. The clash of views reflected opposing political ideologies, but central to each side's attempt to bolster its position was a focus on beginnings. Similar appeals to beginnings for political purposes show up in most legal systems at one time or another.[26]

The same features – a focus on beginnings and a background of political tension – are revealed when we probe the significance of the giving of the Decalogue. However, rather than a clash, as in the history of the common law, between the notion of the law having its origin in the beginnings of the nation as against the idea that it is unmade and from time immemorial, these two perceptions are combined. The nation experiences, at its very inception, a communication that its laws come from the beginning of time. In a way, the view expressed in Rabbinic sources that the creation of the world was conditional on Israel's acceptance of the Law at Sinai makes this point (*Babylonian Shabbath* 88a; *Deuteronomy Rabba* 8:5).

The event at Mount Sinai is the formal beginning of nationhood,[27] but its write-up communicates the notion that the nation's beginning is also a return to the origin of the world. Deuteronomy 4:32, 33 explicitly link the event of the Decalogue's delivery to the creation. Recalling the event at Sinai, Moses addresses the nation:

> For ask now of the days that are past, which were before thee, since the day that God created man upon the earth, and ask from the one side of heaven unto the other, whether there hath been any such thing as this great thing is, or hath been heard like it? Did ever people hear the voice of God speaking out of the midst of the fire, as thou hast heard, and live?

In his praise of creation Ben Sira has the Decalogue delivered to the first humans (Sir 17:1, 11–13).[28] Differently, but along similar lines, Sophocles well expresses the notion that law transcends time and place: 'They are not of yesterday, or to-day, but everlasting, Though where they came from, none of us can tell' (*Antigone*, lines 445–46).

A number of features suggests that the aim of the author who describes events when God delivers the Decalogue is indeed to create an atmosphere that evokes the origin of the world (Exodus 19). There is the explicit point that the deity chooses Israel as his special possession out of all the nations of the earth. The curious role of the trumpet in the story seems to point to the significance associated with the instrument in those texts that describe matters to do with the whole earth and the created order. Thus Isaiah 18:3, 'All you inhabitants of the world, you who dwell on the earth, when a signal is raised on the mountains, look! When a trumpet is blown, hear', and Jeremiah 51:27, 'Set up a standard on the earth, blow the trumpet among the nations'. Trumpets and other instruments played by the inhabitants of the entire earth join nature itself in testifying to God's capacity to judge the peoples of the earth in a just manner (Psalms 98). In Exodus 19 elements of nature – thunder, lightning, and thick cloud – merge with the sound of the trumpet to contribute to the awesome character of the occasion.

The deity descends on to a mountain in order to communicate his pronouncements on the same day, the third, that the dry land and hence the mountains first came into existence (Genesis 1:10). Whereas ordinarily it is

Moses who communicates God's commands in the Pentateuch there are three exceptions: the creation of the world, the renewal of the creation after the Flood, and the giving of the Decalogue. In each of these instances God gives them directly. Moreover, as the tractate of the Mishnah, *Pirqe Aboth* 5:1 (pre-200 CE), pointed out there are ten pronouncements in the Decalogue and there are also ten at the creation of the world.[29]

Less certain, but tantalizing, are some curious features of Exodus 19 that may specifically point back to origins as depicted in the Genesis account of them. The people have to wash their clothes and also refrain from sexual commerce. The action of washing clothes may be to counter the negative implication of the clothing of the first couple. Adam and Eve acquire clothes because their state becomes such that human beings are pitted against the gods on account of knowledge of which the gods claim they alone are the proprietors.[30] Washing them – not removing them, which is out of the question – serves as a ritualistic reminder of that first clash between human-kind and divinity. The injunction that the males should not approach their wives may be similarly motivated. When the first couple acquired knowl-edge they became sexually aware, and this awareness meant that human beings had 'become like one of us [the gods], knowing good and evil' (Genesis 3:22).

While the professed aim of the two requirements about clothing and sexual conduct in Exodus 19 is to separate the people from the divine activity on the mountain, they may also serve symbolically to undo the first, unwanted encroachment of the first humans into the divine realm. In Exodus 19 both humans and animals must not touch the sacred mountain. In Gen-esis 2–4 the serpent, as well as Adam and Eve, offends God by encroaching on the forbidden tree.

What the narrator of Exodus 19 does within the compass of the single occasion when Israel becomes a nation, the compiler of all the events in the Pentateuch does on a grand scale. Its compiler links Israel's formation as a nation, which occurs after the exodus from Egypt (Exodus 1–19), to the preceding history (Genesis 12–50) of the fathers of the nation (Joseph, Jacob, Isaac, and Abraham), and, in turn, to primeval history and the begin-nings of life itself (Genesis 1–11).

The supernatural aura surrounding the giving of the Decalogue is patently an attempt to lend authority to its contents. Every system of law involves such an augmentation of its rules. The word authority comes from the Latin term *auctoritas*, which in turn is from a verb *augere* meaning 'to increase', 'to wax'. The suggestion is of the strength that is added behind the scene. The delivery of the Decalogue is a good example. We have the typical reaching out to higher forces by those with power in order to sanction control over those they rule.

Caution and exactitude appear to be prominent in such attempts to harness these higher powers. Uzzah, a servant of King David, reaches out with his hand to prevent the sacred Ark of the Covenant from falling from the cart in which it is being transported. He dies on the spot, much to David's anger (2 Samuel 6:6, 7). Because the holy order has been disturbed, whoever records the story chooses not to recognize the distinction between unintentional and intentional action. The view is that even an accidental breach of custom has to prove fatal. The weight of divine authority is brought to bear on other legal situations by the use of ordeals (Numbers 5:11–31), oaths (Exodus 22:13), and other magical acts (1 Samuel 14:41). The situations are typically those where the machinery of earthly justice is powerless to cope – for example, when adultery has been committed in secret or when a human court cannot resolve a dispute.

A background of political tension is also a likely feature of the promulgation of the Decalogue. Its first part is a defence of a particular religious ideology. The setting up of golden calves in the shrines in the Northern Kingdom of Israel threatens the authority of the Jerusalem-based Southern Kingdom (1 Kings 12:25–33). In any discussion of the story of the golden calf, critics turn to the struggle between the Judean authorities in Jerusalem and the breakaway tribes of the Northern Kingdom under Jeroboam. The Judeans, the triumphant party, seek to preserve the hegemony of worship at the temple in Jerusalem against the northern threat of the newly established shrines at Bethel and Dan, each with its golden calf as an iconic reminder of the god Yahweh. The dramatic presentation of the Decalogue is an attempt to bolster the Jerusalemite ideological stance.

In an article, 'Law as Mask – Legal Ritual and Relevance', Walter Weyrauch reflected on the influential thesis of John Noonan that forms of legal reasoning can result in dehumanizing persons through the use of conceptual 'legal masks'.[31] The use of the concept of 'property' to enslave human beings is an obvious and notorious example. But no less effective are notions such as 'neutrality' and 'sovereignty', and even the concepts 'fact' and 'reality'. While agreeing with Noonan about the damaging effect of legal masks, Weyrauch argued that they have a positive role as well and, indeed, are crucial for the vitality of any legal system. Broadening the scope of his inquiry beyond contemporary law and taking into account the insights of legal anthropologists about the use of actual masks in traditional rituals, not just the metaphorical ones that Noonan discussed, Weyrauch concluded:

[C]eremonial masks and law perform comparable social functions. Individual decisions are given an institutional or transcendental legitimacy. Those in power can maintain their position by relying on a 'higher authority', protecting themselves from direct criticism. Social conflict can be resolved and defused relatively peacefully. Whether the forces relied upon to achieve these purposes are called the 'ancestors', spirits, deities, or 'objectivity and neutrality', the effect is the same. Both ancient masks and modern law use masking magically and authoritatively to shape social decisions by imposing a set of implicit values on otherwise chaotic reality.[32]

For Weyrauch, then, law is a mask that invokes a higher authority, and the masking seems to satisfy a deeply felt inner need. Emotions and events are made to flow into conduits of fixed styles of reasoning which, while they may well exclude some truth-telling,[33] appeal to the aesthetic sense of those affected and persuade the members of a community that justice is being served. In a way, it is not an insight that should be widely circulated because the result may impact negatively on vital functions of law. It seems to me that all Weyrauch's points are relevant to assessing the religious character of the Decalogue. If the law masks a religious dimension in secular systems, religion, in turn, disguises the characteristic elements of law in God-oriented systems. John MacMurray's maxim quoted at the outset of this chapter, is too radical – although no doubt he intended it to be. We should contribute to law by uncovering its religious side, and we should contribute to religion by stripping away its masks. To overdo this process, however, might not lead to a desirable outcome.

Notes

1   Daube died in California, age 90, on 24 February 1999, while this chapter was being written.
2   David Daube (1947), *Studies in Biblical Law*, (Cambridge: Cambridge University Press), p. 1.
3   R. David and J.E.C. Brierley (1969), *Major Legal Systems in the World Today: An Introduction to Comparative Law*, (1969) (London: Free Press, Collier-Macmillan). I have gathered Daube's views from conversations with him and from unpublished notes held at the Robbins Collection, Law School, University of California, Berkeley. Much discussion has recently centred on how Jewish legal tradition can contribute to issues of authority and interpretation in American constitutional theory. See S.L. Stone (1993), 'In Pursuit of the Counter-Text: The Turn to the Jewish Legal Model in Contemporary American Legal Theory', *Harvard Law Review*, **106**, pp. 813–76.
4   Anton Büchler (1906), *Monatsschrift für Geschichte und Wissenschaft des Judentums*, **50**, pp. 550 ff, 683 ff., and 704 ff. See also David Daube (2000), *Collected Works: New Testament Judaism*, ed. Calum Carmichael, Vol. 2, (Berkeley: Robbins Publications, pp. 617–24).
5   Trials of Christians in Lyons and Vienne in the second century had them charged with 'Oedipodean intercourse', Eusebius, *Ecclesiastical History* 5.1.14; Tacitus, *Histories* 5:5; Athenagoras, *Plea for the Christians* 31.1. See Daube, *Collected Works*, *op. cit.*, Vol 2, p. 475.
6   As I write, the local newspaper in Ithaca, New York, *Ithaca Journal*, 1 January 1999, p.

11A, carries an article by a local Rabbi to assert that this episode requires Jews to give public expression to their religious festivals.

7 See J.N.L. Myres (1960), 'Pelagius and the End of Roman Rule in Britain', *Journal of Roman Studies*, **50**, pp. 21ff.

8 Apart from the issue of what might constitute inclusiveness, they lack a prohibition against lying. The injunction against witnessing falsely against a neighbour – it is the only pronouncement with a decidedly legal flavour – is much narrower in conception than lying *tout court*.

9 See note 29 below.

10 Jean Cocteau's comment is apt: 'History is a truth that in the long run becomes a lie, whereas myth is a lie that in the long run becomes a truth.'

11 See David Daube (1980), 'Greek Forerunners of Simenon', *California Law Review*, **68**, pp. 301–305.

12 Karl Llewellyn (1960) urges students when first handling cases 'to knock your ethics into temporary anesthesia': *The Bramble Bush: On our Law and its Study*, (Dobbs Ferry, NY: Oceana), p. 116. He tells them to immerse themselves in the cases: 'Dig beneath the surface, bring out the story, and you have dramatic tales that stir, that make the cases stick, that weld your law into the whole of culture' (p. 152).

13 The storyteller does not take up the notion expressed after the Flood: 'Whoso sheddeth man's blood, by man shall his blood be shed' (Genesis 9:6).

14 On contemporary developments in the United States, see Stephen Garvey (1998), 'Can Shaming Punishments Educate?', *University of Chicago Law Review*, **65**, pp. 733–94.

15 On protective marks in Egyptian antiquity, see Moshe Weinfeld (1995*), Social Justice in Ancient Israel*, (Jerusalem: Magnes Press), p. 127.

16 The rule that precedes the command to honour parents is the command to honour the Sabbath day. Similar thinking underlies its formulation in the version in Exodus 20:8–11. One sets aside a special day to honour the deity because he created the world and all life in it. See my analysis (1996), *The Spirit of Biblical Law*, (Athens, Georgia: University of Georgia Press), pp. 92–94.

17 The content of Jesus' teaching is typical of moralists at all times and places. They take wrongs known to the law and treat these in a most expansive way because they can ignore the constraints imposed upon the law – for example, evidence acceptable to a court. Around 500 CE Theodoric can declare that to sin against the health of a person constitutes homicide. During the nineteenth century, the French philosopher Proudhon could declare that property is theft, and the contemporary feminist writer Andrea Dworkin could argue that sexual intercourse is rape (of the woman). For Jesus murder is not just physically and wrongfully killing a person. To be angry is also murder. Likewise with adultery: it is not just actual intercourse with the woman, but looking upon her with desire. Anyone involved in the essential emotional element of the wrong known to the law is held culpable. The merit in the moralists' view is the insight that people do indeed murder in the sense of being angry and do indeed commit adultery with their eyes and mind. From this angle, the teaching is progressive in that it highlights attitudes that may be destructive of personal relationships. From another angle, however, the teaching is harmful. For a person under the sway of it the inner desire is as serious as the act. From a modern, psychologically-educated perspective such teaching can pose a threat to emotional stability. It is unhealthy to repress sexual desire and to fail to express feelings of anger: indeed, it may even be wrongful in that not expressing anger may result in dismissing a fellow human as a person.

18 The acceptance of the one sacrifice and not the other is a quite arbitrary act on the part of the deity. The explanation is that the ancient author explores the issue of how human

beings exercise the capacity to discriminate, which Eve and Adam acquired when choosing not to distinguish between the two different kinds of food in the garden. Specifically, how does Cain, endowed with the capacity to discriminate, cope with the deity's decision to distinguish between the two offerings of food. See my discussion (1992), 'The Paradise Myth: Interpreting without Jewish and Christian Spectacles' in Paul Morris and Deborah Sawyer (eds), *A Walk Through the Garden*, (Sheffield: Academic Press), pp. 47–63.

19   W. D. Davies and Dale C. Allison (1988*)*, *The Gospel according to Saint Matthew*, 1, (Edinburgh: T. and T. Clark), pp. 510, 518.

20   Ibid., p. 528.

21   For a major discussion of the ideas underlying Jesus' position on marriage and divorce, see Daube, *Collected Works, op. cit.*, Vol 2, pp. 252–263.

22   I lay out the evidence for the integral connection between the first tablet of the Decalogue and the story of the golden calf in a number of publications, the latest being *The Spirit of Biblical Law, op. cit.*, pp. 83–104.

23   A prime feature of all biblical legal material is that it anticipates, often in a most precise way, what will happen in the future. Thus Moses knows that hundreds of years later Solomon will aggrandize himself by increasing the number of his horses, his wives, and his holdings in silver and gold (Deuteronomy 17:14–20). The religious explanation is that God and Moses are seers and 'know' the future as others do not. The predictive feature in question, however, is not much different from the one Oliver Wendell Holmes set out in his famous essay (1897), 'The Path of the Law', *Harvard Law Review*, **10**, p. 460: 'the prophecies of what the courts will do in fact ... are what I mean by the law'. The predictive element is really about looking back on the past intently and then seeing that such and such is bound to occur.

24   Jewish tradition linked the offence of the golden calf to Adam's offence. See J. Jervell (1960), *Imago Dei: Gen. 1,26f. im Spätjudentum in der Gnosis und in den paulinischen Briefen*, (Göttingen: Vandenhoeck and Ruprecht), pp. 115, 321; and A.J.M. Wedderburn (1978), 'Adam in Paul's Letter to the Romans', *Studia Biblica*, **3**, pp. 413–430.

25   J.G.A. Pocock (1957), *The Ancient Constitution and the Feudal Law: A Study of English Historical Thought in the Seventeenth Century*, (Cambridge: Cambridge University Press).

26   For Athenian law and its beginnings, see David Cohen (1989), 'Greek Law: Problems and Methods,' *Zeitschrift der Savigny-Stiftung für Rechtsgeschichte*, **106**, pp. 96, 101; for Roman law, see H.F. Jolowicz (1952), *Historical Introduction to Roman Law*, (Cambridge: Cambridge University Press), pp. 4, 10; and for Scotland, Hector L. MacQueen (1995), 'Regiam Majestatem, Scots Law and National Identity', *Scottish Historical Review*, **74**, pp. 1–20.

27   In a recently published introduction to the Old Testament, the author states (or rather overstates), 'The book of Exodus ... is Israel's Magna Carta, Declaration of Independence, and national constitution rolled into one. The nation's two root experiences are contained in this book: the miraculous flight from Egypt, called the exodus, and the covenant of Mount Sinai.' See B.L. Bandstra (1999), *Reading the Old Testament. An Introduction to the Hebrew Bible*, (Belmont, CA: Wadsworth Publishing Company), p. 131.

28   The comment on Sir 17:11 in the (1993) *HarperCollins, Study Bible*, (London, HarperCollins), p. 1557 is: 'The law of life refers to the Mosaic law, which is included in the endowments that God "allotted" to humankind, thus collapsing the time between creation and Sinai.'

29   I cannot decide what significance, if any, to give to the curious impression that when

God actually speaks the Decalogue the plain sense of the account, as critics without quite realizing it have noted, suggests that there is no audience for it. They refrain from articulating the matter in this way because they automatically assume that there had to be an audience. With not the slightest encouragement from the textual tradition, they transpose texts (transferring Exodus 20:18–21 about the people's fear of hearing God speak to the beginning of Exodus 20 when God speaks the contents of the Decalogue) so that Moses becomes the sole hearer of them. See J.K. Kuntz (1974), *The People of Ancient Israel. An Introduction to Old Testament Literature, History, and Thought*, (New York: Harper and Row), p. 111. My suggestion is that the curiosity may be tied to the notion that the Decalogue is an echo from the beginning of time. Just as the people hear 'a voice' (Exodus 19:19) that is audible but not intelligible language at the foot of the mountain, so too with the Decalogue itself. The *Mekhilta* (a second-century CE Rabbinic commentary on Exodus) has all ten pronouncements spoken in one utterance, 'something impossible for creatures of flesh and blood', and, I suspect, is puzzling over the odd textual data. See J.Z. Lauterbach (1933), *Mekilta de-Rabbi Ishmael*, vol. 2, (Philadelphia: Jewish Publication Society), p. 228.

30 I have argued that the strange rule in Exodus 20:26 prohibiting ascent by steps to an altar because the worshiper's nakedness may be exposed relates back to God's negative response to Adam's and Eve's awareness of their nakedness. See Calum Carmichael (1992), *The Origins of Biblical Law*, (Ithaca, NY: Cornell University Press), pp. 76, 77.

31 Walter Weyrauch (1978), 'Law as Mask – Legal Ritual and Relevance', *California Law Review*, **66**, pp. 699–726. Noonan's work is J. Noonan (1976), *Persons and Masks of the Law – Cardozo, Holmes, Jefferson, and Wythe as Makers of the Masks*, (Cambridge, MA: Harvard University Press).

32 Weyrauch, 'Law as Mask', *op. cit.*, p. 716.

33 For example, a prosecutor conceals his racial prejudice against black jurors by proffering some neutral explanation for their exclusion. See David Cole (1998), *Race and Class in the American Criminal Justice System*, (New York: The New Press), p. 120 where he cites the finding of a recent study.

3   The United Nations and Freedom of Religion: The Work of the Human Rights Committee

Malcolm D. Evans

Introduction

Within the family of United Nations instruments, freedom of religion is set out in Article 18 of the Universal Declaration on Human Rights (UDHR),[1] Article 18 of the International Covenant on Civil and Political Rights (ICCPR)[2] and in Article 1 of the 1981 Declaration on the Elimination of All Forms of Intolerance and Discrimination Based on Religion or Belief[3] and it is reflected in numerous other United Nations instruments. Freedom of religion has been described as an '"easy case" in the human rights cata- logue'[4] but, whilst it is true that its inclusion in that catalogue has not been particularly controversial, it is not at all easy to understand what is meant by it.

The story of UN activities relating to religious freedom has been told before[5] and it is not necessary to recount it again at length. The broad outline is as follows. Following the adoption of the Universal Declaration in 1948, attention turned to drafting what was to become the 1966 Covenant. Preliminary drafts of an article on freedom of religion already existed but were abandoned in favour of the text of the Universal Declaration which formed the basis for future discussion and, although a number of changes were made, the final text followed its basic pattern. Meanwhile, a second line of development was taking place. In 1956 the UN Sub-Commission on Prevention of Discrimination and Protection of Minorities appointed a Special Rapporteur, Arcot Krishnaswami, whose report, 'Study of Discrimination in

Relation to Religious Rights and Practices', was presented to the Commission on Human Rights in 1960.[6] Despite its title, the Report examined freedom of religion as well as discrimination on the grounds of religion or belief and included a series of 'basic rules' which elaborated on Article 18 of the Universal Declaration. The Sub-Commission itself produced a set of 'Draft Principles on Freedom and Non-Discrimination in the Matter of Religious Rights and Freedoms' which were based on the Krishnaswami Basic Principles and was also placed before the Commission at the same time as his Report.[7]

In 1962 the focus of attention shifted when the UN General Assembly requested the Commission to prepare a Declaration and Convention on the Elimination of Racial Discrimination and, as something of a *quid pro quo*, to do the same as regards the Elimination of Religious Intolerance.[8] By December 1963 the UN Declaration on the Elimination of All Forms of Racial Discrimination had been completed and adopted by the General Assembly[9] and the Convention was adopted in 1965.[10] Progress on the religious instruments was not so swift. In 1963 the Sub-Commission had prepared a draft Declaration which was discussed by the Commission in 1964 but, rather than continue with this, it decided in 1965 to ask the Sub-Commission to prepare a draft Convention for it to consider.[11] During 1966 and 1967 the Commission finalized 12 draft Articles,[12] and at the end of 1967 the Preamble and Article 1 were adopted by the Third Committee of the UN General Assembly.[13] At that point, progress towards a UN Convention on the Elimination of All Forms of Intolerance and of Discrimination Based on Religion or Belief (as it by then had been re-named) came to an abrupt halt and has not been restarted since.[14] In 1974 the Commission resumed its consideration of the draft Declaration and this was finally adopted by the General Assembly in 1981.[15] Article 1 of the 1981 Declaration sets out freedom of religion in terms which are very similar to Articles 18 of the UDHR and the ICCPR but this was only because it proved impossible to forge a consensus around a more detailed formulation. It is, then, clear that this represents the most widely endorsed and most widely acceptable formulation of freedom of religion[16] and provides the structure within which it is to be analysed from a legal perspective – irrespective of the particular instrument in question. Article 18 of the ICCPR provides:

> 1. Everyone shall have the right to freedom of thought, conscience and religion. This right shall include freedom to have or to adopt a religion or belief of his choice, and freedom, either individually or in community with others and in public or in private, to manifest his religion or belief in worship, observance, practice and teaching.

2. No one shall be subject to coercion which would impair his freedom to have or to adopt a religion or belief of his choice.

3. Freedom to manifest one's religion or beliefs may be subject only to such limitations as are prescribed by law and are necessary to protect public safety, order, health, or morals or the fundamental freedoms of others.

4. The States Parties to the present Covenant undertake to have respect for the liberty of parents and, when applicable, legal guardians to ensure the religious and moral education of their children in conformity with their own convictions.[17]

The scheme of protection set out in Article 18 is deceptively simple. Article 18(1) sets out an absolute right to freedom of thought, conscience and religion before articulating two particular aspects of this freedom: the freedom to have or to adopt a religion or belief and the freedom to manifest a religion or belief in a number of ways. Article 18(3) then sets out the grounds on which the freedom to manifest a religion or belief may be restricted. Since Article 18 is included in the list of those articles which may not be derogated from,[18] these are the only forms of restriction permitted by the Covenant.[19] Aspects of freedom of thought, conscience and religion are, of course, also protected indirectly by other articles in the Covenant, such as freedom of association, freedom of private life and freedom of expression. The relationship with freedom of expression is particularly important. To the extent that there is no freedom under Article 18 to 'manifest' thought and conscience, such activities only derive protection to the extent that they amount to a form of expression protected by Article 19(1) and (2), and are subject to the limitations placed on the enjoyment of the freedom of expression by Article 19(3).[20]

This scheme of protection has three key 'pressure points':

1   What forms of belief enjoy the 'freedom to manifest'?
2   What is a 'manifestation'?
3   What is the scope of the legitimate restrictions?

The extent to which religious freedom is enjoyed depends on the interplay between them. It is possible to have a very broad understanding of what constitutes a religion or belief, but to take a narrow view of what forms of activity qualify as a 'manifestation'. Alternatively, one could take a broad view of what counted as a manifestation but grant a state considerable latitude when assessing the legitimacy of restrictions placed on the enjoyment of the right to manifest. It is, then, necessary to assess developments relating to all three 'pressure points' in order to be in a position to assess the extent to which religious freedom is accorded protection and priority within the functioning of the system.

This chapter attempts to contribute towards that task by looking at the work of the Human Rights Committee (HRC) relating to Article 18 of the ICCPR.[21] The HRC is the monitoring body established under the ICCPR and has the task of overseeing its implementation. It comprises 18 independent experts who are elected by the states parties to the Covenant and serve for four-year terms of office, and may be re-elected.[22] All states parties to the Covenant are obliged to submit reports to the HRC on the measures which they have adopted to give effect to the rights contained in the Covenant.[23] These are scrutinized by the HRC in advance of its meeting with representatives of the state concerned at one of its three regular annual sessions. When the state appears before the Committee, it will be questioned on the report and this leads to the adoption of 'Concluding Observations' in which the HRC highlights matters of particular concern and makes some specific recommendations.[24] The reporting process provides an ideal opportunity for the Committee to develop its vision of what is required of states in order to fulfil their Covenant obligations, measure each state's performance against these *desiderata* and recommend what action should be taken to achieve compliance. However, because the outcome of the process is couched in country-specific terms, and focused upon its particular circumstances, it does not provide a suitable vehicle for setting this out in a systematic fashion.[25]

The HRC also has the capacity to consider 'communications' concerning alleged violations of a state's obligations under the Covenant. These may come from one of two sources. Under Article 41 of the Covenant, a state may declare that it is willing for the Committee to consider a complaint made against it by another state that has made a similar declaration but this interstate procedure has never been used. The second source is under the provisions of the First Optional Protocol to the Covenant which permits the HRC to consider communications brought by individuals against those states which are parties to it.[26] Unlike the reporting procedures, the individual communication procedure is quasi-judicial in nature and is more suited to jurisprudential analysis and development. There have been at least nine applications in which issues have been raised by the applicant and addressed to the HRC in terms of Article 18 and which bear directly upon its interpretation. Four are principally concerned with conscientious objection, (three of which raised virtually identical points[27]) one with the definition of religion,[28] two with the nature of a manifestation,[29] one on the scope of limitations on the freedom to manifest a religion,[30] and one concerning religious education.[31] Of these, four were declared admissible but no violations were found.[32]

The HRC has a third form of output, 'General Comments' which, without doubt, provide the most important source of interpretation of Covenant articles. These are adopted by the HRC after an often prolonged process of discussion and revision and set out its understanding of what the various Covenant articles require of states parties. The first draft of what became General Comment No. 22 on Article 18 was prepared by a working group, presented to the Committee in July 1992 and adopted a year later in July 1993.[33] The importance of this General Comment is underscored by the comparative dearth of other forms of authoritative interpretive material from the Committee relating to Article 18 arising from the reporting process and from individual communications.[34] The discussions within the Committee surrounding its adoption provide valuable insights and will be considered in some detail in the following sections.[35]

What Forms of Belief Enjoy Protection?

The first question which needs to be addressed concerns the range of beliefs which qualifies for protection: in other words, what is a 'religion or belief' for the purposes of Article 18? Article 18 opens by expressing the 'bare' right to freedom of 'thought, conscience and religion' and then offers protection to the manifestation of 'religion or belief'. Does the use of the word 'belief' extend the freedom of manifestation to the patterns of 'thought' and 'conscience' mentioned in the opening sentence? Is it merely an alternative way of referring to religious traditions? Or does it refer to a category of beliefs which, whilst not religious in nature, are more than 'thought' and 'conscience'? The answer to this question is critical for both the practical application of this article and the consideration of the other 'pressure points' to be considered below but, unfortunately, the answer is unclear.

The Background to the Text

The drafting history of Articles 18 of both the UDHR and the ICCPR shed some light on why these intrinsically complex issues became intractable. At first, it was taken for granted that these articles were concerned with freedom of religion and the terms 'thought', 'conscience', 'religion' and 'belief' were used in an almost interchangeable fashion – the earliest drafts of Article 18 of the UDHR certainly suggest this[36] and the draft produced by the Commission on Human Rights in December 1947 did not expressly refer to religion at all.[37] However, the combined effect of two particular concerns affected its shape and structure and created the prospect of divergent interpretations being placed upon these terms.

The first concern was the need to protect the interests of non-believers from religious fanaticism. Whilst this could be achieved through restricting the right to manifest religious belief in ways which impinged on the individual rights of others,[38] the Soviet Union also argued that freedom of thought should be viewed separately from freedom of religion, 'in order to promote the development of modern science and which took account of the existence of free-thinkers whose reasoning had led them to discard all old-fashioned beliefs and religious fanaticism'.[39] This was taken up by others in debate and it became accepted – at least in theory – that 'thought' and 'conscience' embraced philosophical and scientific concepts that were not 'religious' in nature[40] and when attention turned to drafting Article 18 of the ICCPR it was generally understood that these terms had to be considered separately.[41]

This still left the central question of whether 'belief' was a synonym for religion unanswered and put into stark relief the uncomfortable fact that there was no general understanding of what any of these separate terms actually meant. The debate was centred on atheism and, whereas most states considered atheism to be included (since it was a pattern of 'thought' or 'conscience'), some still took the view that the Article was principally concerned with freedom of religion and should be read in that light.[42] The Soviet Union, by contrast, argued that 'belief' was broader than religion and so the Article protected the freedom to manifest atheistic beliefs.[43] There was, however, a middle path, since 'belief' could be understood as referring to patterns of thought which, whilst not religious in nature, occupied a similar place in the life of the individual, in the sense of constituting a guiding force. Thus it would embrace Buddhism as well as certain forms of philosophy but not necessarily any set of views – no matter how cogent – which a person held.

If 'religion' is defined so broadly that it encompasses such forms of belief, then this particular problem melts away (although it merely transfers the resulting problems to the next 'pressure point', that of determining the scope of a legitimate manifestation) and, although not put in quite these terms, this was the approach adopted by the influential Krishnaswami study. This said that:

> In view of the difficulty of defining 'religion' the term 'religion and belief' is used on this study to include, in addition to various theistic creeds, such other beliefs as agnosticism, free thought, atheism and rationalism.[44]

Against this background, it is not surprising that the trend has been towards adopting an expansive, inclusive approach which, whilst accepting that not all forms of thought and conscience will count as a 'belief' for the purposes of manifestation, sees the range of beliefs which attracts that right as extending beyond those which are deemed 'religious' in nature.

In order to know what counts as a 'belief' rather than as a 'religion' a definition of a religion must be formulated. However, it might be more profitable to concentrate on the boundary between 'belief' (which clearly included all forms of religious belief) and patterns of 'thought and conscience' which fall short of the protected category.

The Approach of the Human Rights Committee

The approach of the HRC to this question is set out in its General Comment on Article 18, which opens with three paragraphs which address what might be called 'structural' issues. Paragraph 1 provides:

> The right to freedom of thought, conscience and religion (which includes the freedom to hold beliefs) in Article 18(1) is far reaching and profound; it encompasses freedom of thoughts on all matters, personal conviction and the commitment to religion or belief, whether manifested individually or in community with others. The Committee draws the attention of States Parties to the fact that the freedom of thought and the freedom of conscience are protected equally with the freedom of religion and belief. The fundamental character of these freedoms is also reflected in the fact that this provision cannot be derogated from, even in time of public emergency, as stated in article 4(2) of the Covenant.

This paragraph relates only to the opening sentence of Article 18(1), since, as will be seen below, the following paragraphs consider the meaning of, and relationship between, religion and belief and the freedom of manifestation. To that extent, the second sentence of this paragraph is somewhat misleading and it does not mean that the Article *as a whole* protects thought, conscience, religion and belief equally. Indeed, it clearly does not. Two important points should, however, be noted.

First, although this opening paragraph makes it clear that 'belief' is located within the three concepts of thought, conscience and religion, it does not address the problem of which one it is connected with.[45] Second, this paragraph indicates that freedom of thought embraces *'all matters'*. There is, then, no aspect of mental activity which falls beyond the scope of the Article. Inevitably, this means that the process of paring this down falls to the remainder of the Article, justifying the identification of the three 'pressure points' mentioned earlier.

Paragraph 2 of the General Comment provides:

> Article 18 protects theistic, non-theistic and atheistic beliefs, as well as the right not to profess any religion or belief. The terms belief and religion are to be broadly construed. Article 18 is not limited in its application to traditional religions or to religions and beliefs with institutional characteristics or practices

analogous to those of traditional religions. The Committee therefore views with concern any tendency to discriminate against any religion or belief for any reasons, including the fact that they are newly established, or represent religious minorities that may be the subject of hostility by a predominant religious community.

The purpose of this paragraph is to prepare the ground for what follows by identifying those 'freedoms of the mind', the manifestations of which are to be protected. At first sight, it appears to be broadly stated but, although it calls for a broad construction to be placed on the terms 'religion or belief', the remainder of the paragraph seems to take as its starting point the fairly narrow notion of a 'traditional religion' with 'institutional characteristics'. It also cuts against the thrust of the first paragraph by implying that 'belief' is to be associated with religion. The debates surrounding its adoption indicate that its purpose was to ensure that 'all religions and beliefs were protected', the concern being that, in some states, 'certain religions or beliefs were not regarded as such and, in other words, as being entitled to protection', the Baha'i community being given as an example.[46] Against this background, the call for the terms religion and belief to be 'broadly construed' loses much of its initial impact.[47]

The effect of this paragraph is, then, to call on states not to restrict the freedoms associated with religion and belief by refusing to recognize the legitimacy of the claims made by individuals that they are exercising their freedom of religion or belief *when they are in fact doing so*. In other words, it is intended to prevent states from refusing to acknowledge that a form of religion or belief actually *is* a religion or belief:[48] it does not really touch on the question of what is to be considered as a form of religion or belief. To the extent that there are any clues, such as the reference to 'definite religious practices' and 'institutional characteristics', they suggest, paradoxically, a fairly restrictive approach.[49]

The last of these 'structural' paragraphs of the General Comment is paragraph 3, which provides:

> Article 18 distinguishes the freedom of thought, conscience, religion or belief from the freedom to manifest religion or belief. It does not permit any limitations whatsoever on the freedom of thought and conscience or on the freedom to have or adopt a religion or belief of one's choice. These freedoms are protected unconditionally, as is the right of everyone to hold opinions without interference in article 19(1). In accordance with article 18(2) and 17, no one can be compelled to reveal his thoughts or adherence to a religion or belief.

This was intended to underline the distinction between those elements of Article 18 which were absolute in nature and those which were subject to qualification. The underlying premise is that freedom of thought, conscience and religion (and belief) are enjoyed in private[50] and such enjoyment must not be subject to interference, but outside of the private sphere the exercise of all such rights must come under scrutiny. The rubric under which such scrutiny takes place will vary. Any exercise of the freedoms set out in Article 18 that takes place in the public domain will amount to an exercise of the freedom of expression and is protected under Article 19. If the form of expression in question amounts to a manifestation of a religion or belief, it falls for consideration under Article 18[51] but manifestations of thought and conscience are still to be considered under Article 19.[52]

Clearly, this understanding adds nothing to the debate surrounding the distinction between a 'belief' and 'thought' or 'conscience' in that it merely underlines the reasons why the boundary needs to be sought[53] but, despite promising sounding phraseology, the General Comment does not shed much light on this vexed topic. It is clear that the concept 'religion and belief' is narrower than 'thought and conscience', and that 'belief' may encompass more than 'religion', depending on what is understood by 'religion'. In terms of practical guidance, this amounts to lean pickings from 50 years' worth of experience.

Nor does the practice under the reporting process and the consideration of individual communications add a great deal. The issue of conscientious objection to military service has dominated much of the discussions and, for reasons which will become apparent, this will be considered at the end of the following section on what comprises a manifestation. At this point, it is sufficient to note that, although conscientious objection is clearly covered by Article 18 references to 'thought' and 'conscience', it is equally clear that it is not a 'religion'. This immediately generates the problem that needs to be addressed: is it a form of belief which, notwithstanding its non-religious character, may give rise to the freedom of manifestation?[54]

Putting the conscientious objector cases to the side for the moment, there are two individual communications which bear on this problem. The first is *MAB, WAT and J-AYI* v. *Canada*[55] which concerned members of an organization named the 'Assembly of the Church of the Universe' whose beliefs and practices, according to the authors, 'necessarily involve the care, cultivation, possession, distribution, maintenance, integrity and worship of the "Sacrament" of the Church', this being marijuana. The HRC declared the communication inadmissible, noting that 'a belief consisting primarily or exclusively in the worship and distribution of a narcotic drug cannot conceivably be brought within the scope of Article 18 of the Covenant (freedom of religion and conscience)'. This decision was taken just three months before the adoption of the General Comment and certainly reinforces the view that 'religion or belief' should not be interpreted in an overly liberal fashion.[56] No attempt is made to explain why Article 18 does not embrace such patterns of belief, particularly if acts described as 'worship' are involved.[57] Of course, recognizing such beliefs as religious would not preclude the imposition of legitimate restrictions which could easily stretch to dealing with any perceived problem. The point is that it indicates a preference for dealing with such cases at the threshold stage by simply refusing to recognize their status as a form of religion or belief.

This might be contrasted with the earlier decision in *MA* v. *Italy*.[58] The author of the communication argued that his political opinions and freedom of expression had been violated by his conviction for attempting to re-establish the Fascist Party in Italy. The Committee took the view that this restriction on his freedom of expression was justified under Article 19(3) but also commented that Article 18(3) would also have provided a justification. Since Article 18(3) only concerns restrictions on the manifestation of religion or belief, this rather suggests that fascism was a 'belief' for these purposes. Although it is undubitably a form of 'thought', if it was also a 'belief' the scope of Article 18(1) would be dramatically increased. The background to the General Comment does, however, suggest that it would be a mistake to do so. Nevertheless, the outcome of these two contrasting cases indicates that no matter what approach is adopted, the tools exist to produce the desired outcome. These will be considered in the following sections.

What is a Manifestation?

Once it has been decided that a form of belief does qualify as a form of religion or belief for the purposes of Article 18(1) the next question concerns the range of activities which are to be counted as forms of 'manifestation'. Article 18(1) lists 'worship, observance, practice and teaching'. What little light is shed on this question by the *travaux préparatoires* of both the UDHR and the ICCPR is eclipsed by that provided by the General Comment, which considered each of these in turn in paragraph 4. It commences by recalling the words of Article 18(1) that 'The freedom to manifest religion or belief may be exercised "either individually or in community with others and in public or private"' and then goes on to state that 'The freedom to manifest religion or belief in worship, observance, practice and teaching encompasses a broad range of acts'. Once again, however, one should not be misled by this. As it proceeds, it becomes clear that the Comment actually views these categories in a fairly restrictive fashion. This is brought out by comparing the General Comment with the observations made by Nowak in his Commentary to the ICCPR, written just before the Comment was adopted.

Worship

Basing himself on the *travaux préparatoires* and practice at that time, Nowak was of the view that 'By worship ("culte") is meant the typical form of religious prayer and preaching, that is, freedom of ritual. The specific manner in which the ritual is structured depends on the respective religious confession.'[59] Paragraph 4 of the General Comment is couched in very similar terms and provides that:

> The concept of worship extends to ritual and ceremonial acts giving direct expression to belief, as well as various practices integral to such acts, including the building of places of worship, the use of ritual formulae and objects, the display of symbols, and the observance of holidays and days of rest.

Observance

Nowak says that 'This covers processions, wearing of religious clothing or beards, circumcision, prayer and all other customs and rites of the various religions'.[60] Once again, the General Comment is very similar, providing that:

> The observance and practice of religion or belief may include not only ceremonial acts but also such customs as the observance of dietary regulations, the wearing of distinctive clothing or headcoverings, participation in rituals associated with certain stages of life, and the use of a particular language customarily spoken by a group.

In both cases, the General Comment adds further useful illustrations but the general line of thinking is the same. However, this is not true of the remaining two headings, teaching and practice.

Teaching

Nowak considers teaching alongside worship and observance and says:

> Teaching [*l'enseignement*] is understood as every form of imparting the substance of a religion or belief, in particular, in religious schools, in public schools (religious instruction) or by way of various types of non-formal education and missionary work. Such teaching must, however, take place in conformity with the parental right in Article 18(4).[61]

He clearly sees teaching as a form of propagation of religion or belief that extends from the 'private' sphere of the Church itself to the sphere of public proclamation. This is in marked contrast with the General Comment which considers teaching and practice jointly, saying,

> In addition, the practice and teaching of religion or belief includes acts integral to the conduct by religious groups of their basic affairs, such as, inter alia, the freedom to choose their religious leaders, priests and teachers, the freedom to establish seminaries or religious schools and the freedom to prepare and distribute religious texts or publications.

This has a very different focus. It is chiefly inward-looking and is noticeably hesitant on whether teaching extends to missionary-style activities. It refers to the distribution of written materials but not to oral presentation, proclamation or disputation. This seems unduly cautious, as in *JP* v. *Canada*, the HRC had already observed that 'Article 18 certainly protects the right to hold, *express and disseminate* opinions and convictions, including conscientious objection to military service'.[62]

Practice

In the General Comment, 'practice' is considered alongside 'teaching'. Consequently, it has nothing else to say on the subject and does not directly address the difficult question of what is meant by 'practice' which, as Nowak points out, 'could be taken to mean every action or omission motivated by religion or belief'.[63] But the implication is clear – it is to have a restrictive interpretation and should not be used as a vehicle for expanding the scope of the freedom into the public sphere and permit followers of a religion or belief to act in a fashion which is in accordance with their beliefs but cannot be linked to a form of worship, observance or teaching: in short, there would seem to be little room for believers to claim the freedom to 'practise what they preach'.

Is this restrictive approach supported by the Committee's own practice? In a number of cases the Committee has dismissed as unsubstantiated claims by peace activists that Article 18 was violated by the authors having been convicted on charges of violence and criminal damage when their actions were inspired by higher obligations (in these cases, international law).[64] This is relatively uncontroversial. However, the majority of the cases brought before the Committee relating to Article 18 have concerned conscientious objectors, and these have proved problematic.

In *LTK* v. *Finland*[65] the HRC was of the view that 'The Covenant does not provide for the right to conscientious objection; neither article 18 nor article 19, especially taking into account paragraph 3(c)(ii) of article 8, can be construed as implying that right'. This was reiterated on a number of occasions in the context of objection to military service[66] and, in consequence, a number of cases which might otherwise have been brought on the basis of Article 18 were presented and developed from alternative perspectives.[67] The logic of this line of reasoning was applied in a group of cases which were concerned with objections to paying taxes which would be available for expenditure on military purposes, it being noted that 'the refusal to pay taxes on grounds of conscientious objection clearly falls outside the scope of protection of this article'.[68]

Nevertheless, the question of conscientious objection to military service was revisited during the drafting of the General Comment, paragraph 11 of which observes that:

> The Covenant does not explicitly refer to a right of conscientious objection, but the Committee believes that such a right can be derived from article 18, inasmuch as the obligation to use lethal force may seriously conflict with the freedom of conscience and the right to manifest one's religion or belief.

To the extent that this conflicts with its previous case law,[69] the clash is modest and is circumscribed in a fashion that is not obvious from the text itself. In the drafting process, it was suggested that the phrase 'lethal force' be replaced with 'military service', but this drew the response that:

> Some people objected to military service, for example, because they were averse to discipline, restrictions on personal liberty, etc. Conscientious objection was not an objection to military service as such but an objection to killing other human beings. Equating military service with depriving others of their life might be too much for the public, let alone military officers, to swallow. The term 'lethal force' should therefore be retained. If the Committee agreed that such a thing as a right to refuse military service existed, a claim under Article 18 should be accepted only to the extent that it involved the use of dangerous weapons which might entail loss of human life.[70]

Thus, the refusal to act in a fashion which runs counter to one's conscience can find justification under Article 18, albeit on very narrow grounds.[71] What is left quite unclear is whether even this limited degree of recognition is because it is the manifestation of a religion or belief. As was pointed out earlier, categorizing conscientious objection as a form of belief that gives rise to the right to manifest tends to run counter to the general thrust of the interpretation placed upon that term. Assuming that hurdle is overcome, to put that belief into practice by refusing to act in a fashion required by law itself runs counter to the general thrust of the interpretation placed on the headings of manifestation. For both these reasons it is better to consider conscientious objection as something of an anomaly and not to draw conclusions too readily from the conscientious objector cases for the interpretation of the Article as a whole.

As far as the meaning of 'manifestation' is concerned then, it appears that, as with the notion of 'religion or belief' and despite the General Comment's opening invitation to construe it broadly, it is to be understood in a relatively restrictive fashion.[72]

Restrictions

Whatever view is taken, any form of manifestation is potentially subject to restriction under Article 18(3) and this may have the effect of reducing the significance of securing a recognition for a broader range of activities qualifying as manifestations. Indeed, when the Commission was considering the wording of the General Comment concerning the meaning of 'manifestation', some members seemed more anxious to move on to the question of how to prevent certain forms of manifestation from occurring at all. One particularly important exchange concerned the issue of inherent limitations – that is, the argument that freedom of religion or belief was subject to restrictions flowing from the logic of other Covenant articles in addition to those which might be placed on it at the discretion of the state under Article 18(3).[73] Quite how significant this is in practical terms is unclear, since even those who disputed this accepted that the same result could be achieved through the application of Article 18(3).[74] There is, of course, one important difference between these two approaches: states are not *required* to restrict the enjoyment of the freedom of manifestation, but are simply free to do so if they wish. Nevertheless, if a state which endorses forms of manifestation which run counter to the rights of others fails to protect those whose freedoms are thereby infringed, it is potentially liable for that particular breach of the Covenant obligation. This reduces the difference between these two approaches and, for practical purposes, seems to bring them back into line with each other.[75] The debate about inherent limitations could, therefore, be seen as a question of means rather than ends. However, this would be to miss the point, which is that recourse to inherent limitations tends to place the emphasis on the restriction rather than on the right, and this seems to be the Committee's preference.

This preference is further reflected in the simple assumption that if a manifestation 'conflicts' with another Convention right, then it is the manifestation of religion or belief which has to yield.[76] Reference was made to Article 5(1) of the Covenant, which provides that none of its provisions is to be interpreted as implying a right 'to engage in any activity or perform any act aimed at the destruction of any of the rights and freedoms recognized herein...', as demonstrating that Article 18(1) could not permit, for example, human sacrifice.[77] This is an extreme example, but it is clear that little thought has been given to the proposition that if freedom of worship embraces human sacrifice (let us assume, willingly on the part of the 'sacrificee') and this is not frowned upon by the state and so is not restricted under Article 18(3), then Article 5(1) applies equally to the protection of that Convention right. That right should not be restricted by, for example, the application of other Covenant articles, such as Article 2 on the right to life. Moreover, Article 18(3) refers to restrictions imposed with regard to the 'fundamental' freedoms of others. This qualification is not found in the limitation clauses of other Covenant articles, yet this is not dwelt upon nor its consequences considered in the General Comment.[78]

It seems clear, then, that Committee considers the freedom to manifest a religion or belief to be subject to a number of inherent limitations but, with one exception, this was not directly reflected in the General Comment. The exception concerns Article 20, and paragraph 7 of the General Comment provides that 'according to Article 20, no manifestation of religions or beliefs may amount to propaganda for war or advocacy of national, racial or religious hatred that constitutes incitement to discrimination, hostility or violence'. The failure to expressly acknowledge a more expansive approach in the General Comment is, however, of some symbolic significance since it suggests that the state cannot unduly restrict the manifestation of religion or belief by arbitrarily refusing to recognize the validity of an act which is recognized as such by the believers themselves. Of course, this simply throws the matter back to the Committee. Since it takes a fairly restrictive approach to what forms of act fall within the scope of a 'manifestation' and, as will be seen in the remainder of this section, it takes a fairly expansive approach to the range of legitimate restrictions, not much is necessarily gained by the believer or lost by the state.

Having dealt with inherent limitations, it remains to be seen how the Committee approaches Article 18(3) itself. Paragraph 8 of the General Comment is comparatively lengthy and provides:

Article 18(3) permits restrictions on the freedom to manifest religion or belief only if limitations are prescribed by law and are necessary to protect public safety, order, health or morals, or the fundamental rights and freedoms of others. The freedom from coercion to have or to adopt a religion or belief and the liberty of the parents and guardians to ensure religious and moral education cannot be restricted. In interpreting the scope of permissible limitation clauses, States Parties should proceed from the need to protect the rights guaranteed under the Covenant, including the right to equality and non-discrimination on all grounds specified in Articles 2, 3 and 26. Limitations imposed must be established by law and must not be applied in a manner which would vitiate the rights guaranteed in Article 18.

The Committee observes that Article 18(3) is to be strictly interpreted: restrictions are not allowed on grounds not specified there, even if they would be allowed as restrictions to other rights protected in the Covenant, such as national security. Limitations may be applied only for those purposes for which they were prescribed and must be directly related and proportionate to the specific need on which they are predicated. Restrictions may not be imposed for discriminatory purposes or applied in a discriminatory manner. The Committee observes that the concept of morals derives from many social, philosophical and religious traditions; consequently, limitations on the freedom to manifest a religion or belief for the purpose of protecting morals must be based on principles not deriving exclusively from a single tradition. Persons already subject to certain legitimate constraints, such as prisoners, continue to enjoy their rights to manifest their religion or belief to the fullest extent compatible with the specific nature of the constraint. States Parties' reports should provide information on the full scope and effects of limitation under Article 18(3), both as a matter of law and of their application in specific circumstances.

The discussions surrounding the adoption of this paragraph were long and complex and it is impossible to fully review them here.[79] For current purposes, it is sufficient to draw attention to the fact that a number of members thought that states should be *required* to take action under Article 18(3) when manifestations of religion or belief ran counter to the rights of others[80] and this finds reflection in the third sentence of the General Comment. This positive formulation is, for practical purposes, much the same as adopting the view that there are inherent limitations on the scope of a legitimate manifestation. Beyond that, the text as adopted accurately reflects the tenor of the Article, indicating that a strict approach should be taken to assessing the legitimacy of restrictions.[81]

It is probably fruitless to look to the background work for guidance on how this assessment is to be conducted since it is ultimately one of appreciation in each case. There are few concrete examples of the HRC having to consider this matter in practical situations. If however, these examples are a reliable indicator, then it appears that, despite the call for a strict assessment of restrictions, a fairly latitudinous approach has been in evidence as is illustrated by the following cases.[82]

The earliest case to raise this issue was *Delgardo Páez* v. *Colombia*.[83] The author complained that he had been subjected to various forms of persecution because of his 'progressive ideas in theological and social matters' and, in particular, that he had been forced to give up his position as a teacher of religion. It appears that in Colombia at that time it was necessary for those teaching religion in the state system to be certified by the Catholic religious authorities and this had been withdrawn. The Committee laconically observed that:

... the author's right to profess or to manifest his religion has not been violated. The Committee finds, moreover, that Colombia may, without violating this provision of the Covenant, allow the Church authorities to decide who may teach religion and in what manner it should be taught.[84]

It is not clear why the freedom to manifest belief in teaching was not violated by this action, even if the violation was justified under Article 18(3). However, it is equally unclear what head of limitation actually applies. Both issues are rolled up into a general, unreasoned, assessment.[85]

In *K Singh Bhinder* v. *Canada*[86] the author claimed to be a victim of a violation of Article 18. As a Sikh, his religion required him to wear a turban and his refusal to wear protective headgear at work, as required by law, had resulted in the termination of his contract of employment. The HRC considered that 'If the requirement that a hard hat be worn is regarded as raising issues under Article 18, then it is a limitation that is justified by reference to the grounds laid down in Article 18(3)'. The author had argued that the limitation was not necessary to protect public safety since any risk undertaken was his own, but the Committee took the view that 'requiring workers in federal employment be protected from injury and electric shock by the wearing of hard hats is to be regarded as reasonable and directed towards objective purposes that are compatible with the Covenant'.[87] Paternalistic health and safety legislation therefore seems to fall within the scope of legitimate restrictions.[88]

Notably, the Committee did not consider the proportionality of the measure taken to the need, as is now called for by the General Comment. This was also the case in *AR Coriel and MAR Aurik* v. *The Netherlands*[89] which was considered by the Committee at the session following the adoption of the General Comment. The authors had adopted the Hindu religion and wished to change their surnames, claiming that this was necessary if they were to be able to train as Hindu priests. The Committee declared this aspect of the communication inadmissible since 'the regulation of surnames and the change thereof was eminently a matter of public order and restrictions were therefore permissible under paragraph 3 of article 18'.[90] It is almost as if the finding of a legitimate ground for restricting the enjoyment of the freedom of manifestation is sufficient in itself.

None of these cases is particularly satisfactory, and this is an area which clearly needs revisiting. When considering individual communications in the future, it is to be hoped that the Committee will allow itself to be guided by its own General Comment, just as it hopes the Comment will guide the activities of states. For current purposes, it is sufficient to note that, so far, the Committee has not applied Article 18(3) either rigorously or, indeed, even methodically in practice.

Conclusion

It was argued at the outset that, in order to be able to evaluate the approach taken to freedom of thought, conscience and religion under a human rights instrument, it is necessary to look at the three 'pressure points': what qualifies as a religion or belief, what is a manifestation and what forms of restrictions are permitted on manifestations. This examination of the work of the Human Rights Committee suggests that it takes a fairly restrictive approach to all three, despite deploying language which often implies the opposite.[91]

It really does not matter too much whether conscientious objection is or is not a form of belief for the purposes of Article 18 if the concept of a manifestation is so narrowly drawn that it only actually extends to forms of worship or practices associated with its rituals or teaching the elements of the faith. Liberalism at the entry stage of the Article is only relevant if matched by a certain latitude at the other pressure points. Similarly, the cases reviewed in the previous section show that it is relatively harmless to accept a broader approach to forms of manifestation if one is quick to identify the grounds on which it cannot be permitted.

Perhaps the most abiding impression of an examination of the work of the HRC regarding Article 18 is that freedom of religion is, either expressly or by implication, viewed as more of a problem than as an ambition – something which, although doubtless a good thing in principle, is to be viewed with caution. Behind every argument that is based on it there is, one is led to feel, some danger that must be nipped in the bud. It appears that, in both practical and theoretical terms, the 'case' for freedom of religion[92] within the HRC is much more problematic than it first appears.

Notes

1   Gen. Ass. Res. 217A (III), 10 December 1948.
2   999 UNTS 171.
3   Gen. Ass. Res. 36/55 (1981).
4   M. Scheinin (1992), 'Article 18' in A. Eide (ed.), *The Universal Declaration of Human Rights: A Commentary*, (Oslo: Scandinavian University Press), p. 263.
5   For an excellent concise presentation see B. Dickson (1995), 'The United Nations and Freedom of Religion', *International and Comparative Law Quarterly*, **44**, p. 327 and N. Lerner (1996), 'Religious Human Rights Under the United Nations' in J.D. van der Vyver and J. Witte jr (eds), *Religious Human Rights in Global Perspective: Legal Perspectives*, (The Hague: Martinus Nijhoff). For fuller examinations see, *inter alia*, B.G. Tahzib (1996), *Freedom of Religion or Belief*, (The Hague: Martinus Nijhoff); M.D. Evans (1997), *Religious Liberty and International Law in Europe*, (Cambridge: Cambridge University Press). For the documents and drafting of Article 18 of the

International Covenant, see M.J. Bossuyt (1987), *Guide to the Travaux Préparatoires of the International Covenant on Civil and Political Rights*, (Dordrecht: Martinus Nijhoff), pp. 351–371.

6　The Report was subsequently published as E/CN.4/Sub.2/200/Rev.1.

7　See Report of the Commission on Human Rights, 16th Session, 1960, E/CN.4/804, pp. 18–21.

8　Gen. Ass. Res. 1780 (XVII) and 1781 (XVII), 7 December 1962.

9　Gen. Ass. Res. 1904 (XVIII), 20 November 1963.

10　Gen. Ass. Res. 2106 A (XX), 21 December 1965, 660 UNTS 195. See generally N. Lerner (1980), *The UN Convention on the Elimination of all Forms of Racial Discrimination,* 2nd edn, (Alphen ann den Rijn, the Netherlands): Sijhoff & Noordhof; M. Banton (1996), *International Action Against Racial Discrimination*, (Oxford: Clarendon Press).

11　See E/CN.4/882. It is also set out in the *Report of the Commission on Human Rights*, 21st Session, 1965, E/CN.4/891.

12　Report of the Commission on Human Rights, 23rd Session, 1967, E/CN.4/940, Chapter II and Res. 3 (XXIII), Annex A.

13　See GAOR, 22nd Session, 1967, A/C.3/SR.1511. In addition to the general works referred to in note 5 above, see J. Claydon (1972), 'The Treaty Protection of Religious Rights: UN Draft Convention on the Elimination of all Forms of Intolerance and of Discrimination Based on Religion or Belief', *Santa Clara Lawyer*, **12**, p. 403.

14　At the request of the Sub-Commission, a report on this topic was prepared by Theo Van Boven who voiced caution (see E/CN.4/Sub.2/1989/32) as has the current UN Special Rapporteur (E/CN.4/1994/79, para. 11). The Special Rapporteur's most recent report calls for the creation of 'an international coalition around the 1982 Declaration' (E/CN.4/1999/58, para. 126) but there is no mention of renewed work on a Convention. A meeting of experts had in fact taken place in August 1998 in Oslo, at which the 'Oslo Declaration was adopted and led to the establishment of the Oslo Coalition on Freedom of Religion or Belief'. Reports and documentation from the meeting are reproduced in a Special Issue of the Helsinki Monitor, (1998) *Helsinki Monitor*, **9**, Part 3.

15　Gen. Ass. Res. 36/55 (1981).

16　The only difference of substance between the three instruments concerns the freedom to change religion. Although this was controversial, Article 18 of the UDHR expressly provides that freedom of religion 'includes freedom to change his religion or belief'. This was contested by a number of Islamic states and Article 18 of the ICCPR is deliberately more equivocal, providing that 'This right shall include freedom to have or to adopt a religion or belief of his choice'. In the 1981 Declaration, the words 'or to adopt' were dropped, although a new saving Article (Article 8) was added, which provides that 'Nothing in the present Declaration shall be construed as restricting or derogating from any right defined in the UDHR or ICCPR'. Although it is routinely claimed that freedom of religion embraces the freedom to change one's religion or belief and it is claimed that Article 8 of the Declaration preserves the UDHR provision (see D.J. Sullivan (1988), 'Advancing the Freedom of Religion or Belief through the UN Declaration on the Elimination of Religious Intolerance and Discrimination', *American Journal of International Law*, **81**, p. 487 at p. 495), this is still open to doubt (see Evans, *Religious Liberty, op. cit.*, p. 238).

17　Article 18(4) is an example of a special application of freedom of religion. Since the issues that it raises do not relate to the fundamental principles underpinning the basic scheme of protection, it will not be examined in this chapter.

18   ICCPR, Article 4(2). Whether the rights in Article 18(4) are truly non-derogable is open to question.

19   It has been argued that there are inherent limitations upon Article 18 flowing from other Convention rights, such as the right to life, freedom from torture and the obligation under Article 20(1) to prohibit advocacy of national, racial or religious hatred. The alternative, and preferable, view is that these are factors to be taken into account when assessing the validity of a restriction place on the enjoyment of the right under Article 18(3).

20   Article 19 provides: '1. Everyone shall have the right to hold opinions without interference. 2. Everyone shall have the right to freedom of expression; this right shall include freedom to seek, receive and impart information and ideas of all kinds, regardless of frontiers, either orally, in writing or in print, in the form of art, or through any other media of his choice. 3. The exercise of the rights provided for in paragraph 2 of this article carries with it special duties and responsibilities. It may therefore be subject to certain restrictions, but these shall only be such as are provided by law and are necessary: (a) for respect of the rights or reputations of others; (b) for the protection of national security or of public order (*ordre public*), or of public health or morals.'

21   A chapter of this length must inevitably have a limited focus and it must be acknowledged that aspects of freedom of religion and belief can be protected by other elements of the human rights framework, such as the freedom of expression, private and family life, association and non-discrimination, minority rights and groups' rights (such as indigenous peoples' rights) and so on. However, Article 18 (and its analogues) lies at the heart of the protective web and must surely set the standard and the tone. It merits, therefore, careful examination in its own right. It must also be acknowledged that a further rich source of interpretation lies in the 1981 Declaration (and the subsequent reports of the UN Special Rapporteur), particularly in Article 6 which elaborates at length on the forms of manifestation of religion of belief. However, and perhaps surprisingly, there is little evidence of this having any great direct impact on the HRC although this may change following the election of the Special Rapporteur, Mr Abdulfattah Amor, to the HRC with effect from 1 January 1999. Moreover, the Declaration – if not the work of the Special Rapporteur – has been the subject of more thoroughgoing study. See, for example, N. Lerner (1981), 'Toward a Draft Declaration against Religious Intolerance and Discrimination', *Israeli Yearbook of Human Rights*, **11**, p. 82 and (1982) 'The Final Text of the UN Declaration against Intolerance and Discrimination based on Religion or Belief', *Israeli Yearbook of Human Rights*, **12**, p. 185; Sullivan, 'Advancing the Freedom of Religion or Belief', *op. cit.*; Tahzib, *Freedom of Religion or Belief*, *op. cit.*, pp. 165–212; Evans, *Religious Liberty*, *op. cit.*, pp. 227–61. The same is true of Article 9 of the European Convention on Human Rights. See, for example, D.J. Harris, M. O'Boyle and C. Warbrick (1995), *Law of the European Convention on Human Rights*, (London: Butterworths), pp. 357–71; Evans, *Religious Liberty*, *op. cit.*, pp. 281–341. For all these reasons, this chapter concentrates on the HRC alone. For earlier examinations of the work of the HRC relating to Article 18, see M. Nowak (1993), *UN Covenant on Civil and Political Rights: CCPR Commentary*, (Kehl am Rhein: N.P. Engel), pp. 309–34; Tahzib, *Freedom of Religion or Belief*, *op. cit.*, pp. 249–375; Evans, *Religious Liberty*, *op. cit.*, pp. 207–226.

22   ICCPR, Article 32. For an examination of the composition and organization of the HRC see D. McGoldrick (1991), *The Human Rights Committee*, (Oxford: Oxford University Press), ch. 2; T. Opsahl (1992), 'The Human Rights Committee' in P. Alston (ed.), *The United Nations and Human Rights*, (Oxford: Oxford University Press), p. 369 at pp. 372–382.

23 ICCPR, Article 40. The Committee has recently revised its working practices. The most recent set of Rules of Procedure (CCPR/C/3/Rev.5) came into force on 1 August 1997. The committee issued a revised set of 'Consolidated guidelines for State reports under the International Covenant on Civil and Political Rights' in September 1999, to take effect from 31 December 1999. See CCPR/C/66/GUI and HRC Report, 1999, GOAR A/54/50, paras. 39–40.

24 It was in 1992 that the Committee decided to issue 'Concluding Observations' which 'would be adopted reflecting the views of the Committee as a whole at the end of the consideration of each State party report': see HRC Report, 1992, GAOR A/47/40, para. 45. The first was on Algeria (CCPR/C/79/Add.1, adopted on 9 April 1992 and reproduced in HRC Report, 1993, GAOR A/48/40, paras 292–99). Their significance has been magnified by changes in 1994 to the format of the Report of the HRC to the General Assembly which no longer contains summaries of the discussion but only the texts of the concluding observations: See HRC Report, 1994, GAOR A/49/40. The Summary Records of the Committee's meetings, although public documents, are not readily accessible prior to their publication in the *Official Records of the Human Rights Committee* and, at the time of writing, these do not go beyond 1992–93.

25 By the end of 1999 the Committee had issued almost 120 General Comments, the latest being the Concluding Observation on Hong Kong Special Administrative Region CCPR/C/79/Add.103, adopted on 15 November 1999. Although a considerable number do mention freedom of religion, few do so in terms which cast new light on the meaning of freedom of religion, and, in the few cases in which Article 18 has loomed large, the problems have been so egregious that it lends little to an understanding of the scope of the article. This is not to say that the reporting procedure has not had a significant impact on the HRC's understanding of Article 18. The experience of examining state reports obviously feeds into the approach taken by the Committee and finds a reflection in the General Comment, which can be taken as a distillation of the Committee's experience to that point.

26 As at 30 July 1999, 95 of the 145 states parties to the Covenant accept the right of individuals to lodge communications under the Optional Protocol and over 870 individual communications have been registered, concerning some 60 countries.

27 *LTK* v. *Finland*, Comm. No. 185/1984, Decision of 9 July 1985, HRC Report, 1995, GAOR A/40/40, Annex XXI; Selected Decisions, Vol. II, p. 61; (1985), *Human Rights Law Journal*, **7**, p. 267; *JP* v. *Canada*, Comm. No. 446/1991, Decision of 7 November 1992, HRC Report, 1992, GAOR A/47/40, Vol. II, Annex X, Sect. Y; *JvK and CMGvK-S* v. *The Netherlands*, Comm. No. 483/1991, Decision of 23 July 1992, HRC Report, 1992, GAOR A/47/40, Vol. II, Annex X, Sect. CC; *KV and CV* v. *Germany*, Comm. No. 568/1993, Decision of 8 April 1994, HRC Report, 1994, GAOR A/49/40, Annex X, Sect. CC; (1994), *International Human Rights Reports*, **1**(3), p. 54.

28 *MAB, WAT and J-AYT* v. *Canada*, Comm. No. 570/1993, Decision of 8 April 1994, HRC Report, 1994, GAOR A/49/40, Vol. II, Annex X, Sect. DD; (1994), *International Human Rights Reports*, **1**(3), p. 57.

29 *Delgardo Páez* v. *Colombia*, Comm. No 195/1985, Views of 12 July 1990, HRC Report, 1990, GAOR A/45/40, Vol. II, Annex IX, Sect. D; (1990) *Human Rights Law Journal*, **11**, p. 313; *AR Coeriel and MAR Aurik* v. *the Netherlands*, Views of 31 October 1994, HRC Report, 1995, GAOR A/50/40, Vol. II, Annex X, Sect. D (provisionally published in CCPR/C/57/1, p. 43); (1995) *International Human Rights Reports*, **2**, p. 297.

30 *K Singh Bhinder* v. *Canada*, Comm. No. 208/1986, Views of 9 November 1989, HRC Report, 1990, GAOR A/45/50, 1990, Vol. II, Annex IX, Sect. E.

31　*Hartikainen* v. *Finland*, Comm. No. 40/1978, Views of 9 April 1981, A/36/40, Annex XV; *Selected Decisions*, Vol. I, p. 74; (1981), *Human Rights Law Journal*, **2**, p. 133.

32　Precise categorization of cases is difficult. There have been numerous cases in which violations of Article 18 have been alleged but no evidence has been produced to substantiate the claim, several of which will be mentioned later. There has also been a considerable number of cases involving conscientious objection to military or alternative service which, but for previous jurisprudence to the effect that this does not give rise to issues under Article 18 (see *LTK* v. *Finland*, Comm. No 185/1984, *op. cit.*), would doubtless have been couched in such terms and, in the light of the General Comment, might usefully have done so. Tahzib, *Freedom of Religion or Belief, op. cit.*, pp. 276–306, includes several of these within her catalogue list of 14 cases which, to the end of 1994, had raised Article 18 points. Similarly, there are a number of communications which raise issues under Article 26 (non-discrimination) which are germane to Article 18, the most significant being *Järvinen* v. *Finland*, Comm. No. 295/1988, Views of 25 July 1990, HRC Report, 1990, GAOR A/45/40, Annex IX, Sect. L; (1990), *Human Rights Law Journal*, **11**, p. 324; and *HAGM Brinkhoff* v. *The Netherlands*, Comm. No. 402/1990, Views of 27 July 1993, HRC Report, 1993, GAOR A/48/40, Vol. II, Annex XII, Sect. S; (1994) *International Human Rights Reports*, **1**(2), p. 92.

33　General Comment 22 (48) of 23 July 1993. Doc. CCPR/C/21/Rev.1/Add.4. See HRC Report, 1993, GAOR A/48/40, Annex VI; (1994) *Human Rights Law Journal*, **15**, p. 233.

34　Since only two of the nine cases highlighted above were decided after its adoption, the communication procedures provide little further guidance.

35　The General Comment was considered by the HRC at its 45th Session, July 1992, 1162nd and 1166th meetings (the Summary Records of these meetings are reproduced in CCPR/11, *Official Records of the Human Rights Committee 1991/92*, Vol. I, pp. 337–50); 47th Session, April 1993, 1207th, 1209th and 1224–1226th meetings (CCPR/12, *Official Records of the Human Rights Committee 1992/93*, Vol. I, pp. 159–64; 170–75, 222–34); 48th Session, July 1993, 1236th, 1237th and 1247th meetings (ibid., pp. 270–279, 337–40). For ease of citation, subsequent references to these discussions will be to the relevant page number in the Official Records.

36　For example, the Secretariat Outline provided that 'There shall be freedom of conscience and belief and of private and public religious worship' (E/CN.4/AC.1/3, Article 14). The June 1947 proposals of the Drafting Committee provided that 'Individual freedom of thought and conscience, to hold and to change beliefs, is an absolute and sacred right' and then provided for a limited range of limitations upon the 'practice of a private or public worship, religious observances, and manifestations of differing convictions'. The UK had proposed an alternative text which provided that 'every person shall be free to hold any religious or other belief dictated by his conscience and to change his belief' and this was also referred to the Commission by the Drafting Committee (see E/CN.4/21, paras 13–17).

37　Drawing on the texts submitted to it (see previous note) it produced a composite text which provided: '1. Individual freedom of thought and conscience, to hold and change beliefs, is an absolute and sacred right. 2. Every person has the right, either alone or in community with other persons of like mind and in public or private, to manifest his beliefs in worship, observance, teaching and practice.' See *Report of the Commission on Human Rights*, 2nd Session, 1947, E/600, Annex A, Draft Article 16.

38　An amendment to this effect was proposed by Sweden when the Draft was considered by the 3rd Committee of the General Assembly (see UN Doc. A/C.3/252).

39　GAOR, 3rd Session, 1949, Part I, Third Committee, p. 391.

40   See, for example, the reasons given for rejecting a Cuban proposal which was ex-
     pressly limited to the profession of religious faith (ibid., pp. 393–95). This schematizing
     of the draft was also underscored by the Saudi Arabian argument that the Article was
     unbalanced because it only recognized the right to change a religion or belief, and not
     to change 'thought' or 'conscience' (see UN. Doc. A/C.3/247).

41   Hence an early draft of the Covenant text, which predated the final text of the UDHR
     and provided that 'No one shall be denied freedom of thought, belief, conscience and
     religion, including the freedom to hold any religious or other belief, and to change his
     belief' (E/CN.4/95, Article 16 (1)) was now considered inadequate since it could be
     taken to suggest that other 'beliefs' and not 'religion' could be changed – despite the
     fact that the remainder of that draft also implied that 'religion' and 'belief' were one
     and the same thing.

42   For such states, atheism fell outside the scope of the article altogether. See, for exam-
     ple, the views of the Argentinian delegate who argued that 'although thought and
     conscience were also mentioned in the first sentence, they were obviously to be
     interpreted in the light of the third term, religion. The meaning of the first sentence
     was, therefore, that every one should be free to follow his conscience in spiritual
     matters' (GAOR, 15th Session, 1960, A/C.3/SR.1025, para. 22).

43   Ibid., para. 55.

44   Arcot Krishnaswami (1960), 'Study of Discrimination in Relation to Religious Rights
     and Practices', E/CN.4/Sub.2/200/Rev.1.

45   The original draft of the General Comment was phrased rather differently and provided
     that 'the freedom of thought and the freedom of conscience and belief are protected
     equally with the freedom of religion and ... these freedoms extend to all convictions
     and beliefs'. This was criticized since it associated 'belief' with the freedom of thought
     and conscience whereas Article 18 associated it with religion. It was in response to
     this, and other calls to clarify the relationship between these terms, that the draft was
     amended. See CCPR/C/45/CRP.2, para. 1 in *Official Records of the Human Rights
     Committee 1991/92*, Vol. I, p. 337 and Mr Ndiaye, p. 341, and Mr Dimitrijevic (Rap-
     porteur of the Working Group which had produced the draft), p. 342.

46   Mr Dimitrijevic, ibid., p. 343.

47   For example, Mr Dimitrijevic, ibid., p. 344. This is further underlined by his observa-
     tion that 'the intention of the text was to encompass all religions and beliefs in all their
     diversity and to ensure that certain religious groups which regarded themselves as
     religions and had definite religious practices were protected against any move, on the
     part of the authorities or society, to prevent the exercise of their rights because they
     were not regarded as a religion' (ibid).

48   It is important to note that this does not mean that a state is obliged to officially
     recognize all forms of religion or belief. What is required is that a state does not
     prevent those individuals who adhere to a non-recognized religion from enjoying their
     freedom of religion or belief. See Mrs Higgins (ibid., p. 344) who emphasized that
     'care must be taken to avoid any wording which would emphasize respect for religions
     rather than respect for the freedom of religion'.

49   The reference in the second paragraph of the General Comment to 'institutional char-
     acteristics' is, to say the least, ambiguous. Not only is it unclear what such 'characteris-
     tics' are, but it is also unclear whether it means that religions whose institutional
     characteristics are dissimilar to those of traditional religions are nevertheless religions
     for the purposes of Article 18 or that it is unnecessary for a religion to have any
     institutional characteristics at all.

50   See, for instance, Mrs Higgins, *Official Records of the Human Rights Committee 1991/ 92, op. cit.*, Vol. I., p. 343; Mr Lallah, ibid., p. 346.

51   The principal difference between the two is that rights protected under Article 18 are non-derogable in times of emergency and hence have a more fundamental aspect to them, which arguably might be of some significance should the question of balancing competing claims under these two articles arise.

52   A proposal to make this clear in the text of the General Comment was abandoned since it was felt to be unwise to comment on the restriction upon the freedom of expression in a General Comment on another article. However, the discussions suggest that not all forms of manifestations of conscience would necessarily amount to forms of expression. See generally *Official Records of the Human Rights Committee 1992/93*, Vol. I, pp. 174–75. This holds open the prospect that acting in accordance with one's conscience (to the extent that they could be grounded in Article 18(1)) would be an absolute and unrestricted freedom, receiving greater protection than the manifestation of religion or belief. This seems an unlikely outcome and it is more likely that only those forms giving realization to one's conscience which amount to an exercise of the freedom of expression receive protection and are subject to limitation under Article 19(3). Of course, if the pattern of 'conscience' forms a 'belief' for the purposes of Article 18, manifestations are protected by that article in any case.

53   It also raises the question of the boundary between the public and private spheres. Locating this boundary is, if anything, even more problematic but, except to the extent that it is bound up with the notion of a 'manifestation', its consideration lies beyond the scope of this chapter.

54   Alternatively it could be seen as a form of manifestation of a religious belief. The problem with the second approach is that it would mean distinguishing between conscientious objectors to military service according to the motivation for their beliefs.

55   *MAB, WAT and J-AYT* v. *Canada*, Comm No. 570/1993, *op. cit.* For an earlier American example of a marijuana religion, see *United States* v. *Kuch*, 288 F Supp. 438 (1968).

56   It has, however, been pointed out that this decision leaves open the door for those whose worship or belief is not 'primarily or exclusively' centred on drugs. See Tahzib, *Freedom of Religion or Belief, op. cit.*, p. 279.

57   It might be noted that early in the drafting of Article 18 it had been argued by the Nigerian delegate that 'Every individual should have the right to worship as he saw fit, even if he chose to worship a rock or a river': GAOR, 15th Session, 1960, A/C.3/ SR.1023, para. 23.

58   *MA* v. *Italy*, Comm. No. 117/1981, Views of 10 April 1984, HRC Report, 1984, GAOR A/39/40, Annex XIV; *Selected Decisions*, Vol. II, p. 31.

59   Nowak, *UN Covenant, op. cit.*, note 21 above, p. 321.

60   Ibid.

61   Ibid.

62   See *JP* v. *Canada*, Comm. No. 446/1991, *op cit.*, para. 4.2 (emphasis added).

63   Nowak, *UN Covenant, op. cit.*, p. 321.

64   See *Leonardus J De Groot* v. *The Netherlands*, Comm. No. 578/1994, Decision of 14 July 1995, HRC Report, 1995, GAOR A/50/40, Vol. II, Annex XI, Sect. K (provisionally published in CCPR/C/57/1, p. 203); (1996) *International Human Rights Reports*, **3**, p. 1; *Gerrit van der Ent* v. *The Netherlands*, Comm. No. 657/1995, Comm. No. 657/ 1995, Decision of 3 November 1995, HRC Report, 1996, GAOR A/51/40, Vol. II, Annex IX, Sect. I; (1996) *International Human Rights Reports*, **3,** p. 285.

65   *LTK* v. *Finland*, Comm. No. 185/1984, *op. cit.*

66   For example, *RTZ* v. *The Netherlands*, Comm. No. 245/1987, Decision of 24 March 1988, HRC Report, 1988, GAOR A/43/40, Annex VIII, Sect. H; *Selected Decisions*, Vol. II, p. 73; *MJG* v. *The Netherlands*, Comm. No. 267/1987, Decision of 24 March 1988, HRC Report, 1988, GAOR A/43/40, Annex VIII, Sect. K; *Selected Decisions*, Vol. II, p. 74; *HAEdJ* v. *The Netherlands*, Comm. No. 297/1988, Decision of 30 October 1989, HRC Report, 1990, GAOR A/45/40, Annex X, Sect. N; *CBD* v. *The Netherlands*, Comm. No. 394/1990, Decision of 22 July 1992, HRC Report, 1992, GAOR A/47/140, Annex X, Sect. P; *JPK* v. *The Netherlands*, Comm. No. 401/1990, Decision of 7 November 1991, HRC Report, 1992, GAOR A/47/40, Annex X, Sect. T; *TWMB* v. *The Netherlands*, Comm. No. 403/1990, Decision of 7 November 1991, HRC Report, 1992, GAOR A/47/40, Annex X, Sect. U. See also the communications referred to in notes 67 and 68 below, which flow from this position.

67   For example, *Järvienen* v. *Finland*, Comm. No. 295/1988 and *HAGM Brinkhoff* v. *The Netherlands*, Comm. No. 402/1990, *op cit.*

68   See *JP* v. *Canada*, Comm. No. 446/1991, *op. cit.* para. 4.2; *JvK and CMGvKS* v. *The Netherlands*, Comm. No. 583/1991, ibid., *KV and CV* v. *Germany*, Comm. No. 568/1993, ibid.

69   For an argument that they need not be construed as in conflict see Evans, *Religious Liberty*, *op. cit.*, pp. 216–19 but cf. the Summary Records which do indicate that the Committee was aware that it was changing its position.

70   Mr Dimitrijevic, *Official Records of the Human Rights Committee 1992/92*, Vol. I, p. 278.

71   It might be noted that, even in the restrictive formulation, it seems difficult to reconcile with *ARU* v. *The Netherlands*, Comm. No. 509/1992, Decision of 19 October 1993, HRC Report, 1994, GAOR A/49/40, Vol. II, Annex X, Sect. Q; (1994) *International Human Rights Reports*, 1(2), p. 55 in which the applicant had unsuccessfully argued that his objection was not to military service *per se* but to involvement as an accessory to the preparation and use of nuclear weapons. This would rather suggest that only direct involvement in the use of lethal force would be sufficient to ground the claim.

72   But cf. *AR Coriel and MAR Aurik* v. *The Netherlands*, Comm. No. 453/1991, *op. cit.*, above in which, and by implication, the Committee seems to have accepted that seeking to change one's name could be a form of manifesting one's religion or belief. This would be a fairly liberal view of what amounts to a 'manifestation' but given the manner in which it arises – the peremptory dismissal of this aspect of the claim – too much should not be drawn from this. See also the Individual Opinion of Mr Ando, ibid., Appendix, who noted that 'it was not impossible to argue' that a request to change one's family name was a form of manifestation.

73   Thus Mrs Chanet (*Official Records of the Human Rights Committee 1991/92*, Vol. I, pp. 346–7) argued that acts such as human sacrifice and mutilation 'were not authorized as part of the religious observance mentioned in Article 18(1)' and 'freedom to manifest one's religion covered a broad range of acts which could not, however, be contrary to the Covenant'. This drew the protest from Mrs Higgins that this was 'tantamount to allowing the authorities of a State freedom to choose which manifestations of religion should be guaranteed ... it was not the Committee's responsibility to decide what should constitute a manifestation of religion' (ibid., p. 347).

74   Cf. Mrs Higgins, ibid., who, although she 'resolutely opposed the idea that States could have complete latitude to decide what was and what was not a genuine belief [since] [t]he contents of a religion should be defined by the worshippers themselves', accepted that 'it was obviously necessary for the Committee to ensure that there was

no violation of other rights protected by the Covenant ... [but] ... [a] strict application of Article 18(3) would be sufficient'.

75   For example, it may be that the individual does not object to the act in question (say, some form of ritual which could be construed as violating other Covenant rights) and so does not seek to challenge the practice. For the Committee to take this up in the face of acquiescence (or approval) by the erstwhile 'victim' may seem unduly intrusive. The same could, however, be said of the Committee's refusing the accept the validity of the act being seen as a manifestation in the first place.

76   For example, Mr Ndiaye, *Official Records of the Human Rights Committee 1991/92*, Vol. I, p. 348: 'Whether or not the Committee indicated that religious observance and practice should in no circumstances entail a violation of the provisions of the Covenant changed nothing, as that went without saying.'

77   Mr Wennergren, ibid.

78   Indeed, its impact was minimized. In the original draft of the paragraph, the third sentence had enjoined states to proceed from the need to protect the 'fundamental rights', as set out in the text of Article 18(3). However, the word 'fundamental' was removed, to avoid giving the impression that some rights were more important than others (Mr Pocar, *Official Records of the Human Rights Committee 1992/93*, Vol. I, p. 233; Mr Dimitrijevic, ibid.) and, as a consequence, potentially affected the balance between competing claims under the Covenant in a manner not provided for in the text.

79   For a fuller overview see Tahzib, *Freedom of Religion or Belief, op. cit.*, pp.334–343.

80   Ms Evatt, *Official Records of the Human Rights Committee 1992/93*, Vol. I, p. 232; Mr Dimitrijevic, ibid., p. 229.

81   One particular point of controversy should, however, be mentioned. There was considerable concern that state should not be able to justify restriction on the basis of 'morals' if its conception of morality was closely associated with a particular set of beliefs. Clearly, there is a danger that this could become a route through which the attitudes of a majority religion could bear upon others. This is addressed in the General Comment which, in effect, requires the state to refrain from adopting a single concept of morality and to adopt a pluralistic approach. Despite observations to the contrary, it is difficult to see this as being other than as pulling in the direction of a secular form of morality and reinforces the notion that the place for religion or belief is in private rather than public affairs.

82   Cf. Mr Sadi, *Official Records of the Human Rights Committee 1992/93*, Vol. I, p. 229 and Mrs Higgins, ibid., who felt it necessary to remind the Committee that when considering Article 18(3) it was the right and not the limitation which should be kept to the fore.

83   *Delgardo Páez* v. *Colombia*, Comm. No. 195/1985, *op. cit.*

84   Ibid., para. 5.7.

85   It may be that the Committee viewed this as akin to a matter of 'internal' ordering of church affairs and was, therefore, not a matter for state involvement.

86   *K Singh Bhinder* v. *Canada*, Comm. No. 208/1986, *op. cit.*

87   Ibid., para. 6.2. This latter comment was made in the context of the claim of discrimination under Article 26 but it would appear to be equally pertinent to the nature of the restriction under Article 18(3).

88   For discussion see Tahzib, *op. cit.*, note 5 above, pp. 294–300, who also points out that this may raise issues under Article 17 (private life).

89   *AR Coriel and MAR Aurik* v. *The Netherlands*, Comm. No. 453/1991, *op. cit.*

90   Ibid., para. 6.1. The Committee ultimately concluded that there had, however, been a violation of Article 17.

91 This chapter has focused on the HRC. Although this is not intended to be a comparative analysis, it should be pointed out that similar conclusions can be drawn from the experience under the ECHR. See, for example, T. Jeremy Gunn (1996), 'Adjudicating Rights of Conscience under the European Convention on Human Rights' in Van der Vyver and Witte jr, *Religious Human Rights*, *op. cit.*, p. 305. This analysis is supported by more recent developments: For example, *Pendragon* v. *UK*, App. No. 31416/96, Commission Decision of 19 October 1998, unpublished (the failure to address the question of whether Druidism is a religion or belief for the purposes of Article 9 when a legitimate form of restriction offered a less contentious way forward) and Eur. Court HR, *Canea Catholic Church* v. *Greece*, Judgment of 16 December 1997, *Reports of Judgments and Decisions* 1997–VIII, p. 2843, in which the Court declined to consider whether the ability to bring legal proceedings in order to ensure that movable and immovable property could be used in worship and observance was a form of manifestation under Article 9 *per se* (para. 48), the Commission having considered it to be so by a narrow margin (cf. the ten dissenting and two concurring opinions, all of which doubted whether such an inability affected the manifestation of worship or observance at all). For a consideration of recent trends in ECHR Article 9 jurisprudence, see also P. Edge (1998), 'The European Court of Human Rights and Religious Rights', *International and Comparative Law Quarterly*, **47**, p. 680.

92 Cf. note 4 above.

4 Neutrality, Separation and Accommodation: Tensions in American First Amendment Doctrine

Michael W. McConnell

Non-specialists are often surprised at the chaotic, controversial and unpredictable character of the constitutional law of church and state in the United States. Every schoolchild knows that the American founders erected a 'wall of separation between church and state'. In the 200 years since adoption of the Free Exercise and Establishment Clauses, the US Supreme Court has decided scores of cases involving everything from the religious use of peyote to moments of silence in public schools. Surely the basic principles and contours of constitutional doctrine must be clear by now. An examination of constitutional controversies in the courts shows, however, that the law in this field is very much in flux and that, even before the changes of the 1990s, the law was riddled with inconsistencies and incoherence. It is important to understand why, and to ask whether there is any prospect for improvement in the future.

The Sources of Tension

The First Amendment's Religion Clause contains two parts, expressed in a single sentence: 'Congress shall make no law respecting an establishment of religion or prohibiting the free exercise thereof.' (This provision, which originally applied only to Congress, has since been extended to apply to all levels of government – federal, state, and local.) But although most theorists and constitutional historians affirm that the two halves of the Religion

63

Clause are designed to work harmoniously, in service of a consistent constitutional vision, in practice the Supreme Court has interpreted the two provisions independently, in ways that clash with one another.

Much of the problem stems from the fact that the Court has been unable to make up its collective mind about what purposes are to be served by the Religion Clauses. There are at least three candidates. First, there is the separationist ideal: that the Religion Clauses are designed to distinguish between a secular public sphere and a private sphere (family, church, private institutions) in which religion can flourish freely. In this model, the public sphere is strictly secular in nature: laws are based on secular premises, government programmes and activities are strictly secular in nature, and religion is deemed to be irrelevant to determination of the citizens' civic obligations. Religion is protected, but only in a privatized form, stripped of any public dimension. Second, there is an ideal of neutrality: the government must be evenhanded, neither favouring nor disfavouring religion or any particular religion. Religion is understood as one form of voluntary association among many, neither feared nor favoured, and the government draws no distinctions on the basis of religion, whether for the imposition of burdens or for the bestowal of benefits. Government is religion-blind, neutral between religions, and neutral between religion and non-religion. Third, there is an ideal of religious liberty: that the Religion Clauses are designed to protect religious freedom. The Free Exercise Clause protects religious practice from governmental interference, and the Establishment Clause protects against government action that may coerce, induce or (perhaps) even endorse religion. The animating purpose of the Religion Clauses under this interpretation is to enable people of all religious persuasions to be citizens of the commonwealth with the least possible violence to their religious convictions.[1]

While these ideals are compatible at a high level of abstraction, in practice they conflict. In a world in which government has pervasive contact with the institutions of civil society, it is not logically possible to preserve a 'strict separation' and at the same time maintain a scrupulous neutrality. Separation requires special treatment for religion (whether by refraining from providing 'aid' to religious institutions or by protecting them from regulatory impositions). But 'special treatment' is precisely what 'neutrality' forbids. Moreover, a robust protection for the free exercise of religion is neither neutral (in the formal sense) nor entirely compatible with the idea that the government may not give special aid or assistance to religion. Protection of freedom of religion can be seen as a form of aid to religion. Thus, in particular cases and controversies, the Court has been forced to choose between these various understandings. The results have been hopelessly inconsistent.

This inconsistency manifests itself most clearly in the two most frequently litigated areas of constitutional conflict: cases in which religious
institutions and religiously motivated individuals (usually, but not always,
members of minority faiths) seek to be exempted from the requirements of
the general civil or criminal law, and cases in which taxpayers seek to
prevent use of tax money by religious institutions or for the communication
of religious messages. In the former context, the ideal of religious liberty
conflicts with the ideal of formal neutrality. Should we extend special accommodations to religion, or should we adhere to facially-neutral laws? In
the latter context, the ideal of separation is in conflict with the ideal of
neutrality. Should assistance to religious schools or other religious activities
be seen as a form of 'aid' to religion, or merely as equal treatment? The two
contexts can thus be seen as mirror images. In one, the ideal of formal
neutrality competes with the ideal of maximizing religious freedom and, in
the other, formal neutrality competes with the ideal of no-aid separationism.
Let us look at each context more closely.

The Question of Free Exercise Accommodations

One of the great recurring questions of First Amendment doctrine has been
whether to interpret the Free Exercise Clause as protecting the freedom of
individuals and religious institutions to adhere to their religious convictions
even in the face of contrary laws or government policies. Some say that the
principle of free exercise entails some such protection provided exceptions
or accommodations can be made without excessive injury to important
governmental interests. Others say that the free exercise principle goes no
further than protecting believers and religious institutions from discriminatory enactments that single out religion, *qua* religion, for unfavourable
treatment. It is a clash between the ideal of religious liberty on the one hand,
and formal neutrality on the other. The ideal of 'separation' is indeterminate
in this context. Some say Church and state are 'separated' when the state
refrains from regulating religiously significant activity; some say that religious accommodations are a form of 'aid' to religion and embroil the
government in evaluating the strength and importance of various religious
claims. Thus, self-styled 'separationists' can be found on both sides of these
conflicts.

The extent of protection for religious practices that conflict with legal
obligations is one of the oldest questions in American constitutional law. As
early as 1793, the Pennsylvania Supreme Court faced the issue when a Jew
named Jonas Phillips was subpoenaed to give evidence in court on Saturday,
the day of the Jewish sabbath.[2] (In those days, the courts, like most busi-
nesses, operated six days a week.) The trial court fined Phillips ten pounds for

refusing to testify, but an appeal was aborted when the party who subpoenaed Phillips released him from the obligation. In 1813 a New York court held that it is unconstitutional to require a Roman Catholic priest to divulge information learned about criminal activity under seal of the confessional.[3] In 1831 the Pennsylvania Supreme Court declined to follow the New York precedent and held that 'every other obligation shall yield to that of the laws, as to a superior moral force'.[4] According to the Court, any accommodation of religious conscience must be made by the legislature, and cannot be claimed as of right. Courts in three other states faced similar controversies prior to the Civil War: one decided that free exercise requires accommodation; one decided that free exercise requires only neutrality; and one ducked the issue.[5]

For most of its first 150 years, the US Supreme Court rejected all claims for free exercise accommodation, although it did so not on the basis of neutrality theory but on other grounds, most of which have been rejected by modern law. The first claim, involving a Catholic cathedral in New Orleans prohibited under the terms of a municipal health ordinance from performing open casket funerals, was rejected on the ground that the First Amendment does not apply to state and local legislation. The second, by a Mormon polygamist, was rejected on the basis of the belief–conduct distinction. In another case, a state prevented a Jehovah's Witness child from assisting her guardian in the distribution of religious materials, ostensibly as a violation of child labour laws. This action was upheld on the basis of the state's authority to protect children from being martyred to their parents' religious view – a legal doctrine that is legitimate in its place, but was absurd on the facts of the case. A challenge to a requirement that male students at a public university take military instruction was turned aside on the theory that attendance at university is a privilege, not a right.[6] The Court addressed the accommodation–neutrality question squarely for the first time in *Minersville School District* v. *Gobitis*,[7] a 1940 case holding that Jehovah's Witness schoolchildren could be punished for refusing to engage in the flag salute. In an opinion by Justice Frankfurter, the Court held:

> Conscientious scruples have not, in the course of the long struggle for religious toleration, relieved the individual from obedience to a general law not aimed at the promotion or restriction of religious beliefs. The mere possession of religious convictions which contradict the relevant concerns of a political society does not relieve the citizen from the discharge of political responsibilities.[8]

Gobitis, however, was overruled three years later in *West Virginia Board of Education* v. *Barnette*.[9]

The Court confronted the issue with increasing frequency during the final quarter of the twentieth century, producing opinions which vacillated between the free exercise accommodation theory and the formal neutrality theory. In *Sherbert* v. *Verner*,[10] the first, and for a long time the leading, case in the US Supreme Court's modern free exercise jurisprudence, the Court held that the state was required to excuse a Seventh-Day Adventist from the requirement of being available for work on Saturday as a condition of eligibility for unemployment compensation. According to the Court, the requirement of availability for Saturday work was equivalent to imposing a 'fine' for the applicant's religious practice. Where a law burdens the exercise of a religious tenet in this way, the government is required to show that it serves a compelling governmental interest. In the Court's words:

> If, therefore, the decision of the South Carolina Supreme Court is to withstand the appellant's constitutional challenge, it must be either because her disqualification as a beneficiary represents no infringement by the State of her constitutional rights of free exercise, or because any incidental burden on the free exercise of the appellant's religion may be justified by a 'compelling state interest in the regulation of a subject within the State's constitutional power to regulate'.[11]

This means, in effect, that religious reasons for being unavailable for work enjoy a protection that other conscientious reasons do not necessarily receive. The state is 'constitutionally compelled to carve out an exception – and to provide benefits – for those whose unavailability is due to their religious convictions', as Justice Harlan disapprovingly put the point in dissent.[12] Some say that this is a troubling 'favouring' of religion; others find this special treatment inherent in a constitutional text that singles out the free exercise 'of religion' as a constitutional right.

The *Sherbert* decision created the potential for challenges by religious groups and individual believers to a wide range of laws. For example, in the same year that the Court decided *Sherbert*, it overturned the contempt conviction of a religious objector who refused jury service.[13] A decade later, the Court exempted members of the Old Order Amish and the Conservative Amish Mennonite Churches from compulsory education of children beyond the age of sixteen.[14] It also reiterated its unemployment compensation holding in a variety of circumstances.

But although this free-exercise doctrine appeared to embrace the protection of religious freedom as its central ideal, the competing ideal of neutrality continued to influence decisions. Some Justices never became reconciled to the idea of constitutionally compelled religious accommodations, and others applied the doctrine only sparingly. In almost every case outside of the unemployment context, the Court found either that the law placed no cognizable burden on religious exercise or that the government's interest was compelling.

In 1990, in *Employment Division* v. *Smith*,[15] a member of the Native American Church contended that peyote, a hallucinogenic drug banned under the criminal law, could be used in religious ceremonies. Under the *Sherbert* standard, the Court would have had to decide whether this law served a compelling governmental interest. Instead the Court broke from prior precedent and held that 'the right of free exercise does not relieve an individual of the obligation to comply with a valid and neutral law of general applicability on the ground that the law proscribes (or prescribes) conduct that his religion prescribes (or proscribes)'.[16] If the law is 'generally applicable', the government need not show that it serves an important (let alone compelling) purpose, even if its effect – as in *Smith* itself – is to make the practice of a religion virtually impossible. Any religious accommodation from a neutral and generally applicable law must be left to the political process. As the Court explained:

> [T]o say that a nondiscriminatory religious-practice exemption is permitted, or even that it is desirable, is not to say that it is constitutionally required, and that the appropriate occasions for its creation can be discerned by the courts. It may fairly be said that leaving accommodation to the political process will place at a relative disadvantage those religious practices that are not widely engaged in; but that unavoidable consequence of democratic government must be preferred to a system in which each conscience is a law unto itself or in which judges weigh the social importance of all laws against the centrality of all religious beliefs.[17]

The *Smith* decision immediately stirred opposition from religious and civil libertarian groups. In response, Congress passed a statute, the Religious Freedom Restoration Act of 1993, creating a legislative remedy for any action by state, local or federal government that 'substantially burdens' the exercise of religion without 'compelling justification'. Thus, the governing standard in free exercise cases shifted back to the prior test – but only briefly. In *City of Boerne* v. *Flores*,[18] the Court held that the Religious Freedom Restoration Act is unconstitutional, at least as applied to state and local governments. Thus, in a few short years, the constitutional standard flipped from substantive protection for religious freedom (*Sherbert*), to formal neutrality (*Smith*), back to substantive protection (Religious Freedom Restoration Act), and then to a mixture of substantive protection from acts of the federal government and formal neutrality with respect to state and local government (*Boerne*).

In fact, it is even more complicated than that. From colonial times to the present, legislatures have commonly enacted exemptions or accommodations for religious dissenters into the statutory law of the land. These have addressed such disparate religious concerns as conscientious exemption from military conscription, exemption from certain meat inspection standards for kosher butchers, exemption from Social Security for the self-employed Amish, and exemptions from employment discrimination laws for certain religious employers. The constitutionality of these accommodation statutes is frequently challenged under the Establishment Clause, on the theory that they 'favour' religion over non-religion. The US Supreme Court has never accepted that argument in its extreme form, but it has overturned several accommodation statutes on the ground that they go too far – that they effectively 'endorse' religion or provide too 'absolute' a protection or benefit to too narrow a group. Unfortunately, the precise constitutional standard to be applied to these statutes has never been entirely clear.[19] Thus, it appears that the 'neutrality' standard is not compelled in that the political branches may make and enforce classifications on the basis of religious belief where this would accommodate the free exercise of religion, at least in some circumstances.

No-Aid Separationism

Another area of controversy has involved government financial assistance to religiously affiliated social welfare institutions, such as hospitals, schools and homeless shelters. It is generally agreed that it would be unconstitutional for the government to favour religious over non-religious recipients in the distribution of aid, but it is hotly contested whether religious institutions of this sort may receive aid on a neutral basis, as part of generally applicable welfare programmes. The affirmative case was concisely explained by Professor Carl Esbeck:

> Rightly interpreted, the Establishment Clause does not require that faith-based providers censor their religious expression and secularize their identity as conditions of participation in a governmental program. So long as the welfare program has as its object the public purpose of society's betterment – that is, help for the poor and needy – and so long as the program is equally open to all providers, religious and secular, then the First Amendment requirement that the law be neutral as to religion is fully satisfied.[20]

Others contend that subsidizing religious institutions effectively coerces taxpayers to support religion – at least where the religious and secular functions of the recipient cannot be clearly separated, as frequently they cannot.

During the nineteenth century this issue was usually resolved politically. State legislatures frequently provided subsidies to religiously affiliated hospitals, orphanages and other social welfare institutions, with little opposition. Most of these institutions were affiliated with Protestant churches, but Catholic and Jewish institutions received at least formally equal treatment. In its sole nineteenth-century foray into funding issues, the US Supreme Court unanimously held that the fact that a recipient institution (a hospital) was 'conducted under the auspices of the Roman Catholic Church', which 'exercise[d] great and perhaps controlling influence over the management of the hospital', was 'wholly immaterial'.[21] Ever since that time, church-related groups and institutions providing non-educational social services have routinely been recipients of government aid.[22]

Aid to private education, however, was hugely controversial. Until the 1830s, no established system of public education existed, and governmental aid chiefly took the form of grants to charity schools and quasi-private educational institutions, many of them denominational in character. After that time, a combination of the Common School movement, which urged that children of all classes and religions be educated together, and fear of rising levels of Catholic immigrants, led every state in the Union to cease aid to 'sectarian' schools, most of which were Catholic. (Indeed, the term 'sectarian' was effectively a code word for 'Catholic'.[23]) Particularly after the Vatican Decrees of 1870 regarding papal infallibility, many Americans believed that Catholicism was an antidemocratic force and that Catholic education was inimical to American values. This was the primary spur to the no-aid movement.[24] A constitutional amendment, which would have protected (Protestant) prayer in the public schools while denying funds to 'sectarian' alternatives, narrowly failed in the US Senate. Even without a constitutional amendment, however, aid to 'sectarian' schools fell victim to the Common School ideal in combination with anti-Catholic bigotry. After the Second World War, when a few states began to experiment with aid to non-public education, the 'no aid to sectarian schools' tradition was firmly established, and was often considered to be part of the constitutional principle of the Establishment Clause.

The issue first surfaced in the US Supreme Court in 1947, in *Everson* v. *Board of Education*.[25] *Everson* involved a New Jersey statute that paid the cost of school transportation to both public and non-public (including religious) schools. Justice Black's opinion for the Court was uncharacteristically indecisive; it resembled one of those comedy routines in which the good angel whispers in the character's right ear and the naughty devil in the left. Part of the Court's opinion trumpeted an uncompromising vision of no-aid separationism: 'No tax in any amount, large or small, can be levied to support any religious activities or institutions, whatever they may be called, or whatever form they may adopt to teach or practice religion.'[26] The very next paragraph seemed to take it back: 'On the other hand,' the Court stated, 'New Jersey cannot ... exclude individual Catholics, Lutherans, Mohammedans, Baptists, Jews, Methodists, Non-believers, Presbyterians, or the members of any other faith, because of their faith, or lack of it, from receiving the benefits of public welfare legislation.'[27] The Court seemed not to notice that these declarations pointed in opposite directions. If taxes may not be used to support religious institutions, the effect is to deny those who attend religious schools the benefits of public welfare legislation on account of their religious choices. In *Everson*, the Court decided to allow the neutral aid – while warning that this went to 'the verge' of the state's constitutional authority.[28] This warning was a harbinger of cases to come.

In the next decision, *Board of Education* v. *Allen*,[29] over an angry dissent by Justice Black, the Court adhered to the neutrality interpretation, upholding a state law providing secular textbooks to all schoolchildren, in religious as well as public and private secular schools. The Court also held that the Establishment Clause permits states to exempt churches, along with other non-profit charitable organizations, from property taxes.[30] The Court seemed to distinguish, however, between tax exemptions and 'a direct money subsidy' which, the Court implied, would be unconstitutional.

In the 1970s the Court shifted to the no-aid separationist perspective. In the leading case of *Lemon* v. *Kurtzman*[31] the Court struck down state programmes that subsidized teachers' salaries in non-public schools. Although the principal section of the opinion rested on the ground that the statutes, which required the subsidized teachers to eliminate all religious elements from their instruction, was an excessive interference with the religious autonomy of the schools, other sections of the opinion laid the groundwork for invalidating a host of educational aid programmes. In one section of the opinion the Court stated that the government must be 'certain' that aid is not used for religious instruction – a requirement so exacting that it could be enforced only by measures that would be unconstitutional in themselves. In another section, the Court held that the mere 'political divisiveness' of the issue was sufficient ground to hold assistance to religious schools unconstitutional.

Nonetheless, the Justices felt the tug of the neutrality argument and hesitated to deny public benefits to people on the basis of their constitutionally protected decision to attend religious institutions. It was widely assumed, for example, that needy children should be able to obtain federally subsidized school lunches no matter where they went to school; that military veterans should be able to use their 'GI Bill Benefits' to attend religious as well as secular institutions; and that religious institutions would continue to benefit from police, fire, road, mail, and other general public programmes. In addition, the Court never overruled decisions upholding aid to religious education in the form of transportation, textbooks and tax exemptions, nor did it ever extend the logic of the no-aid position to social services outside the field of elementary and secondary education. Thus, the Court articulated a seemingly absolute constitutional theory of no-aid separationism, while implicitly tolerating a multitude of practices that were based on the ideal of neutrality. There seemed to be no logic to when the theory triumphed over the practice, or vice versa.

By the late 1970s the Court had proclaimed that the Establishment Clause forbids any 'substantial aid' to the 'educational function' of 'pervasively religious' institutions.[32] Yet this seemingly absolute standard raised as many questions as it answered. How much aid is 'substantial'? How could the courts distinguish between aid to the 'educational functions of the schools' and to the physical, psychological, social and pedagogical needs of the students? Moreover, how could the courts distinguish between 'pervasively sectarian' and 'non-pervasively sectarian' institutions? The latter question was particularly troublesome, since it forced government agencies to discriminate among religious institutions on the basis of the degree of their religiosity. In practice, the line between institutions that are 'pervasively sectarian' and those that were merely 'religiously affiliated' tended to track the nineteenth-century practice: elementary and secondary schools were automatically 'pervasively sectarian' and everything else (except houses of worship) was merely religious.

The cases from the late 1970s were almost comical in their confusion. Textbooks could be provided to children attending religious schools, but not maps or library books. (What will they do with atlases, which are 'maps in books', wondered Senator Moynihan on the floor of the Senate.) Transportation could be provided to the religious school, but not from the religious school to a secular site for a field trip. Speech, hearing and other diagnostic services could be provided on the premises of religious schools, but not remedial services. Remedial services could not be provided in the religious school building, but could be provided in a portable classroom parked at the kerb. Parents could receive tax credits for the costs of tuition, but not tuition grants. College students could use government loans and scholarships to attend religious colleges and small children could use government grants to attend religiously based day care, but elementary and secondary students were denied the use of government grants or loans to attend religiously affiliated schools. Religiously-oriented social service providers could be given grants to encourage adolescent sexual self-discipline, but public school teachers could not teach remedial maths to students at religious schools. Commentators on and off the Court, from across the jurisprudential spectrum, found the decisions from this era incomprehensible and unprincipled. Constitutional historian Leonard Levy observed that:

... the Court has managed to unite those who stand at polar opposites on the results that the Court reaches; a strict separationist and a zealous accommodationist are likely to agree that the Supreme Court would not recognize an establishment of religion if it took life and bit the Justices.[33]

During the 1970s the neutrality position almost disappeared. The decisions described above were not produced by vacillation between the two theories, but by incoherence in the separationist camp. Some Justices believed that the forms of aid in question were sufficiently secular in character that they did not constitute aid to religion. Other Justices believed that any aid to religiously affiliated ('pervasively sectarian') schools necessarily aided religion or at least generated unconstitutional divisiveness along religious lines. Thus, religious schools either won because they were secular enough or lost because they were irredeemably religious. Almost lost during this period was the idea that the government should not use the religiosity of the recipient as a basis for classification.

Matters began to shift in 1981. The case that precipitated the shift, oddly enough, was not an educational aid case, nor even primarily a Religion Clause case. In *Widmar* v. *Vincent*[34] students at a public university asked to use an empty room to meet for Bible study and prayer, pursuant to a university policy allowing student groups to use the facilities for meetings. Citing the state constitution's policy of separation between Church and state, the university denied the application. The students sued under the Free Speech Clause, citing cases involving radical student groups in which it had been held that the government may not deny access to a public forum to groups based on the content of their speech. As a free speech case, *Widmar* was easy: if political radicals can meet on campus, so can Bible students. Moreover, the Court found the university's Establishment Clause defence unpersuasive: since the 'forum is available to a broad class of nonreligious as well as religious speakers,' the Court observed, 'any benefit to religion is purely "incidental".'[35] There were no dissents on this point. None of the Justices realized that the principle in *Widmar*, if applied generally, is flatly inconsistent with the Court's no-aid cases. Since the aid in those cases was available to a broad class of non-religious, as well as religious, students, any benefit to religion in those cases was also 'incidental'. But the contradiction was not apparent at the time. *Widmar* was a free speech case, and no one could have cause to suspect that the public university, which had tried to exclude the students, was establishing a religion when it relented and treated them evenhandedly.

Over the next 15 years, however, the 'equal access' principle, which is simply formal neutrality under a different name, carried the day in a variety of contexts. The equal access principle was applied to tax credits for educational expenses at public and private schools, to on-campus meetings by high school students, to payment for courses at a religious college on behalf of a blind student, to provision of a sign language interpreter for deaf students in religious as well as non-religious schools, and to receipt of students' activities funds by a religiously-oriented student publication.[36] By 1987 the contradictions in doctrine had become apparent, and the Court overruled two of its earlier no-aid decisions.[37] In the 1999–2000 Term the Court is being asked to overrule two more. Unless the Court strays from its course, no-aid separationism is likely to be replaced by some version of neutrality theory.

The Solutions

In the heyday of no-aid separationism and mandatory free exercise accommodations, the two parts of the Religion Clause were in seemingly irreconcilable conflict. The Free Exercise Clause required the government to make special accommodations or exemptions for religious exercise, at least under some circumstances, and forbade discrimination against religion. The Establishment Clause required government to exclude religious institutions from generally available public benefits, at least under some circumstances, and forbade preferences for religion. In other words, the Free Exercise Clause required what the Establishment Clause forbade; and the Establishment Clause required what the Free Exercise Clause forbade. This internal inconsistency seems at odds with the very notion of constitutionalism, and is surely not a stable position.

What were (and are) the alternatives?

First, the Court could adhere to both interpretations, and decide between them on a case-by-case basis. The consequence of this approach is institutional rather than substantive: it would allow the courts to decide the proper outcome in every case, essentially unconstrained by general principles (since every general principle will be contradicted by an equal and opposite general principle). By the same token, the political branches would have no way to determine whether any particular action will be constitutional. If, for example, a state denies unemployment compensation to a worker who is unavailable for otherwise suitable employment for religious reasons, it imposes a burden on the worker's exercise of religion, in violation of the Free Exercise Clause. That was the holding in *Sherbert*. But if a state amended its unemployment compensation law to give benefits to workers if, and only if, their reasons for unavailability were religious, this could easily be held to be a 'subsidy' for a religious decision and an unconstitutional 'preference for religion over nonreligion' under the Establishment Clause. The legislature could lose either way. However, despite its theoretical incoherence, this combination of positions might produce a desirable practical outcome. On the assumption that courts are more likely than other agencies of government to make religiously significant decisions with an even and tolerant hand, it might be good to maximize judicial discretion. If that is a dubious assumption – as I think it is – or if most decisions must, as a matter of practicality, be made by lower-level officials who need workable standards for judgment, then this approach is highly questionable.

Second, it would be possible for the Court to retreat on both the free exercise and establishment fronts. It could hold that the Free Exercise Clause is satisfied whenever the laws are neutral and generally applicable, leaving accommodations to legislative discretion. That was the holding in *Smith*. At the same time, the Court could conclude that the Establishment Clause does not require exclusion of religious institutions from generally applicable public benefits – which is apparently the trend in recent cases. The effect of this combination of doctrinal positions is to broaden the sphere of legislative discretion. This might be a desirable outcome, on the normative assumption that the people are entitled to resolve issues through representative institutions where there is no clear constitutional answer. One might also argue, on the basis of empirical experience, that legislatures are more hospitable to the claims of religious citizens (both majority and minority) than the courts have been – perhaps because the judiciary is heavily populated by men and women of secular sensibilities. On the other hand, it may deprive religious minorities of a useful backstop when the political process fails. The *Smith* opinion itself observes that 'leaving accommodation to the political process will place at a relative disadvantage those religious practices that are not widely engaged in'.[38] However, if equality of rights is central to the United States' constitutional principles of religious freedom – as I think it is – this may not be an adequate solution.

Third, the Court could abandon its doctrine of mandatory accommodation (as it did in *Smith*), but adhere to its doctrine of no-aid separationism. This would alleviate the constitutional conflict between the two Clauses, since accommodations can be seen as a form of 'aid' to religion. The effect, overall, would be to convert the Religion Clauses into a force for secularization. Religious exercise could not be singled out for protection, but religious institutions would be singled out for exclusion. Religious practices and institutions would be fully subject to governmental interference and regulation, but ineligible for generally available benefits. This outcome could be deemed desirable only if the purpose of the First Amendment is to reduce the incidence of religious practice and influence in society.[39] It would amount to freedom *from* religion, not freedom *of* religion.

Fourth, the Court could adhere to the doctrine of free exercise accommodations, but abandon no-aid separationism in favour of some version of neutrality. This approach would maximize the freedom of religious exercise. All kinds of governmental power – spending decisions as well as regulation – can influence and distort religious choice. When an exercise of the regulatory power proscribes religious exercise, the effect is obvious, and the Free Exercise Clause can be interpreted to require an exemption or accommodation, when possible without undue interference with achievement of an important governmental interest.[40] When government provides public money to private groups to achieve a public purpose, the best way to minimize the effect on religious practice is to allow all groups to participate on a neutral basis. Exclusion of religious groups creates an incentive for the groups to secularize, and for beneficiaries to choose secular over religious provision of the benefit. This combination of doctrines – free exercise accommodations and neutrality in allocation of benefits – would have the effect of minimizing governmental power over religious practice. Adoption of this approach would be desirable if the purpose of the Religion Clauses is to allow people of differing religious views to participate in civil society with the least possible interference with their religious lives. To me, that is a plausible normative assumption, and this is accordingly an attractive doctrinal option.

Alternatively, of course, the Court may hope to muddle through without making a choice between conflicting understandings of the Religion Clauses. In one particularly interesting case, in which the Court ruled that a public university could not exclude a student publication from eligibility for student activities funds on account of its religious viewpoint, Justice Sandra Day O'Connor (who is often the swing Justice in these cases) commented:

> This case lies at the intersection of the principle of government neutrality and the prohibition on state funding of religious activities... . When two bedrock principles so conflict, understandably neither can provide the definitive answer. Reliance on categorical platitudes is unavailing. Resolution instead depends on the hard task of judging – sifting through the details and determining whether the challenged program offends the Establishment Clause. Such judgment requires courts to draw lines, sometimes quite fine, based on the particular facts of each case.[41]

This faith in 'the hard task of judging', I believe, is an impediment to coherent decision-making. It is one thing to be attentive to the specific facts of each case in applying constitutional doctrine, but it is quite another to maintain that two ostensible constitutional principles are in direct conflict, and to refuse to choose between them. When A contradicts B, they cannot both be correct. If A appears to contradict B, it is the interpreter's responsibility to decide that A is correct and not B, that B is correct and not A, or (possibly) to find a synthesis of A and B that combines the best features of both. Simply to vacillate between them on the basis of 'the particular facts of each case' is an invitation to incoherence, and ultimately to perceived illegitimacy. The Court has reached that point in its Religion Clause jurisprudence. It is time to stop 'draw[ing] lines, sometimes quite fine', and to make reasoned judgements about what values and principles the First Amendment stands for. Until the Court faces up to its internal doctrinal inconsistencies, its decisions will be condemned as chaotic, controversial, and unpredictable.

Notes

1   At this point it is necessary to clarify terminology. There are different understandings of 'separation' and there are different understandings of 'neutrality'. Professor Douglas Laycock, for example, argues that it is a mistake to interpret 'separation' as requiring the government to refrain from giving 'aid' to religious institutions, and that 'neutrality' should be defined in terms of the effects on religious practice rather than as forbidding religious classifications. So defined, he says, the concepts cease to be at odds with one another: D. Laycock (1997), 'The Underlying Unity of Separation and Neutrality', *Emory Law Journal*, **46,** p. 43. I do not disagree with his normative position and would be happy to accede to his terminology, but this would not capture the tensions in actual constitutional doctrine as it has been developed by the US Supreme Court. He is correct in maintaining that the Supreme Court has never recognized the inconsistency between its understanding of 'separation' and its understanding of 'neutrality' (ibid., p. 65). Nonetheless, these understandings *were* inconsistent. Where necessary for clarity, I will use the term 'no-aid separationism' to denote the view that the government may not give aid or assistance to religion, and the term 'formal neutrality' to denote the view that the government may not make or enforce religious classifications.

2   *Stansbury* v. *Marks*, 2 US 213 (1793). Since the First Amendment did not apply to the states at this time, this and the next several cases discussed were argued under state constitutional provisions similar, but not identical, to the First Amendment.

3   *People* v. *Philips*, New York City Court of General Sessions (1813), published in W. Sampson (1813), *The Catholic Question in America*, (New York: De Capo Publishers), (photo reprint 1974).

4   *Simon's Executors* v. *Gratz*, 2 Pen. & W. 412, 417 (Pa. 1831).

5   *Commonwealth* v. *Cronin*, 1 QLJ 128 (VA. Richmond Cir. Ct. 1856); *State* v. *Willson*, 13 SCL (2 McCord) 393 (SC 1823); *Commonwealth* v. *Drake*, 15 Mass. (14 (Tyng) 161 (1818). For more detail on the historical background of this issue, see Michael W. McConnell (1990), 'The Origins and Historical Understanding of Free Exercise of Religion', *Harvard Law Review*, **103**, p. 1409; Michael W. McConnell (1998), 'Freedom from Persecution or Protection of the Rights of Conscience? A Critique of Justice Scalia's Historical Arguments in *City of Boerne* v. *Flores*', *William & Mary Law Review*, **39**, p. 819. For a contrasting view, see Philip A. Hamburger (1992), 'A Constitutional Right of Religious Exemption: An Historical Perspective', *George Washington*

Law Review, **60**, p. 915; Gerard V. Bradley (1991), 'Beguiled: Free Exercise Exemptions and the Siren Song of Liberalism', *Hofstra Law Review*, **20**, p. 245.

6   See, respectively, *Permoli* v. *New Orleans*, 44 US (3 How.) 589 (1845); *Reynolds* v. *United States*, 98 US 145 (1879); *Prince* v. *Massachusetts*, 321 US 158 (1944); *Hamilton* v. *Board of Regents*, 293 US 245 (1934).

7   310 US 586 (1940).

8   Ibid., pp. 594–95.

9   319 US 624 (1943).

10   374 US 398 (1963). I pass over *Braunfeld* v. *Brown*, 366 US 599 (1961), an intermediate case providing limited protection for 'indirect' burdens on religious exercise but hinting at broader protections for 'direct' burdens.

11   Ibid., p. 403.

12   Ibid., p. 429.

13   *In re Jenison*, 375 US 14 (1963) (*per curiam*), vacating and remanding *In re Jenison Contempt Proceedings*, 265 Minn. 96 (1963). On remand, see *In re Jenison Contempt Proceedings*, 267 Minn. 136 (1963) (overturning the conviction).

14   *Wisconsin* v. *Yoder*, 406 US 205 (1972).

15   494 US 872 (1990).

16   Ibid., p. 879.

17   Ibid., p. 890.

18   521 US 507 (1997).

19   I have set forth my best understanding of current constitutional standards in Michael W. McConnell (1985), 'Accommodation of Religion', *Supreme Court Review*, **1985**, p. 1, and *idem* (1992), 'Accommodation of Religion: An Update and a Response to the Critics', *George Washington Law Review*, **60**, p. 685.

20   Carl Esbeck (1997), 'A Constitutional Case for Governmental Cooperation with Faith-Based Social Service Providers', *Emory Law Journal*, **46**, p. 1, at p. 40.

21   *Bradfield* v. *Roberts*, 175 US 291, 298–99 (1899). It is probably not coincidental that the target of the litigation was a Catholic institution.

22   Stephen Monsma (1996), *When Sacred and Secular Mix: Religious Non-profit Organizations and Public Money*, (Lanham, Md: Rowman & Littlefield).

23   Horace Mann, the first and greatest leader of the Common School movement, explained that the schools should 'draw the line between those views of religious truth and of Christian faith which are common to all, and may, therefore, with propriety be inculcated in school, and those which, being peculiar to individual sects, are therefore by law excluded'. Quoted in Charles Glenn (1987), *The Myth of the Common School*, p. 164, Amherst, MA: University Press, Massachusetts. From the point of view of Catholics and Jews, the views 'common to all' amounted to watered-down Protestantism.

24   For historical accounts, see Lloyd Jorgenson (1987), *The State and the Non-public School, 1825–1925*, (Columbia, MO: University of Missouri Press), Ward McAfee (1998), *Religion, Race, and Reconstruction: The Public School in the Politics of the 1870s*, Albany, NY: SUNY Press.

25   330 US 1 (1947).

26   Ibid., p. 16.

27   Ibid.

28   Ibid.

29   392 US 236 (1968).

30   *Walz* v. *Tax Commission*, 397 US 664 (1970).

31   403 US 602 (1971).

32 *Meek* v. *Pittenger*, 421 US 349, 365–66 (1975); *Wolman* v. *Walter*, 433 US 229, 250 (1977).
33 Leonard Levy (1986), *The Establishment Clause: Religion and the First Amendment*, (New York: Macmillan), p. 163.
34 454 US 263 (1981).
35 Ibid., p. 274.
36 See, respectively, *Mueller* v. *Allen*, 463 US 388 (1983); *Board of Education* v. *Mergens*, 496 US 226 (1990); *Witters* v. *Department of Services*, 474 US 481 (1996); *Zobrest* v. *Catalina Foothills School Dist*, 509 US 1 (1993); *Rosenberger* v. *Rector & Visitors of the University of Virginia*, 515 US 819 (1995).
37 *Agostini* v. *Felton*, 521 US 203 (1997).
38 494 US at pp. 872, 890.
39 For elaborations of versions of this position, see Marci Hamilton (1999), 'Power, the Establishment Clause, and Vouchers', *Connecticut Law Review*, **31**, p. 807; Suzanna Sherry (1996), 'Enlightening the Religion Clauses', *Journal of Contemporary Legal Issues*, **7**, p. 473.
40 In my opinion, the 'compelling interest' standard of *Sherbert* is probably too exacting to be feasible.
41 *Rosenberger* v. *Rector and Visitors of the University of Virginia*, 515 US 819, 847 (1995). Professor McConnell was the (successful) counsel for the petitioner in this case [editor].

5 Wondering after Babel: Power, Freedom and Ideology in US Supreme Court Interpretations of the Religion Clauses

Marie A. Failinger

Introduction

American Church–state jurisprudence has been particularly lively over the past 20 years, although the causes for increased US Supreme Court review of Religion Clause cases are difficult to isolate. Perhaps the Court's more tumultuous caseload is due to the increasing vocality of religious Americans, from conservative Christians to embattled Muslims, who are more visibly demanding religious accommodations.[1] Perhaps there is more activity because recently appointed Justices have expanded the diversity of the modern Supreme Court's views about the role of religion in public life in their jurisprudence, and the meaning of the Religion Clauses seems more open to contest by litigants right through the political spectrum.

The increase in Church–state litigation may, of course, represent Americans' fascination with litigation, wedded to what some claim is increased social polarization on moral issues such as abortion and school choice, described by Justice Scalia as America's *Kulturkampf*.[2] Finally, the plethora of ways in which local, state and federal agencies now regulate most major arenas of human endeavour, from schools to workplaces, has led to more clashes between the state and individuals asserting their interests.

In recent times the Court has engaged a varied First Amendment docket, ranging from challenges to crèches on public property to unemployment compensation rules that bar peyote-using workers to zoning regulations dictating the use of church buildings.[3] These cases have left the Supreme Court scrambling for new theoretical frameworks that effectively account for emerging constitutional problems in an increasingly religiously pluralistic culture.

While longstanding academic conflicts on how judges should interpret the Constitution account for a small part of the disorder, this is much less true in Religion Clauses litigation than in other constitutional rights cases. For instance, the Religion Clause cases defy the interpretative rule of thumb that originalists or intentionalists (who generally believe that the Bill of Rights is limited by the plain meaning of the text or the intent of the Framers in their own historical context) will normally have a narrow view of civil liberties and that non-originalists/non-intentionalists (who believe that the constitutional text should be generously interpreted to account for new historical circumstances) will protect a broader spectrum of human rights. Recent Religion Clause 'liberals', such as Justices Sandra Day O'Connor and David Souter, have taken great pains to address the original understanding of the Religion Clauses, often to justify a hard line against any government action that resembles an establishment or restricts religious freedom.[4] Even commentators seem to accept the proposition that historical concerns should inform a reading of the Religion Clauses to a greater extent than for free speech or other protected rights.

The first part of this chapter will briefly describe how the Supreme Court has been travelling in somewhat of a doctrinal circle since the jurisprudence that opened the way to First Amendment religion challenges to state law in the 1940s and 1950s. However, a focus on the Court's doctrine may obscure some of the deeper issues that have troubled American Church–state jurisprudence since the very beginning – issues often not explicitly raised by divided Court opinions and academic commentary. I will summarize these battles by organizing them into three concerns that have competed for domination in American Church–state jurisprudence, each with its own idea-map about the role of religion in public life: a concern about the allocation of power (including the equality principle); the changing concept of individual freedom; and the effect of traditional, liberal and postmodern ideological social influences on First Amendment doctrine.

These concerns forge interesting alliances between judges and commentators who otherwise would be found on opposite ends of the political spectrum, but they are perhaps more important for those new to American constitutional debates than doctrinal solutions to the problems they embrace. A fair, complex treatment of these three concerns would yield tensions between them and sometimes other 'American' values. For instance, when a religious believer asks for an exemption from a regulation that will be applied to everyone but him (such as the wartime draft or the payment of taxes) the value of freedom conflicts with the value of equal treatment, and both courts and commentators must find a way to either prioritize or reconcile these values.[5] Such tensions, which cannot be resolved here but which must be resolved in 'real life', in some cases account for the apparently muddled picture of Religion Clauses jurisprudence perceived if only doctrinal arguments were attended to.

The Modern Doctrinal Circle in Religion Clause Jurisprudence

To oversimplify, the Supreme Court's discussion of the Free Exercise and Establishment Clauses of the First Amendment might be imagined as a debate over what the Amendment requires of the state and federal governments along the following spectrum:

Discrimination–Burden–Neutrality–Accommodation–Preference

At one end of the spectrum, as the *Church of the Lukumi Babalu Aye* case confirmed, in striking down a city ordinance preventing Santeria believers from sacrificing animals as part of their worship, the government may not intentionally set out to discriminate, i.e. to harm some religions or disadvantage believers in the exercise of their religious beliefs as compared with other religions.[6] Thus, the Supreme Court has condemned the punishment of individuals for their beliefs or religious exercise.[7] Condemnation reaches its peak in what is, for Americans, the most virulent form of discrimination, *coercion* – that is, forcing persons into a profession of belief or religious behaviour at odds with their conscience or choice. In the landmark case of *Everson* v. *Board of Education*[8] the Supreme Court described the coercion that the First Amendment was intended to prevent – forcing individuals to go to or stay away from church, or to profess belief or disbelief in a particular religion, or to support any religious activities or institutions through taxation. This holding has been a cornerstone of the Court's jurisprudence, in both Free Exercise and Establishment Clause cases.

Beyond such 'negative' discrimination, the modern Court has stated emphatically that the government may not exercise positive discrimination – intentionally *preferring* one religion over another, all religion to non-religion, or secular ideology over religion.[9] The Court has held that such preferences constitute an establishment of religion, although an easy case could be made under the Free Exercise Clause as well. The negative discrimination cases most often involve minority religions, embracing the principle that majorities may not take away some precious rights from a

minority, even in a democratic society. The positive discrimination or preference cases, by contrast, originally inferred that majoritarian Christianity
may not be singled out for special advantages, either financial or symbolic.
In recent jurisprudence, however, the Court has held that even minority
religions such as Satmar Hasidism may not be granted political advantages
that do not accrue to other religious bodies.[10]

Most of the debate within the Court and the academic world is about
defining and applying the concepts of *burden*, *neutrality* and *accommodation*, the middle positions between these ends of the spectrum. On the
Establishment Clause side, the conflict has been over whether the state must
be scrupulously neutral where religions are concerned or whether the state
may accommodate religious minorities by granting exemptions from uniform, neutrally applicable statutes without running foul of the Clause. This
debate about neutrality versus accommodation, however, embraces many
more questions than the language suggests, depending on what baseline for
comparison is used as a starting point.

Some theorists – although their numbers are waning in the academic
world – have argued that the only way in which the state can be neutral,
neither establishing nor infringing on religion, is through more or less *strict
separation*. Strict separation would prohibit the state from interacting in any
way, either by regulating the behaviour of religious institutions and individuals or by providing even modest state or federal funding even to apparently 'secular' day care programmes, hospitals, or teenage pregnancy
counselling. For example, Laurence Tribe suggests that separatism or

> ... the 'noninvolvement' or 'nonentanglement' principle... calls for much more
> than the institutional separation of church and state; it means that the state
> should not be involved in religious affairs or derive its claim to authority from
> religious sources...and – perhaps – that sectarian differences should not be
> allowed unduly to fragment the body politic...[as well as] that under no circum-
> stance should religion be financially supported by public taxation... .[11]

Many who support separation focus on the principle of voluntarism which
operates practically to prevent political or economic support from flowing
from the state to the Church.[12] Those who have taken up this debate on the
other side have argued that functional or *institutional separation*, prohibiting Church and state from exerting organizational authority or control, or
exercising programmatic influence over the institutions of the other, is sufficient to avoid real establishment problems.[13]

'Neutrality' may also refer to the position taken by Phillip Kurland and
others that the state may not use religion as a basis for either action or
in-action.[14] This position has come to be known as *formal neutrality* or

'religion-blindness' – that is, the state must interact with a religious individual without 'seeing' the individual's religion. In religion-blind neutrality, the state may regulate a believer's conduct on the same basis as any other person's conduct, even if it violates his faith; yet it may also make grants to religious institutions, including schools, that perform the same functions that a secular entity might, not 'seeing' their religious activities or orientation. Opponents of 'religion-blind' neutrality include, on one side, separationists who believe that this theory grants too much licence for the state to support religious institutions, albeit for their secular purposes[15] and, on the other, accommodationists who argue that the Free Exercise Clause requires the government to waive rules that conflict with religious beliefs in all but the most compelling cases, which Professor Douglas Laycock has labelled *substantive neutrality*.[16]

A third argument about state neutrality, reborn in recent years, is over *non-preferentialism* – that is, whether constitutional neutrality is simply a type of equality principle that permits state aid to religions so long as it is equally distributed to all.[17] Some non-preferentialists are what Carl Esbeck terms 'restorationists', persons who want to restore the United States to its place as a 'Christian nation',[18] while others side with those who believe that the Religion Clauses are simply another manifestation of the United States' commitment to the equal citizenship of groups and individuals.[19] Non-preferentialists are opposed by nearly all other theorists who think that non-preferentialism goes too far towards an establishment of religion and the preference for religious over non-religious citizens, including many who consider that there is no historical or textual foundation for a non-preferential position.[20] Non-preferentialists may not always agree with *religious equality* theorists on issues of tangible aid to religion, such as parochial school funding[21] or on symbolic support, such as publicly sponsored religious ceremonies, which some equality principle theorists argue constitutes state endorsement or disapproval of religion in violation of the Establishment Clause.[22] Non-preferentialists who are largely concerned about majoritarian religious interests see no such endorsement, while strict religious egalitarians and accommodationists concerned about minority religious interests tend to disagree.

On the Free Exercise side, the conflict over the states duties *vis-à-vis* the burden – neutrality – accommodations spectrum has largely centred on two issues. The first concerns what type and how much of a disadvantage a religious believer must incur before his or her burden is constitutionally impermissible, triggering 'strict scrutiny' of a state law. State regulation that is *coercive*, forcing a believer to choose between the principles of his faith and a tremendous harm, such as imprisonment or the loss of livelihood, has been sufficient to trigger constitutional scrutiny,[23] although the *Smith* case has added the requirement that such coercive regulation be also targeted at religious practice before the Court can intervene.[24] Many decisions have suggested that lesser burdens, so long as they are 'substantial', should also call forth constitutional protection.[25] Second, commentators have quibbled about whether the Constitution demands, permits or prevents the state from accommodating believers by exempting them from generally applicable laws not targeted at harming a religion.[26] Inherent in that debate is the question whether a scheme of religious neutrality that might impose higher burdens on some faiths than others better ensures religious freedom than a patchwork of exemptions for particular religious groups that might result in preferential treatment for some religious people.

Viewing the modern Court's work through the lens of history, the record discloses something of a half-century circle in the Court's jurisprudence, beginning with *Everson* v. *Board of Education* (1947)[27] and ending in *Agostini* v. *Felton* (1997)[28] in Establishment Clause jurisprudence, and with cases such as *Prince* v. *Massachusetts* (1944)[29] and ending with *Smith* (1990)[30] and *Church of Lukumi Babalu Aye* (1993)[31] on the Free Exercise Clause side.

In Establishment Clause jurisprudence the Court moved from 'coercion' to 'neutrality' and back, and in the Free Exercise cases, from coercion to accommodation and back. On the Establishment Clause side, the *Everson* case established the principle that government may neither coerce religious profession or action, nor may it aid religion, although this particular case applied the 'no-aid' formula pragmatically rather than rigidly.[32] Then, from at least 1963 to the early 1980s, the Court focused on governmental neutrality towards religion under the Establishment Clause, largely utilizing the Lemon test[33] which focused not only on 'excessive entanglement' of Church and state pursuant to the separationists' concerns, but also the 'neutrality' of the law's aim and its primary impact, neither favouring nor harming religion.

Some Justices, such as Justice Brennan and Justice Marshall, have tended toward a strict separationist view of neutrality,[34] while others concentrated on more pragmatic questions of whether there was significant tangible aid or symbolic endorsement flowing to religious entities.[35] The result of the emphasis on neutrality in Establishment Clause cases was uneven: some symbolic government activity was invalidated as being too purely religious while other activity was upheld as being primarily secular.[36] Similarly, government funding for religious primary and junior educational institutions was largely invalidated,[37] while funding directed to other religious institutions accomplishing more 'secular' tasks such as higher education and social services was preserved.[38]

On the Free Exercise Clause side, the few cases from the 1940s era similarly seemed to assume that the Constitution largely protected believers against religious compulsion, turning back claims that non-targeted rules such as child labour and public health laws which violated minority religious beliefs were constitutionally invalid.[39] By the 1960s, while neutrality reigned in Establishment cases,[40] *mandatory accommodation* was the principal theme in free exercise cases, particularly for minority groups who complained to the Court that they were forced to choose between a religious tenet and a severe disadvantage under neutrally-intended, generally applicable laws.[41] However, religious minorities often lost even under an accommodation regime, particularly in two types of case. First, minority religions that did not follow Western paradigms, most notably American Indians, were unsuccessful in convincing the Court to protect them, especially in matters where the state's active cooperation was required, such as setting aside state lands for religious observance[42] or avoiding the use of a Social Security number.[43] Second, religious claimants tended to lose cases in which the Justices felt that there might be some incentive for free-riders to falsify religious duties to exempt themselves from statutory hardships or gain an advantage at the expense of other citizens, such as cases requesting exemptions from duties to pay Social Security tax,[44] drug abuse laws[45] and Sunday closing laws.[46]

While the theme of neutrality still has a significant following on the Court in Establishment Clause cases, particularly as it embraces symbolic neutrality or the non-endorsement principle, other Justices have diverged from this path. Most notably, in cases such as *Employment Division* v. *Smith*,[47] Justice Scalia has had some success in arguing for a return to the mid-twentieth-century (and he would claim original) understanding that the Religion Clauses prevent only coercion by the state and not well intentioned, generally applicable laws that unintentionally burden minority religions. Justice Souter has generally taken a practical separationist viewpoint, following in Justice Brennan's footsteps,[48] while Justice Thomas has argued for non-preferentialism.[49] Other Justices, whilst not willing to commit to a particular theory of constitutional law, have nevertheless repudiated strict separation, permitting states wide latitude in supporting parochial education through parental tax deductions for private education in *Mueller*, and specialized educational services provided by public employees at private schools in *Agostini*.[50]

With regard to the Free Exercise Clause the accommodation principle of the 1960s and 1980s has been all but eviscerated by *Employment Division* v. *Smith*. *Smith* evinces a return to the Court's regime during the 1940s and earlier, which held that neutrally-intended, generally applicable laws should be upheld even if they impose harsh burdens on religious practice, including proselytization and worship.[51] Thus, the neutrality principle with its emphasis solely on coercive or intentionally discriminatory practices, rather than its strict separation or non-preferential guise, has won the day on free exercise, although some Justices continue to nip at its heels.[52]

This historical circle of constitutional theory, however, is dynamic rather than static, as evidenced by the divergence among members of the Court about the appropriate theory to apply. It is difficult to predict the directions in which the Court will move in the twenty-first century without taking account of the problems of power, freedom and ideology that have continued to inform Church–state jurisprudence in the United States.

The Problem of Power in First Amendment Law

Most American constitutionalists are agreed that the problem of power significantly animated the Religion Clauses, citing founder James Madison's views as paradigmatic. From this perspective Madison's pragmatic objective was to deconcentrate power on two fronts. First, by encouraging the separation of powers between federal and state governments he hoped to limit the growth of massive official power centres whose coercive abilities could not be matched.[53] Thus, one original (although contested) rationale for the First Amendment Religion Clauses was that they preserved to the individual states any decisions about the extent of both religious establishments and free exercise, while broadly prohibiting the federal government from establishing a Church or crushing the diversity of religious beliefs into a national religion. This balance of powers rationale became constitutionally extinct when the Supreme Court incorporated the Religion Clauses in the 1940s, holding that they applied to state governments as well as federal governments as an aspect of the liberty protected by the post-Civil War Fourteenth Amendment.[54] Since the 1980s a new set of largely conservative commentators and a few lower court judges have risen up to challenge the Court's decision to incorporate the Free Exercise and Establishment Clauses, but so far they have met with little success.[55]

Just as importantly for this discussion, Madison touted religious factionalism as a positive state of affairs – a way of ensuring that no religion was able to gain *de facto* governmental power nor impose its religious beliefs and practices upon adherents of minority religions.[56] Beyond the immediate problem of religious coercion, the generally accepted justifications for separating clerical from governmental power were to ensure the purity of the Church against the worldly corruptions that accompany the grant of worldly power over others (attributed to Roger Williams[57]) and to ensure that public policy debate would be conducted along rational, non-self-interested Enlightenment principles instead of irrational, loyalist religious lines (attributed to Thomas Jefferson[58]). That is, in the standard historical account (also contested) both Williams and Jefferson hoped that they could, to some extent, remove their cherished institutions from the influence of power, which was conceived of as inherently a corruption of spiritual–intellectual human nature.

Yet, while theorists – particularly liberal legal academics – have held on to the vision of human community divorced from power struggle, Madison's more pragmatic vision has seemed to win the day in constitutional jurisprudence; the Court has been fine-tuning power balances between the branches of government as it has perceived the power of one branch to be growing disproportionately to its responsibility. For example, in recent years, the Court's concern with the power of the presidency (that was so visible in jurisprudence in the 1950s through the 1970s) has been replaced with the concern that Congress is federalizing issues that properly belong to the states, such as gun control and violence against women.

In terms of religious freedom, for most of the period after incorporation in the 1940s, Madison's concern for the balance of power between federal and state governments was largely ignored by the Supreme Court and by Congress, although occasionally someone like Justice Harlan might suggest that states had wide discretion over whether to accommodate religious dissenters.[59] For instance, Congress passed some laws which gave religious freedom rights nationally, without concern for possibly diverging state interests in the matter, such as Title VII's prohibition against religious discrimination in 'secular' workplaces.[60] Moreover, Congress has, on occasion, 'rectified' the results of a federal court case boding adverse consequences for religious claimants by passing a statute granting religious dissenters statutory protection that, according to the Court, the Constitution could not be made to grant. One such example was when Congress passed legislation evincing its desire to protect specific religious practices of American Indians that had not received protection from the courts, such as the use of peyote in religious ceremonies, the gathering of eagle feathers banned under wildlife protection laws and permission to hold sweatlodge ceremonies in prisons.[61] It also responded to problems encountered by schoolchildren trying to form religious groups at school – efforts not always supported by the courts – by passing the Equal Access Act, which permits religious groups to meet on an equal basis with secular student groups.[62]

In 1997, however, in a surprising twist to the power-balancing story, the Supreme Court held that Congress was not authorized to pass the Religious Freedom Restoration Act, a law which struck at both the Supreme Court's power to interpret the Constitution and the states' power to make laws incidentally burdening believers. In *City of Boerne* v. *Flores*, the Court ruled that Congress' legislative attempt to restore the *Sherbert* Free Exercise accommodation test (which had been wiped out by *Smith*) not only invaded the Court's power to interpret the Constitution, but also exceeded Congress' authorization under the Fourteenth Amendment to remedy state violations of constitutional rights.[63] Thus, the debate over power-balancing between the federal branches and the state and federal government has gained new life in the religious freedom area, as it has in other areas.[64] Yet, it is far from clear that the Court is prepared to grant states greater latitude than the federal government to concoct their own brew of establishment and religious freedom theory.[65]

In terms of power-balancing between Church and state, very few scholars or judges would seriously entertain the possibility that the United States might return to any juridical fusion between a church body and a branch of American government. Nevertheless, there has been a substantial debate about two forms of religious involvement in American public life. One debate centres on whether it is proper at all for religious individuals or institutions to exercise their political muscle based on overtly theological grounds. At one extreme, theorists argue that all religious language is inappropriate in a religiously diverse political community; on the other, it is argued that any religious argument, even one that is inaccessible to non-adherents, is appropriately expressing religious individuals' most authentic selves and should be permitted.[66] Theorists in the middle have attempted to describe conditions for the ethical use of religious arguments in political debate and the grounding of political decisions,[67] but they are far from agreed.

The second question affecting the power-balancing issue more directly concerns the First Amendment: it asks whether any governmental tangible or symbolic aid that makes it more possible for religious bodies to exercise their social and political power in the political process violates the Establishment Clause. In strong separation and neutrality arguments, both religious influence that appears to have governmental approval, such as the use of a vague religious symbol (for example, 'In God We Trust' on currency) and indirect aid, such as tax deductions for parochial school expenses are impermissible. By contrast, non-preferentialists favour robust (even self-interested) religious participation in political decision-making and encourage governmental aid for all religious exercises, particularly those of the majority, which they see as being constricted by a separation regime.

Third, power-balancing finds expression in the religious equality principle which some believe to be the priority value driving free exercise and establishment law. Harkening back to Madison, religious egalitarians go beyond arguing that power-balancing among the sects is a way of avoiding the hegemony of any particular sect, and thus political corruption. They argue that the equality principle reassures minority groups that they will not be persecuted in the exercise of their most central religious practices by majorities who dislike their participation in political decision-making and, conversely, that they will not be politically disenfranchized because of their religious or non-religious beliefs.[68] As Justice O'Connor puts it, the Establishment Clause prevents the government from endorsing or disapproving of religion – that is, communicating to one group that they are political outsiders and to another group that they are political insiders based on their religious beliefs.[69] The implication of disapproval is that minorities will internalize their outsider status and opt out of the political process or start from an attitude of defeat, weakening their political will. Meanwhile, endorsement will encourage insiders to believe that their politics should prevail by virtue of their status and political muscle, not by virtue of the correctness or usefulness of their ideas for the common good – a situation which would defeat the critical political value of equal regard.[70]

The problem of power is of particular concern in a nation-state which was formed in some sense as an anticultural culture – that is, a nation in which the values of individual freedom, diversity of culture, equality of persons and the rule of law define culture, rather than a distinct ethnic history and set of moral, religious or economic values. Cultures with a developed, complex narrative and norms may treat power in one of two principal ways: they will either authenticate longstanding power abuses, resulting in unjust but stable traditions; or they will check the abuse/usurpation of power by appealing to cultural values that the powermongers cannot publicly gainsay in the long run, however adept they may be in culturally justifying their abuses in the short run. But in an anticultural or (perhaps more correctly) multicultural culture like that of the United States, the reality of who holds power is not checked by history or culture, it is counterbalanced only by opposing power or by values such as freedom and equality that simply serve as limiting or checking mechanisms, not offering a positive vision of the good. Thus, the equality of religious and secular beliefs, undergirded by separationism, is promoted by Americans who want to limit majoritarian religious influence on the political scene, while religious freedom is the battlecry for those who want to curb the power dominance of secularism or minority religious influence.

Justice Scalia, however, has enunciated yet a fourth power dynamic in Free Exercise Clause cases that reflects the influence of modern and postmodern debates. In *Smith*, he identifies the most important power struggle as that between the state and the individual. He argues that effects of the Court's liberal insistence on accommodations will be to make the individual autonomous – a law unto himself – resulting in anarchy.[71] Scalia hopes to put the state, which represents the majority as the American community of moral concern, back into its proper place in the hierarchy above the individual. *Smith* achieves the objective of putting the individual in his place by sacrificing individuals' religious freedom of action to all but a limited number of state regulations.

It is unclear why Justice Scalia, for one, imagines that religious exemptions so radically invert the liberal power paradigm accepted by many Americans across the political spectrum, from conservatives fighting gun control and taxation to liberals fighting police abuse and discrimination against gays. These Americans are united in the belief that the major power dynamic to be feared is that the massive bureaucracy of the state will crush the individual. Justice Scalia's concern might perhaps be explained as an echo of the popular fear that the United States stands on the brink of moral and social chaos. This fear, traceable to the civil rights era and the Vietnam War when the country felt threatened by hippies and anti-war protesters, has never been displaced in the popular mind and places the potential responsibility for chaos at the feet of unlicensed freedom and its consequences.

Justice Scalia's argument also gives a traditional answer to the two questions plaguing political architects from time immemorial. Is the human person innately good or innately evil, or both? And is evil to be feared more from the individual or the institution? While Madison's solution suggests that individuals and small groups, left to themselves, will at least do less evil than powerful individuals and institutions,[72] Justice Scalia comes to the opposite conclusion: that the community is necessary to restrain the evil of the human person, and it is the community where the common good is perceived and instantiated. The American layperson's interpretation of the Constitution has, in some ways, celebrated both the possibility of the human person and his or her possible corruption. That interpretation reflects a great optimism about the ability of government to 'provide for the general welfare' and a deep suspicion that the government will abuse its power and waste its moral and economic goods, which are more safely held in the hands of individuals and private corporations. Even though the Court's jurisprudence never strays far from the issue of human nature in the relationship between freedom and the common good, very rarely has any Justice confronted it so directly as Justice Scalia.

The Problem of Freedom of Conscience

If American culture had to be characterized by only one value, it would undoubtedly be that of personal freedom. Yet, as previously suggested, while American concern for freedom celebrates the limitation of state power in favour of the individual (contra Justice Scalia), freedom also embraces a host of other values, including opportunity, progress, success, authenticity and self-fulfilment, to name just a few. Nearly all 'American' stories are characterized by an emphasis on freedom of action and the right to think for oneself; these range from the story of settlement of the continent to the stories of American heroes, from James Madison to John F. Kennedy Jr, who succeeded by going their own way in business, in the arts and sciences, and even in politics. The story told about religion in the United States is no different: even the smallest children are taught that the Pilgrims and others settled the country as dissenters, in order to protect their right to decide for themselves how to worship their God and to live out of their beliefs.

However, the argument for freedom of conscience has undergone a significant transition from the original arguments proposed by James Madison in his *Remonstrance* to the modern-day Supreme Court's description of the nature of religious freedom. Conservative critics of the Court's religion opinions have been quick to point out that, in justifying religious freedom, Madison and Jefferson relied on theological as well as secular arguments – arguments that most members of the Court would never consider using today in a culture of religious pluralism.[73] Indeed, argued Madison, 'in matters of Religion, no man's right is abridged by the institution of Civil Society and ... Religion is wholly exempt from its cognizance'.[74] Madison's and Jefferson's rhetoric seems to be directed at a polity that they, at least, believed did not question the existence of God. Thus, some of their key arguments for religious freedom proposed that human beings were created by God precisely to be free-thinking and free-willing, to make choices, including the choice for God, of their own will and not under coercion from anyone else. Madison claimed that not only did it go against human nature to coerce religious belief but also, because no one could know what relationship God expected to have with different human beings, coercing religious belief or behaviour might threaten the Divine Plan.[75] Moreover, religious coercion was positively dangerous to the moral fabric of the New World, for it would breed vices, such as hypocrisy, that would undermine the American polity.[76] (In a culture that has always esteemed sincerity, honesty and directness as the highest of virtues, hypocrisy has conversely been among the chief vices of the new republic.)

What began as an argument that government must ensure a free response by the individual called distinctively by the Divine within each unique religious tradition has, in modern-day cases, become an argument for the protection of human autonomy and the right to choose one's religion. While the Founding documents emphasized the value of discernment and choice within the already existing constraints of religious and moral communities, modern-day cases have largely abandoned that background in describing the right to religious freedom.

In the early 1960s, as individuals raised non-theist claims of conscientious objection to military service in cases such as *United States* v. *Seeger*,[77] the Supreme Court was faced with a dilemma that it could not resolve. If the Court defined religion to include only longstanding theist traditions, it would violate the rule of equality which suggested that there are no objective standards to judge the comparable worth of one religious tradition against another, or even one individual's idiosyncratic construal of religious doctrine. On the other hand, if the Court failed to define religion, it would be impossible to separate religious dissent from a wide variety of conscientiously held beliefs that war, or certain wars, or the subsidy of wars through taxes, were wrong. Beliefs that depended on political, social, pragmatic or even ethical assessments that were not grounded in traditional religion could not have been excluded. Failure to define religion would thus rob the Religion Clauses of any specific meaning, and wreak havoc with legal enforcement of generally applicable duties such as taxation and conscription because of the many exemptions for people who claim that their 'religion' demanded one.

The Supreme Court's response was to hedge on defining religion, declaring the exemption available to any person who objected to serving in the military because of a 'sincere and meaningful belief which occupies in the life of its possessor a place parallel to that filled by the God of those admittedly qualifying for the exemption'.[78] However, once this can of worms was open, the Court was unable to go back and consider whether there was a defensible way of defining religion that did not fall prey to equality concerns while preserving some distinct meaning to the constitutional amendment. Perhaps as a result, in the modern cases, the Court often uses the notion of freedom in a very atomistic way: religious freedom is the right of a person to select his or her religious faith and to choose what it will mean to him or her, whether his or her beliefs are shared by any other person, whether they grow out of any relationship with the external world including a transcendent being, whether they are based on a thoughtful argument or are simply the individual's whim.[79] This dynamic has resulted in criticism in recent years that American society, and particularly the Court, has 'privatized' and trivialized religion by conceiving of it a personal 'taste' of the individual[80] rather than an important truth about human existence. While the word 'conscience' is still used, it has come to mean very little beyond the notion of personal existential decision-making in the Court's direct jurisprudence. Conversely, the Court's inability to frame a definition of religion that will meet both equality and freedom concerns has resulted, on the Establishment Clause side, in numerous court challenges to public school textbooks and curricula on the ground that the values which they promote establish a 'religion' of secular humanism.[81]

Meanwhile, despite its failure to define violations of conscience, since the 1960s the Court has tended to apply religious freedom principles in a way that suggests that old distinctions are being made between 'real' religions and those which are not real. For instance, the Amish, who could cite a longstanding, complex and clear religious tradition that pervasively governed their lives, and whose values and behaviour were consistent with American ideals, were allowed an exemption from compulsory schooling requirements,[82] while Indian peoples who claimed that they were in a personal relationship with the sacred living being Earth (which happened to be government real estate) were shouldered aside.[83] New religions to America, such as Hare Krishnas or Scientologists, or even adherents of ancient religions who happened to be suspect, such as prison inmates trying to exercise their religious rights, would often lose their court cases.[84]

The transmutation of religious conscience into a type of human choice has given ammunition to conservatives, such as Justice Scalia, who see libertinism, rather than government oppression, posing a major threat to the American community. Rather than try to mount a defensible definition of religion – a task which admittedly may be impossible in a culture that cannot transcend postmodernity – the courts have resorted to neutrality and other tests which have left religions that are unquestionably authentic even by Western definitions, such as Orthodox Judaism and Catholicism, scrambling to defend core practices. Thus, religious freedom battles in the United States are centring around such issues as whether a *minyan* of Jews may meet in a private residence to celebrate Shabbat,[85] or whether a Christian church can run a homeless shelter in violation of residential zoning laws,[86] or even whether a child may write about Jesus in a public school essay.[87] Such a problem cannot be resolved unless it is possible for at least a majority of the Court to come to some consensus about the types of belief and practice that are worthy of protection as religious, and what things of value religious experience brings to the life of the individual and the polity. Although the theological arguments of Madison and Jefferson may not be open to the Court in their attempts to define what religious beliefs and actions are protected (because of the diversity of American religious traditions and the influence of liberalism), many analogous secular arguments may be. The Founders, for instance, did not simply rely on theological arguments to ground the justification of religious principles; they used insights about human nature commonly available to people of all faiths. They argued, for instance, that people who are forced to profess what they do not believe will become roguish hypocrites; that people are naturally questioning and self-defining creatures, so it is against their nature to force them to accept core beliefs about anything; and that coercion breeds vice in the person who has the power to coerce, as some examples.

The Problem of Ideology

Recent Supreme Court decisions have also reflected a struggle over what ideology will govern American social and political thought in the future. Although there are many ideological positions struggling for acceptance in the Religion Clause cases, three of the principal 'schools' might be described as traditional, liberal and postmodern, although this typology may obscure as many important differences as it highlights. These larger differences are often coloured by the historical lens through which courts and commentators have viewed Church–state issues.

A few judges and commentators view the problem of religious freedom through the lens of historical nostalgia – the notion that the United States would be better off if it could return to American Christendom. Others have viewed the problem of church and state through what one might call the lens of 'future shock', the concern that the United States could end up like its nemesis, Russia; they differ only on whether the Russia to be feared is the American image of a godless Soviet Union or of *The Brothers Karamazov*. Still a third set of thinkers attempts to resolve Church–state problems by focusing on the present, using a contextual approach that tries to discern the current landscape of freedom for minority religions, and argues for a regime that will protect believers from immediate persecution or hardship while permitting the public discourse to be free of the pernicious influence of ideologies of any kind, whether they be triumphalist Christian or secularist.

Traditional ideology, most often embraced by political conservatives, understands establishment and, to some extent, free exercise values as a necessary evil – a limited protection against an unusual derogation by majoritarian political institutions from the basic moral values of American society. In traditional constitutional ideology, the United States has a sound, identifiable moral culture, based loosely on Protestant (and at least some would include Catholic) religious tradition. Some traditionalists are indeed restorationist, hoping to return the continent to the 'moral footings' of past generations, including distinct Christian traditions.[88] Others are, like Madison, more openly pragmatic about religion as a necessary moral base for a thriving society; they would be open to including other religious expressions that have similar moral traditions, such as Judaism and Islam, in the moral tradition they wish to bring back to public schools and public life.[89]

In the traditionalist's view, religious freedom permits comfortable deviations by minority religions, such as the Amish, whose strongly held religious beliefs make them ill-fitting participants in the moral culture. By contrast, religions whose worldview presents a strong challenge to basic American moral tenets or the organization of its economic and social life – from hierarchical religious orthodoxies that regulate their adherents' lives to religious collectives that preach deviations from certain American social values – are tolerated only when they do not present the possibility of a substantial upset.[90] Historically, for example, the Mormon practice of polygamy, characterized as 'a barbaric practice that violated natural law and attacked the moral foundation of "civilized society"' was not even considered to be religiously motivated,[91] and Mormons were vigorously persecuted by the government with the endorsement of the courts.[92] In modern times, American Indians who reject the moral view that human beings are masters over the living world created for their benefit present a major constitutional culture clash for a society built on the right to property,[93] as do absolute pacifists in a nation which perceives itself as the world's policeman.

To many traditionalists, the Establishment Clause is a checking device reserved only for displays of sectarian religious hegemony or actions clearly oppressive to the religious freedom of minorities.[94] It may, for instance, usefully prevent power struggles between evangelical and mainline Protestants, or prevent communities from persecuting Jews or Muslims. Otherwise, for traditionalists, some toleration of minorities is sufficient to satisfy the establishment concern. Traditionalists give the benefit of the doubt to the good faith of the majority and the soundness of a moral culture which is now, in their view, either threatened or lost.

The objective of many traditionalists is to restore the vital place of religious institutions in American culture. Some approach the problem of religious freedom somewhat nostalgically; they want to return to those days when, as they believe, Christian culture undergirded a common American moral and religious perspective on life that permitted morally healthy relationships within the community.[95] Others have been motivated more by a sense of dread about the future: the threat of moral chaos in American life animates their concern for the involvement of religion in public life[96] – moral chaos that, for some, displays human disloyalty toward the Divine.[97]

For still others, the threat of a non-religious culture is understood as political. Even in the waning days of Soviet power, traditionalists such as Ronald Reagan and George Bush were motivated to define the difference between the United States and its nemesis in religious terms: the difference, Reagan said, is that in America, we believe in God.[98] From this perspective, secularism necessarily leads to totalitarianism; the state becomes not only an idol but also an omnipotent and omnipresent force for evil in individual and corporate private endeavours. Thus, many traditionalists are relatively unconcerned about possible Establishment Clause violations, hoping that religious institutions will be restored to a prominent place in American life. On the other hand, viewing anarchy as a threat at the opposite end of the spectrum, many traditionalists can be surprisingly 'hard' on emerging Free

Exercise Clause claims, particularly of newer religions, as aspects of human corruption of freedom.

Liberal ideology, by contrast, continues to hold fast to the notion that the individual is the unit of constitutional concern, and that the value of individual freedom and self-government (autonomy) is the highest moral value in American life.[99] Liberals suffer attacks from both traditional and postmodern theorists who agree that human beings are constituted by, and situated in, communities.[100] For a liberal, religious freedom and establishment can be consistently read to disable the government from doing anything to support any institutions, whether state or religious, that threaten the freedom of individual conscience or social peace.[101] For many, the Church is as much to be feared as the state, given its (perceived) communitarian–authoritarian streak and the history of human suffering at the hands of religious combatants.[102] Thus Establishment Clause issues that threaten to fuse Church and state oppression of individuality are of particular concern.

Free exercise issues that raise the problem of the religious individual in an authoritarian religious culture are particularly problematic for liberals: witness Justice Douglas' plea in *Wisconsin* v. *Yoder* that the Supreme Court should be more concerned about the futures and choices of the Amish children who were kept out of high school by their parents than by the violations of the parents' religious freedom to protect their children against the world.[103] Some less doctrinally liberal judges, such as Justice Brennan, have grasped the fundamental conflict that free exercise liberalism raises, however. In *Corporation of Presiding Bishop* v. *Amos*, involving a church body's refusal of employment to a person who was not a faithful member, he acknowledges both that the employee has suffered a violation of his religious freedom, and that religious bodies need freedom to choose their members and set church discipline, even when their choices are at odds with liberal principles.[104] Without that right to choose, they cannot be effective participants in a liberal democracy.

Shades of a postmodern constitutional ideology also appear in constitutional commentary, and occasionally even in the cases, although the implications of postmodernism lead to strange bedfellows. On the one hand, the postmodernist emphasis on the futility of searches for 'objective' and coherent truth, which has been taken up by constitutional theorists such as Steven Smith,[105] refutes traditionalists who work for a return to a single moral culture undergirded by religious faiths. On the other, the postmodernist emphasis on the situatedness of the individual within community and the value of diversity can be read to support symbolic non-preferentialism, in line with traditionalists who are often willing to acknowledge the need to extend religious aid to all religious traditions as a means of obtaining aid for the dominant ones.

Often, postmodernism is revealed in contextual or pragmatic approaches to the problem of religious freedom – a focus that emphasizes what is happening to religious people in today's culture, whatever the past or the future. Some theorists have argued that a contextual, or at least a non-principled or non-theoretical, approach is the only sensible one given a sea of uncertainty about the Founders' intent, the clash between establishment and free exercise principles in some cases, and the radical pluralism of the American religious experience.[106] Justice O'Connor has become a contextual, pragmatic advocate for religious freedom, dissenting in both the *Smith* and *City of Boerne* cases, while taking a more moderate approach in some cases attacking symbolic aid to religions, such as Christmas displays on public property.[107] In these cases, she has talked about the positive benefits of acknowledging the United States's religious traditions and the diversity of religious beliefs that characterize modern American culture. Moreover, she has demanded that the context of a symbolic religious display be considered, for example, in determining its constitutionality: for her, the placement of a crèche in the town square may or may not be constitutional, depending on what is surrounding the crèche and depending on how the objective observer might react to the entire display. Rather than a return to a monolithic Protestant moral–religious culture, she seems to herald a new age where a melting-pot of religious traditions will inject new life into American moral culture.

Postmodern ideology also has pushed religious equality to the forefront of Religion Clause concerns. A number of Justices have seen the granting of exemptions as an affront to the American value of equality, permitting some religious groups to do what others cannot, or allowing religions relief from a legal burden that non-religious people cannot obtain. For instance, in *Goldman* v. *Weinberger*, involving an Orthodox Jewish chaplain's free exercise request to wear a yarmulke (skullcap) with his Air Force uniform, both Justice Blackmun and Justice Stevens suggest that the religious equality principle would demand that Rastafarians be permitted to wear their dreadlocks in uniform, and Sikhs their turbans.[108] Their strict formal equality is postmodern in tone: like many postmodernists and liberals, they suggest that there is no objective, reasoned way in which to distinguish a yarmulke from dreadlocks or robes; thus, every political dividing line involving religion is based on incommensurable values and relativist judgements that cannot be defended.

The battle over public schools, one of the most fiercely fought under the Religion Clauses, is the clear testing ground for these ideologies, because proponents of each ideology understand how critical the public school can be in inculcating, and thus entrenching, an ideology as an accepted truth by the next generation. Traditionalists seek by court decision and constitutional amendment to return prayer, sacred texts and moral education to public schools, and oppose 'secular humanism' in textbooks and teacher lectures because they believe that Christian moral values need to be taught to every schoolchild whose parents do not object on religious grounds. Liberals just as strenuously seek strict separation in the schools, in terms of both tangible aid and symbolic endorsement. They are concerned that children will be taught traditional ideology instead of a more secular version reflecting American values such as equal dignity, individual freedom and the rule of law. Postmodernists tend to argue for a curriculum which teaches about religions in all of their diversity. Where a strict traditionalist might want children to read the Bible, and a pure secularist might want to strip the public school setting of Christmas traditions in favour of 'winter solstice' celebrations and banish references to the religious beliefs of the Pilgrims from textbooks, postmodernists favour classes that teach about the beliefs of many religions and a school celebration calendar that introduces students to the rituals of Ramadan and the Passover as well as Christmas.[109]

In the United States, Christians are probably as divided as anyone else along the spectrum of traditionalism, liberalism and postmodern ideologies. While some conservative and moderate Christian theorists are traditionalists urging a non-preferentialist approach in order to strengthen religion as a 'mediating institution', other conservative and moderate Christians come from denominations that have traditionally espoused separation from the world, lining them up with strict separation liberals. Christians who are theologically as well as socially liberal retain a strong lobby within liberalism. Many Christians, including those in dwindling mainstream denominations, are waking up to the fact that Christendom has passed, some (always suspicious of the intermingling of faith and culture) with relief. Others are uneasy about what kind of new Church–state relationship needs to be developed to enable religious institutions to regain their social health.

As I have suggested, perhaps now more than ever, these three ideologies compete for hegemony in the American constitutional story. Whereas liberal ideology held sway for most of the 1960s and 1970s in the Court's religion cases, resulting in many Establishment Clause invalidations as well as at least some Free Exercise Clause victories, the outcome of the ideological battle is far from certain and may depend to some extent on the perceived success of either traditionalists or liberals in other political and social arenas. It does, however, suggest that the 'American story' on religion and the state has yet to be reframed by the Supreme Court.

Notes

1   For instance, conservative Christians have raised challenges to 'secular humanist' textbooks: see *Smith* v. *Board of School Commissioners of Mobile County*, 655 F. Supp. 939 (SD Ala. 1987); *Mozert* v. *Hawkins Co. Bd. of Education* 827 F.2d 1058 (6th Cir. 1987), cert. denied 484 US 1066 (1988). They have demanded accommodations for home schooling: see *New Life Baptist Church Academy* v. *East Longmeadow*, 666 F. Supp. 293 (D. Mass. 1987). Muslims have fought for the rights of female workers and schoolchildren not to be required to wear immodest clothing; see A. McCloud (1995–96), 'American Muslim Women and U.S. Society', *Journal of Law and Religion*, XII, pp. 51–59.

2   See *Romer* v. *Evans*, 517 US 620, 636 (1996) (Scalia J dissenting) and J. Hoffman (1998), 'Denominational Influences on Socially Divisive Issues: Polarization or Continuity?', *Journal for the Scientific Study of Religion*, 37, p. 528.

3   For examples, see *County of Allegheny* v. *American Civil Liberties Union*, 492 US 573 (1989) (challenge to crèche in county courthouse); *Employment Div.* v. *Smith*, 494 US 872 (1990) (unemployment compensation disqualification for American Indians smoking peyote in religious ceremony); *City of Boerne* v. *Flores* 521 US 507 (1997) (Church challenge under Religious Freedom Restoration Act to city historic preservation policy).

4   See, for example, *Lee* v. *Weisman*, 505 US 577, 612–617 (1991) (Souter J concurring); *City of Boerne* v. *Flores*, ibid. (O'Connor J concurring).

5   See, for example, *United States* v. *Seeger*, 380 US 163 (1965) (attempting to define religion for purposes of draft exemption for conscientious objectors); *United States* v. *Lee*, 455 US 252 (1982) (denying Social Security tax exemption for objecting Amish employers).

6   *Church of Lukumi Babalu Aye Inc.* v. *City of Hialeah*, 508 US 520, 533 (1993).

7   See *Everson* v. *Board of Education*, 330 US 1, 15–16 (1947).

8   Ibid.

9   *Everson*'s formulation is that the state or federal government may not 'pass laws which aid one religion, aid all religions, or prefer one religion over another' (330 US at p. 15), but subsequent cases have explicitly said that aiding religion over non-religion, or vice versa, also runs foul of the Establishment Clause, although there is strong disagreement about whether aid to all religions, or 'non-preferentialism', violates the First Amendment. Compare discussion in *Lee* v. *Weisman*, 505 US 577, 612 (1991) (Souter J concurring) with *Wallace* v. *Jaffree*, 472 US 38, 103–106 (Rehnquist J dissenting).

10   See *Bd. of Educ. of Kiryas Joel Village School Dist.* v. *Grumet*, 512 US 687 (1994) holding that the state of New York could not form a special education public school district composed entirely of Hasidic Jewish children so the children would not have to face humiliation and hostility from public schoolchildren because of their different appearance and behaviour.

11   L. Tribe (1988), *American Constitutional Law*, 2nd edn, (Mineola, NY: Foundation Press), pp. 1160–61.

12   Ibid.

13   Frederick Gedicks follows James Davison Hunter in identifying a lobby for functional or institutional separationism among 'religious communitarians, who include "orthodox", cultural conservatives who are committed to "an external, definable, and transcendent authority"' as opposed to "secular individualists", who require religious neutrality'. F. Gedicks (1995), *The Rhetoric of Church and State: A Critical Analysis*

of Religion Clause Jurisprudence, (Durham, NC: Duke University Press), pp.10–13. See also A. Adams and C. Emmerich (1990), *A Nation Dedicated to Religious Liberty: The Constitutional of the Religion Clauses*, (Philadelphia: University of Pennsylvania Press), pp. 51–53.

14 See P. Kurland (1961), 'Of Church and State and the Supreme Court', *University of Chicago Law Review*, **29**, pp. 1, 96. Douglas Laycock notes that hardly anyone but Mark Tushnet, a critical legal studies scholar, has endorsed Kurland's position for a generation. D. Laycock (1990), 'Formal, Substantive, and Disaggregated Neutrality Toward Religion', *DePaul Law Review*, **39**, p. 1000. However, some scholars have argued for similar results using the theory of religious equality: see, for example, I. Lupu (1991), 'Reconstructing the Establishment Clause: The Case Against Discretionary Accommodation of Religion', *University of Pennsylvania Law Review*, **140**, pp. 580–603.

15 Laycock notes that under formal neutrality, Congress could have banned the use of communion wine during Prohibition. Laycock, 'Formal, Substantive and Disaggregated Neutrality', *op. cit.*, pp. 1000–1001.

16 Ibid.

17 See discussions in *Lee* v. *Weisman*, 505 US 577, 612 (1992) (Souter J concurring) and *Rosenberger* v. *Rector and Visitors of University of Virginia*, 515 US 819, 853–57 (1995) (Thomas J concurring).

18 C. Esbeck (1994), 'A Typology of Church–State Relations in Current American Thought', in L. Lugo (ed.), *Religion, Public Life and the American Polity*, (Knoxville, TN: University of Tennessee Press), pp. 21–22.

19 See, for example, principles of religious equality espoused in *Lynch* v. *Donnelly*, 465 US 668, 687–89 (1984) (O'Connor, J, concurring). Justice O'Connor has not directly embraced non-preferentialism in her opinions.

20 See, for example, *Lee* v. *Weisman*, 505 US 577, 612–618 (1992) (Souter, J, concurring)

21 See the cases cited in note 34 below.

22 See cases such as *Lynch* v. *Donnelly*, 465 US 668, 695–97 (1984) (Brennan, J, dissenting) (upholding propriety of displaying a city-owned creche along with secular Christmas symbols in the town square); *County of Allegheny* v. *American Civil Liberties Union*, 492 US 573 (1989) (invalidating display of crèche and tree on courthouse steps as an establishment, while upholding the City of Pittsburgh's display of a menorah, Christmas tree and sign entitled 'Salute to Liberty').

23 See, for example, *Wisconsin* v. *Yoder*, 406 US 205 (1972) (Amish successfully challenged a criminal compulsory school law violating their beliefs that children should not attend school after the eighth grade) and *Sherbert* v. *Verner*, 374 US 398 (1963) (Seventh-Day Adventist successfully challenged unemployment compensation law denying benefits to persons unwilling to work on Saturday).

24 See *Employment Div.* v. *Smith*, 494 US 872, 877–79 (1990).

25 See *Thomas* v. *Review Bd. of Indiana Employment Security Div.*, 450 US 707, 718 (1981) (granting employment benefits to a Jehovah's Witness who refused to go to his new work assignment making weapons); *McDaniel* v. *Paty*, 435 US 618, 626–29 (1978) (striking down state law barring ministers from serving in the state legislature); *Wisconsin* v. *Yoder*, 406 US 205, 215 (1972).

26 See, for example, *Sherbert* v. *Verner*, 374 US 398, 422–23 (1963), where Justice Harlan argued that the state could permissibly accommodate religious minorities if it wished, but that it was not required to 'carve out an exception to its general rule of eligibility...'. See also Laycock, 'Formal Substantive and Disaggregated Neutrality',

op. cit., pp. 1001–6, in which Laycock proposes a form of partial mandatory accommodation which he calls 'substantive neutrality' or the principle that government must 'minimize the extent to which it either encourages or discourages religious belief or disbelief, practice or nonpractice, observance or nonobservance'.

27   *Everson* v. *Board of Ed. of Ewing Tp.*, 330 US 1 (1947).

28   *Agostini* v. *Felton*, 521 US 203 (1997).

29   *Prince* v. *Commonwealth of Massachusetts*, 321 US 158 (1943).

30   *Employment Div.* v. *Smith*, 494 US 872 (1990).

31   *Church of Lukumi Babalu Aye, Inc.* v. *City of Hialeah*, 508 US 520 (1993).

32   In *Everson*, 330 US 1, 16 (1947), even though the Court, quoting *Reynolds* v. *United States*, 98 US 145, 164 (1868), recited Madison's language in his letter to the Danbury Baptist Church that the First Amendment had erected a 'wall of separation' between Church and state so that no tax could be levied to support any religious activities, the Court went on to hold that state provision of transportation to school did not violate the Establishment Clause because it was a general programme similar to other government services. The *Everson* holding prepared the way for two themes that would recur in the 1980s and 1990s challenges to government aid for parochial schools: first, the notion that the government must be neutral to religion, not its adversary, and should not hamper religion by denying the general protections of government. Second, the opinion focused on the fact that the programme helped not the institution but the individual students, who could not be precluded from receiving 'the benefits of public welfare legislation' – a theme that would return in *Mueller* v. *Allen*, 462 US 388, 399 (1983) (upholding state tax deduction for school expenses for both public and parochial schoolchildren because parents elected the deductions, not the school), and *Witters* v. *Washington Department of Services for the Blind*, 474 US 481, 488–89 (1986) (arguing that any benefit to religion from a rehabilitation programme that permitted a blind student to attend a religious seminary occurred 'only as a result of the genuinely independent and private choices' of the student).

33   *Lemon* v. *Kurtzman*, 403 US 602, 612 (1971), a case challenging parochial teacher salary supplements for secular subjects and other direct aid to the schools. The *Lemon* test requires courts to ask whether there was a secular purpose for legislation (thus demanding neutrality of legislative intent), whether the primary effect of the law was to advance or inhibit religion (thus demanding neutrality of effect, although not strictly so), and whether the law excessively entangled the Church and state (thus demanding institutional separation).

34   See, for example, *Aguilar* v. *Felton*, 473 US 402 (1985) (Brennan opinion striking down financial assistance for educationally deprived children in parochial schools, such as remedial classes and guidance services provided by public school employees, a case later overruled in *Agostini* v. *Felton*, 521 US 203 (1997)); *Mueller* v. *Allen*, 463 US 388, 406–408, 416 (1983) (Marshall dissent, joined by Brennan, arguing that the benefit of a tax deduction primarily benefits parochial schools).

35   See, for example, *Zobrest* v. *Catalina Foothills School Dist*, 509 US 1 (1993) (Rehnquist majority opinion upholding the provision of a state-paid sign-language interpreter for a deaf parochial student, arguing that no funds traceable to the government found their way into church institutions and the benefit did not give parents an incentive to send their children to parochial schools); *Capitol Square Review and Advisory Board* v. *Pinette*, 515 US 753 (1995) (holding that a Klan display of a cross on public land did not violate the Establishment Clause simply because some viewer might mistakenly take the cross for a government endorsement of Christianity).

36   Cf. *McGowan* v. *Maryland*, 366 US 420 (1961) (holding that Sunday closing laws are

secular rather than religious in character) with *Lee* v. *Weisman*, 505 US 577 (1992) (holding that non-denominational prayers at a public high school graduation are still religious and therefore unconstitutional, and noting that the government may not even foster a 'civic religion' denuded of sectarian references).

37   See H. Abraham and B. Perry (1998), *Freedom and the Court: Civil Rights and Liberties in the United States*, (New York: Oxford University Press), pp. 305–9 (includes table of cases where Supreme Court found Establishment Clause violations). For a list of US Supreme Court cases on religious liberty prepared by constitutional scholar, Carl Esbeck, consult the web page of *The Journal of Law and Religion*, http://www.hamline.edu/law/jlr/.

38   See, for example, *Tilton* v. *Richardson*, 403 US 672 (1971) (allowing government construction grants to private religious colleges for secular education building); subsequent cases include *Hunt* v. *McNair*, 413 US 734 (1973) (permitting the state to provide tax-free bonds); and *Roemer* v. *Board of Public Works of Maryland*, 426 US 736 (1976) (permitting non-categorical grants to parochial universities); *Bowen* v. *Kendrick*, 487 US 589 (1988) (permitting federal funding for social services programmes to prevent teenage pregnancies to be given to religious agencies).

39   For example, in *Prince* v. *Commonwealth of Massachusetts*, 321 US 158, 167–68 (1943), the Court held that a child's welfare was a paramount interest to her free exercise of her religion by proselytizing and selling periodicals on the street, turning back the parents' argument that the state would be required to show a 'clear and present danger' of harm to the child. The Court noting that the state as *parens patriae* could override parental control, even that grounded in religious belief, in matters such as school attendance, child labour 'and in many other ways'. Justice Jackson's concurring argument emphasizes the necessity of state neutrality in religion. By contrast, see *Fowler* v. *Rhode Island*, 345 US 67 (1953), where the Court used the religious neutrality argument to protect the right of Jehovah's Witnesses to worship on public land.

40   See, for example, *Abington School Dist.* v. *Schempp*, 374 US 203 (1963) (striking down state programme of Bible readings on neutrality grounds); *McGowan* v. *Maryland*, 366 US 420 (1961) (upholding Sunday closing law as a secular rule); *Board of Education* v. *Allen*, 392 US 236 (1968) (upholding state loan of secular textbooks to children in parochial schools).

41   The key case is *Sherbert* v. *Verner*, 374 US 398 (1963) (denying the state the right to disqualify an unemployment benefits claimant who could not work on Saturdays due to her religious beliefs).

42   In *Lyng* v. *Northwest Indian Cemetery Protective Association*, 485 US 439 (1988) the Supreme Court turned back a Free Exercise Clause challenge by American Indians who claimed that the federal government's decision to expand a logging road in the national forest would disturb their sacred lands, holding that free exercise claimants could not force the government to use its lands for their benefit. The irony of the method by which the federal government acquired many of its lands, by conquest or unconscionable purchase agreements with American Indians, was apparently lost on the Court.

43   In *Bowen* v. *Roy*, 476 US 693 (1986), the Supreme Court held that a Native parent could not demand that the state agency not use a Social Security number for his daughter in tracking the family's public benefits because of his religious belief that it would harm her spirit, while intimating that the state might violate the Free Exercise Clause if it tried to force the parent to use the number himself.

44   See *United States* v. *Lee*, 455 US 252 (1982) (Amish denied free exercise exemption

from compulsory Social Security payments, though they violated the Amish belief that the community should take care of its own elderly and disabled workers). See also Gedicks, *The Rhetoric of Church and State, op. cit.*, pp. 106–7.

45 *Employment Division* v. *Smith*, 494 US 872 (1990).

46 *Braunfeld* v. *Brown*, 366 US. 599 (1961), holding that Sunday closing laws did not violate free exercise rights. The Court rejected the Orthodox Jewish claimant's suggestion that religious objectors be permitted to close another day a week, on the theory that such objectors might reap an economic advantage over competitors, and others would fraudulently assert that their religious belief forced them to close on their least profitable day. See also *McGowan* v. *Maryland*, 366 US 420 (1961) (upholding Sunday closing laws against an Establishment Clause challenge), and *Two Guys from Harrison Allentown Inc.* v. *McGinley*, 366 US 582 (1961) (upholding Sunday closing laws).

47 494 US 872, 877 (1990).

48 See, for example, his opinion in *Lee* v. *Weisman*, 505 US 577, 612–17 (1991).

49 See, for example, his discussion in *Rosenberger* v. *Rectors and Visitors of the University of Virginia*, 515 US 819, 853–57 (1995) (Thomas J concurring).

50 *Agostini* v. *Felton*, 521 US 203 (1997) permitted school districts to provide remedial education assistance to children on-site in parochial schools using public employees instructed not to participate in the religious aspects of the parochial school programme. While this case is remarkable in that it virtually overrules a fairly recent case, *Aguilar* v. *Felton*, 473 US 402 (1985), the Court's decision is not surprising in light of the cases that led up to it, including *Zobrest* v. *Catalina Foothills School Dist.*, 509 US 1 (1993) and *Witters* v. *Washington Dept. of Services for the Blind*, 474 US 481 (1986).

51 The line of cases from 1879–1946 involving punishment of Mormons for polygamy, including the most famous one, *Reynolds* v. *United States*, 98 US 145 (1879), are one example of the application of apparently neutral laws to harm religious exercise. However, the Court also rejected claims of objectors to oaths, *In re Summers*, 325 US 561, 572–73 (1945), and salute of the American flag, *Minersville School Dist.* v. *Gobitis*, 310 US 586 (1940) reversed in *West Virginia Board of Education* v. *Barnette*, 319 US 624 (1943). Commentators such as Marci Hamilton have noted that *Smith* does not destroy all Free Exercise Clause protection. The clause is still potentially available to reach cases of proven intentional discrimination against particular religious bodies, cases in which the religious freedom right is coupled with some other fundamental right such as the right to direct the upbringing of one's children, and cases in which the statutory scheme already includes a process for obtaining exemptions for non-religious reasons. See M. Hamilton (1998), 'The Constitutional Rhetoric of Religion', *University of Arkansas at Little Rock Law Journal*, **20**, p. 630.

52 For instance, several dissenting justices in *City of Boerne* v. *Flores*, suggested that *Smith* was improperly decided or that it should be reconsidered: see 117 S.Ct. 2176, 2186 (1997).

53 W.L. Miller (1985), *The First Liberty: Religion and the American Republic*, (New York: Paragon House Publishers), pp. 114–17; J. Madison, 'The Federalist No. 10', in G. Wills (ed.) (1982), *The Federalist Papers by Alexander Hamilton, James Madison, and John Jay*, (New York: Bantam Books), pp. 42–49.

54 See *Cantwell* v. *Connecticut*, 310 US 296 (1940), applying the protections of the Free Exercise Clause to state legislation and *Everson* v. *Board of Education*, 330 US 1 (1947), holding that the Establishment Clause also applies to the states.

55   See, for example, A.R. Amar (1996), 'Some Notes on the Establishment Clause',
      Roger Williams University Law Review, **2**, p. 1; W. Lietzau (1990), 'Rediscovering the
      Establishment Clause: Federalism and the Rollback of Incorporation', *DePaul Law
      Review*, 39, p. 1191ff; Adams and Emmerich, *A Nation Dedicated, op.cit.*, pp. 43–45.

56   Ibid., p. 47.

57   Miller, *The First Liberty, op. cit.*, pp. 163–66, 175, 177–80, 188–90; Tribe, *American
      Constitutional Law, op. cit.*, pp. 1158–60.

58   Tribe, *American Constitutional Law, op. cit.*, p. 1159. For another view, see D.
      Dreisbach, 'In Pursuit of Religious Freedom: Thomas Jefferson's Church–State Views
      Revisited', in Lugo, *Religion, op. cit.*, pp. 74–96.

59   See *Sherbert* v. *Verner*, 374 US 398, 422–23 (1963) (Harlan, J, dissenting).

60   Title VII, 42 USC §. 2000e-1(a) gives a limited exemption to religious institution
      employers to prefer members of their own faith, but employers who are not within the
      auspices of the Church proper may not similarly discriminate, even if they believe in
      creating pervasively religious atmospheres in their places of business.

61   See, especially, the American Indian Religious Freedom Act, Act of 11 August 1978,
      Pub. L. No. 95–341, 92 Stat. 469 (1978) as amended Pub. L. 103–344 §1, 6 October,
      1984, 108 Stat. 3125 (codified in part as 42 USC §. 1996).

62   Equal Access Act, Pub. L. No. 98–377 §802, 98 Stat. 1302 (codified at 20 USC §4071
      (1988). The result in *Goldman* v. *Weinberger*, 475 US 503 (1986) was also overturned
      by congressional statute in 1987.

63   521 US 507 (1997).

64   For instance, during the 1990s the Supreme Court has turned back federal attempts to
      require state and local governments to assist it in conducting background checks of
      prospective handgun purchasers under the Brady Handgun Violence Prevention Act,
      Printz v. *United States*, 521 US 98 (1997), and attempts by Congress to prevent
      handguns from being brought into school zones under its Commerce Clause author-
      ity, *United States* v. *Lopez*, 514 US 549 (1995).

65   However, the Supreme Court has permitted states to provide more protection and/or
      accommodation for religious freedom claims under their state constitutions than the
      federal constitution provides: see, for example, A. Carmella (1993), 'State Constitu-
      tional Protection of Religious Exercise: An Emerging Post-*Smith* Jurisprudence',
      Brigham Young University Law Review, **1993**, pp. 284–93.

66   See the discussion of the position that law-makers should not rely on religious
      reasons in making a political decision, even if they are motivated by religious con-
      cerns, in M. Perry (1991), *Love and Power: The Role of Religion and Morality in
      American Politics*, (New York: Oxford University Press), pp. 9–28 and Perry's later
      argument that religious arguments supporting public decisions should be tested in
      public political debate but that law-makers should still proffer an independent secular
      ground for their decisions on human well-being in M. Perry (1998), 'Liberal Democ-
      racy and Religious Morality', *DePaul Law Review*, **48**, pp. 5, 20; see also M. Perry,
      Religion in Politics: Constitutional and Moral Perspectives (1997), (New York: Ox-
      ford University Press), pp. 102–4; *Love and Power, op. cit.*, at pp. 32–33. See also D.
      Conkle (1993–94), 'Differing Religions, Different Politics: Evaluating the Role of
      Competing Religious Traditions in American Politics and Law', *Journal of Law and
      Religion*, **10**, p. 1; F. Gamwell (1985), 'Religion and Reason in American Politics,'
      Journal of Law and Religion, **2**, p. 325; W. Marshall (1993), 'The Other Side of
      Religion', *Hastings Law Journal*, **44**, pp. 843–63 (arguing that religious argument
      must be constrained in the public square, using the story of the Grand Inquisitor).

67   Perry, *Love and Power, op. cit.*, pp. 99–106. Perry called for an ecumenical politics

that is publicly intelligible and accessible to those who speak different religious or moral languages, respectful, empathetic, honest and sincere, and attentive in speaking with the other. He also argued that those in dialogue must embrace fallibilism or self-critical rationality, and the pluralistic understanding that difference 'can be a more fertile source of deepening moral insight'.

68   For a discussion of interest group politics affecting religious liberty, see D. Laycock (1993), 'The Religious Freedom Restoration Act', *Brigham Young University Law Review* **1993**, pp. 224–31 (describing harm to culturally conservative churches as well as recent Hmong, Jehovah's Witness and the Cornerstone Bible Church encounters with government).

69   *Lynch* v. *Donnelly*, 465 US 668, 694 (1994) (O'Connor J concurring).

70   See C. Eisgruber and L. Sager (1996), 'Unthinking Religious Freedom', *Texas Law Review*, **74**, pp. 600–16.

71   *Employment Div.* v. *Smith*, 494 US 872, 888 (1990). See also the discussion of the pietist–separatists' view that temporal authorities must prevail over individual consciences, Adams and Emmerich, *A Nation Dedicated*, *op. cit.*, p. 57.

72   Madison, 'The Federalist No. 10', *op. cit.*

73   For example, in Madison's *Remonstrance to the Virginia General Assembly*, in an argument which is adopted in parts in the Declaration of Independence, he argued:

The Religion then of every man must be left to the conviction of conscience of every man; and it is the right of every man to exercise it as these may dictate. This right is in its nature an unalienable right. It is unalienable, because the opinions of men, depending only on the evidence contemplated by their own minds cannot follow the dictates of other men: It is unalienable also, because what is here a right towards men, is a duty towards the Creator. It is the duty of every man to render to the Creator such homage and such only as he believes to be acceptable to him. This duty is precedent, both in order of time and in degree of obligation, to the claims of Civil Society. (Miller, *The First Liberty*, *op. cit.*, p. 359).

74   J. Madison (1785) 'To the Honorable the General Assembly of the Commonwealth of Virginia: A Memorial and Remonstrance' in ibid., p.359 (Appendix II).

75   Ibid.

76   Ibid.

77   380 US 163 (1965).

78   Ibid., p. 166.

79   See Gedicks, *The Rhetoric of Church and State*, *op.cit.*, p. 111.

80   See, for example, F. Gedicks (1992), 'Public Life and Hostility to Religion,' *Virginia Law Review*, **78**, pp. 671–76, 682. Perhaps the most well known book that makes this claim is that of Stephen Carter (1993), *The Culture of Disbelief*, (New York: Basic Books), pp. 51–52, 68.

81   See, for example, *Smith* v. *Board of School Commissioners of Mobile County*, 655 F. Supp. 939 (S.D.Ala. 1987) (holding that public school texts violated the Establishment Clause); *Mozert* v. *Hawkins Co. Bd. of Education*, 827 F.2d 1058 (6th Cir. 1987), cert. denied, 484 US 1066 (1998) (parents unsuccessfully asserted that books taught secular humanism).

82   *Wisconsin* v. *Yoder*, 405 US 205, 209–17, 235 (1972).

83   *Lyng* v. *Northwest Indian Cemetery Protective Assn*, 485 US 439 (1988).

84   See, for example, *International Society for Krishna Consciousness* v. *Lee*, 505 US 672 (1992) (one of several court cases in which members of the Hare Krishna religion were

prohibited from proselytizing through the sale of merchandise and literature, at state fairs, airports, and in other public places); upheld by the Court; *O'Lone* v. *Estate of Shabazz* 482 US 342 (1987) (prisoner prevented from practicing religious food rituals).

85   See, for example, *In the Matter of Harrison Orthodox Minyan, Inc.* v. *Town Bd. of Harrison*, 159 AD 2d 572, 552 NYS.2d 434 (App. Div. 1990).

86   See, for example, *St. John's Evang. Luth. Church* v. *City of Hoboken*, 95 NJ Super. 414, 479 A.2d 935 (1983).

87   See, for example, *Settle* v. *Dickson County School Board*, 53 F.3d 152 (6th Cir.), cert. denied, 116 S.Ct. 518 (1995), described in M. Paulsen and S. Johnson (1997), 'Scalia's Sermonette', *Notre Dame Law Review*, **72**, pp. 877–80.

88   Esbeck 'A Typology of Church–State Relations', *op. cit.*, pp. 21–22.

89   Adams and Emmerich, *A Nation Dedicated, op. cit.*, pp. 95–96; Gedicks, *The Rhetoric of Church and State, op. cit.*, pp. 11–12; cf. Esbeck, 'A Typology of Church–State Relations', *op. cit.*, note 18 above, pp. 15–17 (discussing structural pluralism).

90   Ibid.

91   Ibid., p. 17.

92   See E. Firmage (1989), 'Free Exercise of Religion in Nineteenth Century America: The Mormon Cases', *Journal of Law and Religion*, **VII**, p. 281.

93   See R. Michaelsen (1988), 'Is the Miner's Canary Silent? Implications of the Supreme Court's Denial of American Indian Free Exercise of Religion Claims', *Journal of Law and Religion*, **VII**, p. 97.

94   See, for example, Lietzau, 'Rediscovering the Establishment Clause', *op. cit.*, pp. 1196, 1208–10, 1224–26 on the intended place of non-establishment in the protection of minority liberties, and the current improper use of the establishment doctrine to favour the interests of minority secularists.

95   See, for example, 'Letter to the Editor' (4 July, 1998), *The Harrisburg Patriot and Evening News*, p. A07, 1998 Westlaw 6471726; A. Weaver, 'The Religious Right's Sectarian Future?: Drop-out Christianity', *Christian Century*, **116**, p. 300, 1999 Westlaw 10269130; on the Christian nation ideal, see also M. Frankel (1992), 'Religion in Public Life – Reasons for Minimal Access', *George Washington Law Review*, **60**, pp. 633–35.

96   See descriptions by critics of such concerns: for example, A. Walen (1997), 'The "Defense of Marriage Act" and Authoritarian Morality', *William and Mary Bill of Rights Journal*, **5**, pp. 621, 639.

97   See, for example, the plea of Judge Brevard Hand, one of the few judges who has recognized 'secular humanism' as a religion, on affirmative action:

> We have been the recipients of the choicest bounties of Heaven; we have grown in numbers, wealth and power as no other nation has ever grown. But we have forgotten God… . [W]e have vainly imagined, in the deceitfulness of our hearts, that all these blessings were produced by some superior wisdom and virtue of our own. Intoxicated with unbroken success, we have become too self-sufficient to feel the necessity of redeeming and preserving grace, too proud to pay to the God that made us… . Our government is operating today under a phoney interpretation of our governing law. Can it be that we have given power where it should not have been reposed? (B. Hand (1997), 'Affirmative Action: A Mort de la Republique? A Second Cry from the Wilderness', *Alabama Law Review*, **48**, p. 858).

98   N. Dorsen (1986), 'The Religion Clauses and Nonbelievers', *William and Mary Law Review*, **27**, pp. 864–66.

99 See Gedicks, *The Rhetoric of Church and State*, *op. cit.*, pp. 52–56 (discussing school financing).

100 See, for example, J. Garvey (1996) 'An Anti-Liberal Argument for Religious Freedom', *Journal of Contemporary Legal Issues*, **7**, p. 275 (arguing, against liberalism, that religion is not simply an aspect of autonomy but a public good).

101 See, for example, D. Laycock (1996), 'Religious Liberty as Liberty', *Journal of Contemporary Legal Issues*, **7**, p. 313.

102 Ibid., M. McConnell (1993), 'God is Dead and We Have Killed Him! Freedom of Religion in the Postmodern Age', *Brigham Young University Law Review*, **1993**, pp. 172–76; E. Gaffney (1993), 'The Religion Clause: A Double Guarantee of Religious Liberty', *Brigham Young University Law Review*, **1993**, pp. 189–94 (criticizing the argument that religions account for civil strife).

103 See, for example, *Wisconsin* v. *Yoder*, 406 US 205, 243 (1972) (Douglas J dissenting) in which Justice Douglas argued that only one of the individual child plaintiffs had explicitly acknowledged her desire to follow her faith tradition's ban on attending public school after the 8th grade.

104 In *Amos* 483 US 327 (1987), the Court held that a congressional exemption from employment discrimination laws that permitted church bodies to hire individuals based on their religious affiliation and compliance with religious doctrine was not a violation of the Establishment Clause because it allowed churches to advance their religious beliefs.

105 See, for example, S. Smith (1998), 'Is a Coherent Theory of Religious Freedom Possible?', *Constitutional Commentary*, **15**, pp. 73–74 (suggesting that religious argument can only be a *modus vivendi* – something 'in the nature of a negotiated and perhaps messy, truce'); S. Smith (1996), 'Unprincipled Religious Freedom', *Journal of Contemporary Legal Issues*, **7**, pp. 497ff; McConnell, 'God is Dead', *op. cit.*, pp. 186–87 (noting the unmasking of liberal theory, once supposed to be the 'neutral arbiter among competing understandings of the good life').

106 See the discussion of Douglas Laycock's and Michael McConnell's views, offering a 'pluralistic' approach to religious freedom questions, and Steven Smith and Frederick Gedicks who express scepticism about a theoretical approach in T. Berg (1997), 'Religion Clause Anti-Theories', *Notre Dame Law Review*, **72**, pp. 703–38; R. Teitel (1993), 'Postmodernist Architectures in the Law of Religion', *Brigham Young University Law Review*, **1993**, pp. 106–13 (focusing on the postmodern value of pluralistic equality).

107 Ibid., pp. 695–701; *Lynch* v. *Donnelly*, 465 US 668, 688–694 (1984) (O'Connor J concurring).

108 475 US 503, 512–13 (Stevens J concurring) and 526–27 (Blackmun J dissenting).

109 For example E.G. Wallace (1998–99), 'Beyond Neutrality: Equal Access and the Meaning of Religious Freedom', *University of Arkansas Little Rock Law Journal*, **12**, p. 335, at pp. 380–90; *County of Allegheny* v. *American Civil Liberties Union*, 492 US 573, 692 (O'Connor J concurring). See also *Clever* v. *Cherry Hill Township Bd. of Education*, 838 F. Supp. 929 (D. NJ 1993) (upholding district policy requiring acknowledgement of religious holidays of diverse traditions); *Florey* v. *Sioux Falls School District*, 619 F.2d 1311 (8th Cir. 1980) (same).

6   Discretion and Discrimination in Legal Cases involving Controversial Religious Groups and Allegations of Ritual Abuse

James T. Richardson

Introduction

Legal systems are pervaded by discretion. Choices are made by those in authority about such issues as who to detain, who to arrest, what charges are brought, whether the defendant is guilty and, if so, of what crime. Similarly, civil legal systems also involve the use of discretion at virtually every point in a suit. Judges are particularly empowered to exercise considerable discretion in order to achieve justice.

But courts are also normative institutions which have as a major function the enforcement of norms of belief and behaviour that are deemed important in a given society. This confluence of normative and justice concerns within the same institution can sometimes lead to serious problems in which normative concerns override justice considerations. This has happened in American history – for instance, with the treatment of minorities in the legal system. Many observers believe that the American legal system has been used as a social control device for black males, and that justice has not always been achieved in cases involving such parties. Such was also the case for decades in South Africa.

A similar argument can be made about legal actions involving controversial religious groups or personages. If triers of fact – judges and jurors – are imbued with certain values and beliefs about minority faiths, then, as these

111

decision-makers exercise their legal responsibilities to decide issues relevant to cases, should it be surprising that those values and beliefs are sometimes acted out, perhaps to the detriment of justice concerns? There is some evidence for this idea, as research on the impact of such considerations demonstrates.[1]

This chapter will focus on how legal systems sometimes operate in ways detrimental to unpopular religious groups. I will discuss the ways in which courts deal with evidence and other key decisions in cases involving unpopular religions or alleged objectionable practices. As will be shown, there are sometimes serious problems concerning the kinds of evidence offered, and accepted, in cases involving controversial religious groups or other types of case with religious overtones (for instance, those involving allegations of satanic activity). Decisions to admit or not admit evidence can be determinative, as anyone familiar with legal systems knows.

I will discuss some American cases involving new religious groups, sometimes referred to pejoratively as 'cults',[2] paying particular attention to so-called 'cult/brainwashing' cases. I will also relate evidentiary problems in two notorious Australian cases involving minority religions. Finally, I will comment on evidentiary problems associated with cases dealing with allegations of satanic ritual abuse in the United States and elsewhere.

My thesis is a simple one: problems of quality of evidence arise in cases involving controversial groups or practices because courts may allow questionable evidence in such cases. Decisions are sometimes made to admit evidence that would not be admitted under other, more normal, circumstances. In addition, jurors (in societies and cases which make use of juries) are prone to accept questionable evidence when it supports biases and prejudices they hold about minority religious groups and alleged practices.[3] First, however, I will discuss so-called 'cult/brainwashing' cases in the United States and elsewhere.

'Cult/Brainwashing' Cases

In recent decades the United States has witnessed a significant number of cases involving new religions accused of 'brainwashing' participants and using so-called 'mind control' to retain members. This simplistic 'brainwashing' theory of why people participate in such groups is a negotiated 'account' that serves the interest of those offering it and seems to be undergirded by the idea that no right-thinking person would ever participate in such strange groups unless they were tricked or under some sort of mental control.[4] Why some young people would give up promising futures to participate seems beyond the ability of some parents and others to grasp or accept. A popular 'account' of the situation is that something must have happened involving powerful psycho-technologies that were beyond the control of the young person and which somehow overcame years of socialization and training. Therefore, the threat that has apparently overcome the 'free will' of many young people is defined as a major problem requiring strong responses from society's institutional structures, including the justice system.

Civil actions have been brought in which ex-members have sued the former group for large sums of money using a brainwashing-based theory. The legal basis of such cases has been tortious, comprising claims of false imprisonment, fraud, intentional infliction of emotional distress or related torts. Much of the discussion in court has been based on popular theories of brainwashing and mind control. A sizeable number of such cases have been brought in recent years, often by people who have been forcibly 'deprogrammed'. Several such cases have resulted in multimillion dollar jury awards, mostly in the form of punitive damages awarded to punish behaviour (thought by the triers of fact to be especially egregious) and to make an example of the offender.[5]

These brainwashing-based claims have also arisen in a few criminal cases in which people have used such theories to help establish a kind of 'diminished capacity' defence to criminal charges, saying, in effect, that they would not have broken the law had they not been brainwashed. Such claims have been raised as a defence in kidnapping or assault cases brought against 'deprogrammers' who have forcibly removed adult members from new religious groups and then used rigorous methods with the 'deprogramee' in an effort to make them recant their beliefs and withdraw allegiance from the group. The issue of brainwashing has also arisen in civil actions resulting from attempted deprogrammings, when deprogrammers (and those who hired them) have been sued by the deprogramming target.

For a time, the use of brainwashing-based claims in civil actions was rather successful, as has been the use of such claims as part of the defence in cases where deprogrammers were being charged with kidnapping or assault. However, such claims in diminished capacity defences in criminal cases have not worked well.[6] Family court uses of brainwashing-based claims flourished for a while as a basis for conservatorship hearings brought by parents of adult children. However, adverse appeal court rulings have limited such uses in recent times.[7]

In the kidnapping cases, brainwashing claims have sometimes been a part of what in the United States is called the 'necessity' or 'choice of evils' defence. The idea is a simple one, but fraught with the possibility of abuse. Supposedly, the person was taken from the group because it was necessary to do so or he or she would have suffered a greater harm than that of being kidnapped. Such use of a necessity or choice of evils defence is not routinely allowed in American courts, but it can be raised and allowed by the court where deemed relevant. When dealing with a strange, even hated and feared new religious group, it is easy to see a judge allowing such testimony. This has happened with direct rulings to allow such defences, or more indirectly by the judge allowing considerable leeway in discussions of motives for the commission of the alleged crime of kidnapping or assault.[8]

In civil actions against a group of former members, brainwashing-based testimony has often also been admitted under the rationale that the plaintiff must be allowed to explain what it is about the group that was so bad as to constitute a valid claim of false imprisonment, fraud or intentional infliction of emotional distress. Thus, in some cases, judges and jurors have heard days, even weeks, of often slanted testimony about the beliefs and practices of an unconventional religious group in an effort to support tort claims against it.

Such decisions in criminal and civil matters have had the effect of allowing very questionable testimony from a few self-designated 'experts' who are willing to say that the particular group in question does brainwash its members, and that life in the group is heinous and revolting. They claim that the group is so bad that merely being a member causes mental problems that require treatment and warrant damages and that people should be rescued at all costs, if necessary by kidnapping them against their will.

These experts ignore the volitional nature of virtually all decisions to participate, as well as the very high attrition rates that such groups suffer, since most participants decide, after a short time, to move on to something else. Such 'experts' also ignore a huge scholarly literature demonstrating that participation in such groups usually has an ameliorative function, and that many people have a quite positive experience in such groups.[9]

Thus, in the United States, although there is a Bill of Rights supposedly guaranteeing freedom of religion, we may see problematic testimony about the beliefs and practices of a given religious group placed on the record for the jury's consideration. This can also occur in other countries, including some that guarantee freedom of religion either through national or international governing documents. Testimony that seems a clear violation of freedom of religion guarantees may thus be introduced through the 'backdoor' under the guise of explaining why allowing a person to remain in the group would have been a greater evil than kidnapping them, or how the person was supposedly tricked into participating in such a strange group.

The very fact that judges allow such testimony at all would not be lost on jurors who, of course, also bring their own biases and prejudices to the court. The political and normative nature of judicial systems is thus well illustrated by cases involving new and controversial religious groups. When so-called scientific experts are allowed to testify in ways that reinforce the normal biases and misinformation found in many jury pools, the court needs to be especially mindful of possible problems and be alert to decisions to allow what is plainly questionable testimony. Both in the United States and elsewhere it is fashionable to oppose the so-called 'cult menace', but it may not be good legal and judicial practice to allow such considerations to govern decisions about the type of evidence and defences allowed in court.

Australian Cases Involving Controversial Religious Groups

Australia has not experienced the same volume of civil and criminal actions concerning new religious groups as the United States, at least to date. Brainwashing-based claims were implicit in family court proceedings instituted in the early 1990s concerning over 240 children taken into custody from their parents who were members of a controversial new religion known as 'The Family' (formerly known as the 'Children of God').[10] Also, there has been a concerted attempt to develop more American-style litigation concerning so-called 'cults', as part of an effort at social control by private groups of citizens.[11] This effort will certainly involve implicit, if not explicit, claims related to brainwashing and its synonyms.

The lack of brainwashing-based claims in ordinary court proceedings in Australia does not mean that there have been no problems associated with legal actions involving newer and minority religious groups in that country, however. I will describe briefly two important cases, both of which received considerable publicity at the time of their occurrence. One such instance of very questionable evidence being allowed was the famous 'Hilton bombing' case, involving members of the Ananda Marga religion. A second is the Lindy Chamberlain case resulting from the disappearance of her baby at Ayers Rock (Uhuru) about 20 years ago – a case so notable that a movie, with the American title *Cry in the Dark* and starring Meryl Streep and Sam Neill, was made of the episode and its aftermath.[12] First, I will comment on the Hilton bombing case.

In 1981 a bomb went off outside the Hilton Hotel in Sydney, killing two workers and injuring several others. It was thought that the bomb was designed to disrupt an important political conference taking place at that time in Sydney and, later, once the police and media had fixated on a group that supposedly placed the bomb, the idea developed that the bomb might even have been directly targeted at a specific visiting dignitary, the Prime Minister of India.

Almost immediately after the bombing, the press began to speculate that the Ananda Marga group, a radical Hindu sect, was possibly linked to the bombing. In the news stories this group was associated with some violent political actions overseas, including in India, and had been the focus of an investigation by the Australian federal authorities for several months at the time of the bombing. Three of its members in Sydney were arrested on other charges, but almost immediately the press was full of stories that those arrested were implicated in the Hilton bombing, via statements made by a police informant.[13]

A police informer who had allegedly infiltrated the group told wild tales of the planning of the bombing and other matters. Other police informants came forward later with tales of what they had heard the defendants say while imprisoned with them after the bombing. The testimony of police informants in this case was obviously problematic, simply because the informants would claim things that were physically impossible (some of those making claims were not even in the same prison), and the testimony was often internally illogical and inconsistent. In hindsight the evidence from the infiltrator of the Ananda Marga group looks more like a systematic effort to entrap the defendants than to observe them and report back to authorities.

Just as problematic was the use of so-called 'police verbals' which were written notes of what defendants allegedly said to police. Again, such evidence failed tests of simple logic and internal consistency and seems, after the passage of time, to have been manufactured just to secure a conviction.

Problems with this testimony were pointed out at trial, but they were ignored by the media and apparently forgotten by most of the judges who dealt with the case, as well as by the jurors. The media wrote articles as if convictions were a foregone conclusion, ignoring the evidentiary problems. Virtually everyone, including media representatives, seemed to think that they 'had their men'.

One major problem arose because the defendants were unable to gain access to some key evidence against them – evidence that turned out to have a significant exculpatory effect when finally reviewed by a special commission, and which led eventually to their release from prison. The battle over access to certain types of evidence was carried all the way to the Australian High Court, and lost on a split vote against the defendant's right of access. This decision probably contributed greatly to the convictions of those charged, and clearly shows the impact of judicial discretion in cases involving unpopular groups.

As indicated, the three defendants were eventually released, and were even paid a relatively meagre amount of compensation for their trouble, *but only after serving seven years in prison*. One of them, Tim Anderson, was even put through another trial for the bombing (he was found not guilty this time) – an action that some commentators suggested was brought by some authorities (embarrassed) in the first case in an effort to get even.

With hindsight, the lessons of this case seem obvious. The police and some federal governmental agencies, as well as the judiciary, can sometimes became so influenced by mass hysteria that good judgement is clouded, and wrong, even tragic, decisions are made.[14] Clearly, justice was not served by the Hilton bombing case, and we still do not know for certain why it happened or who did it. The defendants appeared to be convenient scape-goats, and their scapegoating was almost completely successful.

The defendants' participation in an unpopular minority religious sect played a major role in how they were treated by governmental agencies and the legal system, as well as by the media. They were politically weak and were thus vulnerable to allegations about their connection with the bomb-ing. Once the accusations were made, a tidal wave of media prejudice washed away all hope that the defendants might receive a fair trial. And the Australian legal system failed at virtually every turn to allow a fair trial that would have led to justice being done in this case.

Similar comments can be made about the Lindy Chamberlain matter. When her baby disappeared it seemed at first like a routine, if tragic, incident at an isolated spot in the middle of Australia. There had been recent reports of dingos attacking humans in that very area, including in which a mother engaged in a tug-of-war with a dingo attacking her small boy before the dingo gave up and went away. Just the day before a dingo had grabbed the arm of an adolescent girl in the campsite adjacent to that of the Chamber-lains. An official in the area had become sufficiently concerned about dingo behaviour around Ayers Rock (Uhuru) to write a report recommending measures to curtail dingo–human contact. Contact with humans who in-sisted on feeding the wild animals and trying to pet them was radically altering the behaviour of the local dingos and making them unpredictable and dangerous.

The first inquest into the baby's disappearance resulted in a ruling that the baby had disappeared for reasons unknown, but the media, fed by rumours about the strange rituals and beliefs of the Seventh Day Adventist Church to which Lindy and her husband Michael belonged, did not let the matter rest, and neither did police officials. Particularly noteworthy was the media 'feed-ing frenzy' that developed around rumours that the baby's name, Azaria, meant 'sacrifice in the wilderness'. Consequently, the idea that Lindy had murdered her baby in some sort of bizarre religious ritual took root in the mass media and thus in the public consciousness, fuelled by police officials who refused to agree that Mrs Chamberlain was innocent. Thus, the Chamber-lain's participation in, and strong beliefs about, their religion, and the way in which the courts dealt with such matters, contributed to what happened next.[15]

A second inquest was held after scientific evidence was obtained from a Professor James Cameron, a well known UK Professor of Forensic

Medicine, who was asked by the police almost immediately after the first inquest to examine the baby's clothes and other evidence, including the skull of a dingo (apparently to discern whether the dingo could open its jaws wide enough to hold a baby), and render a report about the possible cause of death. Cameron, who had apparently never seen a dingo, decided that the baby had died from having its throat cut (reported as decapitation in the media), with the baby's suit then cut to make it appear that a dingo had done the killing. He also claimed to be able to see, under ultraviolet light, a handprint in blood on the baby's suit – a print from a small hand such as that of Lindy Chamberlain.

It turned out later that Professor Cameron, who was obviously much too quick to jump to conclusions about what had happened, was also in part misled by the police. He was told, for instance, that the baby's clothes were snapped shut except for the top two snaps (which was not true) and he was also told that the baby's clothes had been found in a neat bundle (instead of scattered about the area as they actually were). The police apparently decided, in their discretion, to withhold these inconvenient facts from the professor.

The eventual decision of the second inquest was that the baby was murdered – a decision based wholly on forensic circumstantial evidence furnished by Dr Cameron. Lindy Chamberlain was indicted for the crime, and her husband Michael was also charged as an accessory for having tried to shield his wife after the alleged deed had been done.

Mrs Chamberlain was eventually found guilty of murdering her baby in one of the most sensationalized trials of the century – a trial which received considerable international media coverage. She was sentenced to life imprisonment, a decision upheld on a three-to-two vote of the Australian High Court, of which two members expressed serious concerns about the quality of the forensic evidence used to convict her. (Michael Chamberlain received a sentence of 18 months, as well, which was suspended on the posting of a bond.)[16] In the event, Lindy Chamberlain served *five years'* imprisonment until released after a special commission was appointed to examine some new evidence, and after a prolonged campaign by people who believed that justice had not been done.

Baby Azaria's jacket was eventually found at Ayers Rock – a fact that was used to justify reconsideration of the case in a very unusual way. The Police Commissioner of the Northern Territory had recommended reopening the case on the basis of new evidence, but the Northern Territory cabinet declined. Federal members of the cabinet intervened and secured the release of Lindy Chamberlain from prison. A special Judicial Commission was then appointed to review the evidence in the case, the report of which was extremely critical of the forensic evidence used to convict. The Commission recommended a pardon for both Chamberlains, which was then granted by Royal Prerogative.

The Commission found that the evidence on which her conviction was based to be sadly wanting. Spray paint underneath the dashboard of the family car (present since the original painting of the vehicle) had been testified to as blood from the 'arterial spray' emanating from the baby as her throat was cut in the car. Blood samples had been tested using plainly improper methods, and conclusions from the tests were presented in ways that fitted the apparent beliefs of the individual carrying out the tests.[17] Tears on clothing had been testified to by the famous visiting English forensic scientist as definitely not having been made by a dingo's teeth, but more likely by a pair of scissors.

The Commission's findings raise a profound question. If the evidence was so weak, why was this not discovered during the trial by the judge, who should have disallowed it, or by the jury, whose job it was to assess the evidence?

The defence team did a reasonably competent job of pointing out problems with the evidence, but they were ignored by the judge, by the media, and eventually by the jurors. The persistence of police and the Northern Territory justice officials paid off, particularly when they obtained the unequivocal statement from Professor Cameron that led to the second inquest. Professor Cameron's credentials, coupled with his sensational conclusions, doomed the Chamberlains. The media made much of the speculation about the baby's cut throat, linking it with supposed rituals of the Adventists. The Chamberlains' stoicism in the face of tragedy, an apparent product of their deep and rather fatalistic faith, was misinterpreted by many as an uncaring attitude towards Azaria's death.

The Chamberlains, who eventually divorced under the stress of the trial and its aftermath, might have been found guilty of the charges even if they were not Adventists. However, a serious question can be raised about whether the second inquest that led to their being charged would have ever taken place had the case not been given impetus by so many media-fed rumours linking their religion to what had supposedly happened. It now seems safe to say that most people accept the 'dingo theory' of the case, but it seems that the judicial system failed in the face of strong efforts to convict, including efforts by supposedly objective scientists and technicians who were allowed considerable leeway by the court in expressing their personal opinions. Such a breakdown in the judicial system, both initiated and then exploited by a media frenzy almost unparalleled in Australian journalism, should give all who desire a fair justice system considerable pause for thought.

Satanic Ritual Abuse Allegations

There is nothing more heinous, given today's values in European-derived societies, than child abuse, and child sexual abuse is usually defined as the worst sort of such abuse. This high level of concern has had a significant impact on the functioning of the justice system, as will be shown by examining the apparent epidemic of cases during the 1980s and early 1990s in the United States and elsewhere. Many of these notorious cases involved allegations of a considerable degree of child sexual abuse in child care centres and small communities – accusations often accompanied by claims that the abuse was part of some satanic ritual involving ritualized sacrifices and sexual behaviour. (Hence the term 'ritual abuse' that has become so popular in stories about such claims.)

The outbreak of child sex abuse cases in the United States yielded varying results.[18] Some of the most notorious resulted in the absolution of those accused (such as in the famous *McMartin* case in California which went through two lengthy and very expensive trials without one conviction), or the dismissal of charges. However, some cases led to convictions of individuals whose guilt was later questioned, mainly because of the type of evidence brought to bear in such cases, and judicial decisions to allow the problematic evidence. A number of cases involving such accusations have been overturned on appeal, including the notorious *Kelly Michaels* case in New Jersey, which, after the *McMartin* case in California,[19] was the most publicized such case in the United States.

The UK has also witnessed a major outbreak of ritual abuse cases, with similar results. Jenkins thoroughly analyses the causes and history of this 'moral panic' in the UK and discusses major cases such as that in the Orkney Islands, and the Cleveland case, both of which fell apart under scrutiny, but only after disrupting the lives of dozens, if not hundreds, of people.[20] He also details the crucial involvement of American 'missionaries' of satanic ritual abuse who brought the ideas to the UK through printed matter and videotapes, as well as personal visits.

In New Zealand there has also been at least one major child sex abuse case which attracted the attention of scholars, and which also involved the work of American 'anti-satanist missionaries'.[21] The case developed in Christchurch at a civic crèche which was abruptly closed in the autumn of 1992 following allegations of child sexual abuse arising in circumstances quite similar to those in some major American cases, such as *McMartin*. However, in the *Ellis* case, a conviction was obtained in what has become a controversial verdict within New Zealand.[22] The controversy is largely based on the same issue raised in other such cases – the quality of the evidence and the exercise of discretion by those in authority within the legal and judicial systems.

Since the end of the 1980s the high level of concern about child sexual abuse has led to the development in the United States, the UK and other countries, including Australia and New Zealand, of special laws designed to make it easier to prosecute such cases. Those laws have had two principal impacts. One of these is to lower usual bulwarks against hearsay testimony to allow others to testify to what the child allegedly told them in investigative or therapeutic sessions, or even in conversations with family members and friends.

The other major change in how such cases are handled has been for the purpose of affording the child greater protection from being traumatized by the events of the trial. For instance, some new laws have allowed the child to avoid being in the presence of the accused – a clear departure from traditional guarantees that an accused should be allowed to confront their accusers. The courts now frequently allow children to testify via videotape, or closed circuit television, or from behind screens, shielded from the view of the accused. Indeed, sometimes courts have allowed children not to testify at all, if it is thought likely to traumatize them too much. Furthermore, often defendants have not even been allowed to cross-examine the children, on the basis that to do so would result in further unnecessary trauma. Thus, sometimes the only testimony used to convict has been hearsay testimony from adults who themselves are deeply involved in the case in ways that make their testimony somewhat suspect and even self-serving.

These changes in law and procedure were made by well-meaning individuals, but they seem to overlook other important considerations. For instance, what impact do such elaborate measures to protect witnesses from the accused have on jurors? They may serve to convince jurors that the accused must be an extremely wicked individual if the authorities are so afraid for a child witness's welfare.[23] Also, when a defendant cannot be allowed any access at all to his or her accuser for the purposes of investigation or cross-examination, what is the effect on the concept of a fair trial?

Even more problematic has been the way in which key testimony, whether offered by the child directly or by other hearsay witnesses, has been developed. Courageous work by some judges and some extremely creative research by a few scientists has made us aware of severe problems with evidence offered in some child sexual abuse cases. Some judges have simply allowed any type of testimony about possible abuse, apparently giving up the field (and the notion of judicial autonomy) to the new laws passed by concerned legislatures. Others have attempted a gatekeeping function, and screened such evidence for reliability and validity, sometimes at great political and personal cost.[24] They have reviewed, or had others review on the judge's own motion, video- or audiotapes or transcripts of therapy or investigative sessions with the children. Such reviews of key testimony have sometimes found the testimony sorely wanting in reliability and validity. Leading and persistent questioning by investigators and/or therapists (who obviously believed such charges to be true) have led to the children agreeing with the investigator, sometimes just to get them 'off their back'. Furthermore, sometimes the children themselves have come to believe what the adults questioning them so obviously believed to be the case.

In one case overturned a few years ago by the Supreme Court of Nevada, two individuals had been accused of ritual child sexual abuse.[25] After an initial report from one mother that her daughter had said some things suggesting that she had been abused at the day care centre which she attended, the authorities took it upon themselves to notify all the parents of the other children at the centre that such abuse was possibly taking place and that parents should talk to their children about it or take them to a therapist (at the state's expense). The notification provoked great concern within the community and led to innumerable sessions with therapists. Eventually, after much questioning, nine children were thought by the authorities to have been abused, although most strongly denied it initially and recanted later (including on the witness stand), and some of the claims were so bizarre as to be completely unbelievable. Nevertheless, 21 charges of sexual abuse were eventually lodged, involving the nine children, and the case was brought to trial. The two defendants were found guilty on only four of the 21 counts (the rest were dismissed at trial because of believable recantations done on the stand by the other children), but one was sentenced to three consecutive terms of life imprisonment, while the other received one term of life imprisonment.

The convictions were based on claims brought concerning only two young girls, one of whom was six years old at the time of the trial and three and one half when the abuse was claimed to have occurred. This young girl made the initial statement that led to the case being brought which turned into the most expensive and longest-running case in the history of that area (lasting six months). She also claimed that she had been hung in a closet for four hours by the neck, had been forced to drink gasoline and dog's urine, that the defendants had inserted penises, knives, long fingernails and knitting needles into her vagina, and that they had plucked her eyebrows out. Eventually, under therapy, she remembered pigs, goats, calves and horses, along with an entire family of four, being killed and buried in the back yard, and claimed that she and other children were forced to drink the blood of these animals, which was drained into a big container. Prior to the initial statement made to her mother two and one half years after she left the day care centre she had never mentioned any of this. Nor was any physical evidence ever found for the claims (after much digging of back yards and such), nor had her mother noticed anything unusual during the girl's time at the day care centre (such as the smell of gasoline, rope burns on the neck, or vaginal soreness or bleeding).

The other young girl around whom the convictions were based did not testify at trial because it was claimed that to do so would traumatize her too much. Instead, her testimony was entered through adults who had interviewed her, including, in particular, one therapist who had been brought into the case, and was paid for by the state. The second girl was involved in 98 therapy sessions, during *only two* of which she admitted, under heavy persistent questioning, that the two defendants had done certain things to her that might constitute child sexual abuse. Videotapes of these sessions and of other such sessions with other children were shown in court several times to jurors. The young girl had spent a total of 22 hours alone with the therapist in such sessions, some of which involved use of anatomically correct dolls. Under questioning, the therapist admitted using leading questions and discouraging 'wrong' answers. She also admitted discounting denials by the young girl that nothing had happened.[26]

Such questioning techniques are extremely prejudicial and can result in the clear manufacturing of evidence. Well-meaning therapists throughout the United States and elsewhere have been engaged in such efforts, simply because of a widely shared belief that child sexual abuse is at epidemic levels, and that children often wrongfully deny that it has occurred. A *New York Times* report stated that 20 000 children a year testify in child abuse trials in the United States, and thousands of such cases have been brought in recent years.[27] One cannot help but wonder how many such cases involved contaminated testimony that should not have been allowed. The famous *Kelly Michaels* case in New Jersey, mentioned earlier, was also overturned on appeal, mainly because of the way in which the therapist and other investigators conducted their questioning of the children. Indeed, one child was asked the same question *38 times in a row* by the therapist, until the child 'admitted' what the therapist obviously wanted her to say.

There has been some very creative relevant research done on this topic by Drs Stephen Ceci and Maggie Bruck, psychologists at Cornell University, who were motivated to do their own research into the suggestibility of children and the accuracy of their memories after reading the transcript of the testimony that was used to convict Kelly Michaels of 115 counts of sexual abuse against 19 children.[28] For the research Ceci and Bruck developed a list of ten events for each of a number of children, in conjunction with their parents. Two of the events had happened to the child but eight had not. Then they simply started to ask the children in short, two- or three-minute sessions each week if these events had happened to them. Fifty-six per cent of the children ended up admitting at least one false event, and some of the children admitted all of the false events.

Then, in a stroke of genius, Ceci and Bruck showed videotapes of the children's accounts to over 1000 professionals engaged in child abuse, including lawyers, social workers and psychiatrists, and asked them to assess the veracity of what the children were saying. The experts were accurate in *only one-third* of their assessments as to which children were telling the truth, which is considerably less than chance.

Later, Ceci and his colleagues undertook another piece of outstanding research. They videotaped a group of children undergoing a standard pediatric examination in which half of them were given a genital examination and half not. Using anatomically correct dolls, they then asked both sets of children (by pointing at the genital area of the doll) if the doctor had touched them there. Thirty-eight per cent of those not given a genital exam said 'yes' to the question. A more leading version of the question, using the child's own terms for genitals, led to 70 per cent of those not given the examination agreeing that it had in fact occurred.[29]

My examination of procedural changes and judicial discretion in child sexual abuse cases does not mean that I believe child abuse does not occur or that children can never be expected to give valid testimony. It is my best guess that there is much less child sexual abuse than claimed by some, and that the amount of ritual abuse associated with satanic groups is itself minuscule. However, the amount of child sexual abuse is difficult to discern, given both the levels of hysteria about the topic and the way in which investigations of alleged cases of ritual abuse have been carried out. If we are ever to understand this phenomenon then those in positions of authority in justice systems need to review the research on the suggestibility of children, and think carefully about what is happening as families and communities are torn apart by these cases. Such cases can be brought because our society has said, through its political leaders, that they should be, and because of the discretion being exercised by judges and others with authority. A more cautious approach to the issue of child sexual abuse may be needed – one which might lead to finding out how much abuse is actually occurring, thus allowing us to tackle the problem more realistically.

Analysis and Conclusions

I have laid out a series of types of case in which evidentiary and discretional problems have arisen, in part, I think, because the cases involved politically weak and unpopular religious groups, or the claims involved allegations of activities deemed unacceptable to normal society. In a sense, just characterizing the groups and alleged victims offers an explanation about why such problems occur. However, I want to be more specific about why my principal thesis has been borne out by the examination offered herein.

First, judges and others in authority in justice systems are human, sharing the same prejudices and misinformation as most members of the general public, and they may be just as prone to be influenced by the latest 'fashion' in cultural values. Judges read newspapers and watch television, and are influenced thereby as are other citizens. Often they, like members of the general public, depend on media presentations to learn about new phenomena. What they learn through that medium is, of course, not always factual, and may be seriously coloured by bias and misinformation on the part of media personnel, or even by deliberate attempts to manipulate.[30]

Second, strong forces can sometimes be allied against some particular group or practice which seems outside the mainstream, and those forces make it seem important to 'do something' to control such an obvious (to some) menace to society. Courts do have an important role to fulfil in terms of social control. They are a major bastion of authority in civilized human societies, and citizens rightfully look to the courts to enforce the law and help maintain social order. If order is not maintained, then supposedly chaos will result, and maintaining order requires social control of deviant groups and making examples of people who do unacceptable things.

When certain groups or practices are deemed as threatening to social order, then the courts may be called upon to exert authority on behalf of the society in order to control the new menace – be it communism, the Moonies, or satanists. Thus courts help define what is and is not acceptable behaviour in a given society. When something that seems a gross violation of society's norms and values is alleged to have occurred, criminal charges may be brought against someone, or the civil or family courts may be allowed to be used in ways that allow exertion of social control over the strange group or alleged practices.

Jurors also live in and act out the basic normative structure of a society. They pay attention to media discussions of new developments, especially if they are strange and controversial and seem to call into question some of society's basic values. Jurors may act on their values in ways that do not promote justice, even as their actions reinforce normative values in the society. Moreover, if the judge, who is a significant opinion leader and a figure of social stature, says or does things that seem to indicate that he or she thinks a person is guilty, or that a group or individual is liable in a civil action and should be punished, this can seriously influence jurors' beliefs and actions. Regrettably, sometimes judges do, by word or action, overtly suggest their opinion as to the proper outcome in a case.

However, on the whole, such overt bias is probably relatively rare, and therefore it is not the principal focus of my concern. Instead, I am concerned both about the decisions of legislative bodies that dramatically change the rules of the judicial game and about judges allowing certain types of questionable expert testimony in controversial cases – specifically those involving exotic religious practices or beliefs. It is these less transparent situations that threaten justice in controversial cases such as those discussed.

In the United States and other Western countries judges decide what evidence is to be presented in court. They are, of course, bound by statute, and sometimes those statutes reflect values in such a way as to force the admission of questionable testimony: newer laws designed to allow more successful prosecutions of alleged child abuse offenders are an example. However, generally, the judge makes key decisions about what should and should not be said in open court. These decisions are crucial because they can dramatically influence the outcome of a given case.[31]

If evidence is allowed, then it is safe to say that many, if not most, jurors would treat it as sound, and use it in their decision-making. Granted, the adversarial system found in the United States and some other societies is supposed to be able to deal with this problem through the offering of rebuttal witnesses and cross-examination. However, such a simplistic assumption about the social psychology of the trial situation, and the interaction of juror biases and misinformation with available evidence, entails several difficulties.[32]

First, balance may be difficult to maintain through good cross-examination and by offering rebuttal witnesses. Trial lawyers may not be trained in a given field to the depth necessary to understand problems with certain types of testimony. Indeed, they may even personally share misin–formation or biases that make it difficult for them to handle certain issues. Thus, they may not cross-examine effectively on a given topic. Effective rebuttal witnesses may be difficult to find, particularly if the issue is quite controversial. If, for example, it is not 'politically correct' to oppose certain types of testimony, possible rebuttal witnesses may be reluctant to offer testimony.[33]

Even if good rebuttal witnesses are found, there is no guarantee that such evidence will be heeded, or even attended to, by the jurors. Indeed, there is some solid evidence indicating that jurors pick and choose from available evidence about which they have previously formed opinions, and that they select out items that reinforce their previously held views.[34] The notion of an open-minded and neutral juror is, in fact, quite problematic in cases involving controversial issues and principles. This problem should be recognized and dealt with as far as possible by those in charge of the legal system. Judges ought to be cognizant of such research results as they direct the proceedings in their courtrooms.

However, another significant point is that judges themselves may not be trained in areas relevant to crucial decisions they are called upon to make in the course of a trial. For instance, few, if any, American law schools require students to take more than a traditional evidence class focusing on topics such as the hearsay rule and other general rules and procedures. Bar examinations in America do not require special expertise in, for instance, scientific methodology. There is instead a built-in structural dependence on expert witnesses to offer specialized testimony where this is required to resolve a dispute or deal with a criminal charge. But such a dependency begs the question of who should be allowed to testify – a question that has become a major controversy in American law.

In 1993 the US Supreme Court, in the landmark *Daubert* case, established new groundrules concerning expert scientific testimony – rules which place a great burden on judges (as gatekeepers) to protect jurors from questionable scientific opinion.[35] The Court overruled a 70 year-old precedent – the 'general acceptance' doctrine derived from the 1923 *Frye* case, a criminal case involving the attempted use of the early polygraph or lie detector (a device which was not allowed).[36] The new *Daubert* guidelines include:

1 the 'falsifiability' of a theory;
2 whether the findings have been subject to peer review and publication;
3 known or potential error rates of the techniques used; and
4 whether the findings are generally acceptable in relevant areas of science.

Thus the *Frye* rule was subsumed into the new criteria, but much was added as well.

The 'general acceptance' test simply said that before scientific testimony could be offered in court, the principles and methodology undergirding the scientific finding had to be generally accepted within the relevant discipline(s). This rule was controversial, and was not followed by all courts. However, it was the dominant position in most American courts, especially when applied to scientific findings from the so-called 'hard' sciences offered in criminal cases.[37] A similar criterion has been used in most other Western societies and is usually justified on a relevancy basis.[38]

It seems apparent that a 'general acceptance' rule, as well as the other criteria such as those laid out in the *Daubert* decision from the United States, should be enforced, particularly in cases involving questionable science and controversial parties and issues. Clearly, the kinds of allegedly scientific evidence discussed here do not generally meet either *Frye* or *Daubert* standards. Therefore, if such standards are used, and those in decision-making positions within judicial systems can, and will, exercise their discretion and authority properly, justice may yet be served, even in such controversial areas as those discussed above.[39]

Notes

1 See J. Richardson (1992), 'Public Opinion in the Tax Evasion Trial of Reverend Moon', *Behavioral Sciences & the Law*, **10**, p. 53 for strong evidence of bias against one controversial new religious group that arguably would make it difficult for the group to be treated fairly in a court. Also, see J. Pfeifer (1992), 'The Psychological Framing of Cults: Schematic Representations and Cult Evaluations', *Journal of Applied Social Psychology*, **22**, p. 531 whose careful experimental research demonstrates that many people have extremely negative attitudes towards both cults and satanic cults and J. DeWitt, J. Richardson and L. Warner (1997), 'Novel Scientific Evidence and Controversial Cases: A Social Psychological Examination', *Law & Psychology Review*, **21**, p. 1 for a clear demonstration of the effects of anti-cult bias existing among potential jurors.

2 For discussions of this problematic term see J. Richardson (1993), 'Definitions of Cult: From Sociological–Technical to Popular–Negative', *Review of Religious Research*, **34**, p. 348 and J. Dillon and J. Richardson (1994), 'The "Cult" Concept: A Politics of Representation Analysis', *SYZYGY: Journal of Alternative Religion and Culture*, **3**, p. 185.

3 See J. DeWitt, J. Richardson and L. Warner (1997), 'Novel Scientific Evidence and Controversial Cases: A Social Psychological Examination', *Law & Psychology Review*, **21**, p. 1 for experimental evidence on this point that is quite germane to this chapter.

4 For a thorough critique of 'brainwashing' claims in legal cases see J. Richardson (1993), ' A Social Psychological Critique of Brainwashing Claims about Recruitment to New Religions', in J. Hadden and D. Bromley (eds), *The Handbook of Cults and Sects in America*, (Greenwich, CT: JAI Press), pp. 75–97. Also see D. Anthony (1990), 'Religious Movements and Brainwashing Testimony: Evaluating Key Testimony' in T. Robbins and D. Anthony (eds), *In Gods We Trust*, (New Brunswick, NJ: Transaction Books), pp. 295–344; E. Barker (1984), *The Making of a Moonie: Brainwashing or Choice?*, (Oxford: Basil Blackwell); and J. Richardson and B. Kilbourne (1983), 'Classical and Contemporary Brainwashing Models: A Comparison and Critique', in D. Bromley and J. Richardson (eds), *The Brainwashing/Deprogramming Controversy*, (New Brunswick, NJ: Transaction Books), pp. 29–45. For a discussion of the notion of 'accounts' as applied to new religions, see J. Richardson, J. van der Lans and F. Derks (1986), 'Leaving and Labeling: Voluntary and Coerced Disaffiliation from Religious Social Movements', in K. Land, G. Lang and L. Kriesberg (eds), *Research in Social Movements, Conflicts and Change*, Vol. 9, (Greenwich, CT: JAIN Press), pp. 97–126.

5 See J. Richardson (1991), 'Cult/Brainwashing Cases and Freedom of Religion', *Journal of Church and State,* **33**, p. 55 for a discussion of one major US case, and J. Richardson (1996), 'Brainwashing Claims and Minority Religions outside the United States: Cultural Diffusion of a Questionable Legal Concept', *Brigham Young University Law Review*, p.873 for coverage of such cases outside the United States. Also see D. Anthony and T. Robbins (1998), 'Negligence, Coercion, and the Protection of Religious Belief', *Journal of Church and State*, **37**, p. 509 for a thorough discussion of most American cases involving brainwashing and mind control claims.

6 See Anthony and Robbins, 'Negligence', *op. cit.*, for a good discussion of the precedent-setting *Fishman* case in a US federal court where such a defence was disallowed (*United States* v. *Fishman*, 743 F.Supp. 713 (N.Dist. Cal., 1990)). This case has had a significant negative impact on civil uses of brainwashing-based claims, as well, although it seems clear that judges and juries are more prone to accept such notions in civil actions for damages than they are in criminal cases where to do so would excuse criminal behaviour.

7   See chapters by J. LeMoult and D. Bromley in D. Bromley and J. Richardson (eds), *The Brainwashing/Deprogramming Controversy*, (New York: Edwin Mellin Press).

8   See J. Richardson (1995), 'Legal Status of Minority Religions in the United States', *Social Compass*, **42**, p. 249; T. Robbins and D. Bromley (1993), 'The Role of Government in Regulating New and Nonconventional Religions', in J. Wood and D. Davis (eds), *The Role of Government in Monitoring and Regulating Religion in Public Life*, (Waco, TX: Dawson Institute for Church–State Relations), pp. 205–40, and K. Pierson (1981), 'Cults, Deprogrammers, and the Necessity Defense', *Michigan Law Review*, **80**, p. 271. Note that in a Colorado case written about by Robbins and Bromley and in which this author testified, the Colorado Supreme Court eventually reversed itself (after the deprogrammers were found not guilty of kidnapping charges), disallowing necessity defences in such cases in the future.

9   See especially Richardson, 'A Social Psychological Critique', *op. cit.*, for a review of the generally accepted criticisms of brainwashing theories.

10   See the discussion of this and related cases in other countries in J. Richardson (1999), 'Social Control of New Religions: From "Brainwashing" Claims to Child Sex Abuse Accusations', in S. Palmer and C. Hardman (eds), *Children in the New Religions*, (New Brunswick, NJ: Rutgers University Press), pp. 172–186.

11   See a discussion of this effort in J. Richardson (1996), 'Journalistic Bias toward New Religious Movements in Australia', *Journal of Contemporary Religion*, **11**, p. 289.

12   See the fascinating book about this event, from which the movie was derived: J. Bryson (1986), *Evil Angels*, (Ringwood, Victoria: Penguin Books).

13   This case led to a number of publications, including one by a defendant, T. Anderson (1992), *Take Two: The Criminal Justice System Revisited*, (Sydney: Bantam Books), which has a very thoughtful analysis of the role played by the media in his case. See J. Richardson, 'Journalistic Bias', *op. cit.*, for more analysis, as well as J. Richardson (1995), 'Minority Religions ("Cults") and the Law: Comparisons of the United States, Europe, and Australia', *University of Queensland Law Journal*, **18**, p. 181. Other treatments of the Hilton bombing case are: J. Hocking (1993), *Beyond Terrorism: The Development of the Australian Security State*, (Sydney: Allen & Unwin); and T. Molomby (1986), *Spies, Bombs, and the Path of Bliss*, (Sydney: Potoroo Press).

14   That statement is actually much kinder than some accusations made in publications about this matter; see Anderson, *Take Two*, *op. cit.*; Hocking, *Beyond Terrorism*, *op. cit.*; and Molomby, *Spies, Bombs*, *op. cit.* Some accept the view that police agents themselves might have planted the bomb, in an effort to gain support for budget requests being considered at that time by the Australian government. This view is fuelled by considerable foot-dragging by the authorities that went on for years (the case is still officially unsolved), and by the ready acceptance of problematic evidence, some of which, in hindsight, was obviously manufactured. This interpretation of the events simply defines the Ananda Marga as a target of convenience used by the authorities once the bomb went off and killed people. The media were, according to Anderson and others, quite willing to serve as the delivery method for the story that had Anderson and others as the responsible parties, in exchange for access to authorities and information.

15   See Richardson, 'Journalistic Bias' and 'Minority Religious', *op. cit.*, which also discuss the Chamberlain case. Adrian Howe, a feminist criminologist at La Trobe University, has written a fascinating play about the Chamberlain case, using almost totally the exact words of journalists who covered the story. This play, *Chamberlain Revisited: The Case against the Media* (presented on 24 October 1993 at the Athenaeum

Theatre, Melbourne), clearly reveals the bias of supposedly objective journalists. Also, see K. Crispin (1995), 'An Australian Witchhunt', *The Weekend Australian*, 16–17 December, p. 23. Crispin was the QC who represented Lindy Chamberlain in the commission that eventually exonerated her, but only after she served five years in prison and saw her family torn apart by the pressures of the case.

16   *Chamberlain* v. *R* (1984) 51 ALR 255.

17   See the thoughtful discussion of the blood tests and other matters in this case offered by R. Harding (1998), 'Jury Performance in Complex Cases', in M. Findlay and P. Duff (eds), *The Jury Under Attack*, (Sydney: Butterworths), pp. 74–94. Harding's principal point in discussing this case and other notorious Australian ones in which problematic decisions were made is that it is not the jury which is to blame, but that instead (p. 83), '*jury malfeasance is invariably a direct function of legal and scientific malfeasance*' (emphasis in original). By this, he means that the legal system breaks down and cannot handle certain kinds of cases well, especially ones involving complex evidence. Thus his thesis supports my own that the legal and judicial systems find it difficult to deal with cases involving controversial religious groups.

18   See discussions of some of these cases in J. Richardson, J. Best and D. Bromley (eds) (1991), *The Satanism Scare*, (New York: Aldine de Gruyter), especially the chapter by Nathan on the *McMartin* and other well known cases, as well as chapters by Best, by Jenkins and Maier-Katkin, by Mulhern, by Hicks, and by Crouch and Damphouse, the latter two of which elucidate how the police come to accept accusations of satanic activity. Also see J. Richardson (1997), 'The Social Construction of Satanism: Understanding an International Social Problem', *Australian Journal of Social Issues*, **32**, p. 61 for a social constructionist perspective on the rapid spread of satanic accusations and claims around the Western world.

19   *State of New Jersey* v. *Michaels*, 625 A.2d 489 (NJ Super. AD 1993). See the discussion of this and similar cases in J. Richardson, G. Ginsburg, S. Gatowski and S. Dobbin (1995), 'Problems Applying *Daubert* to Psychological Syndrome Evidence', *Judicature*, **79**, p. 10 – an article in which the underlying scientific basis for much evidence offered in child sexual abuse cases is questioned.

20   See Philip Jenkins (1992), *Intimate Enemies: Moral Panic in Britain*, (New York: Aldine de Gruyter).

21   See examinations of this case in light of sociological deviance theories in M. Hill and J. Barnett (1994), 'Religion and Deviance', in P. Green (ed.) *New Zealand Social Problems*, 2nd edn, (Palmerston North: Dunmore Press), pp. 231–49; J. Barnett and M. Hill (1993), 'When the Devil comes to Christchurch', *Australian Religious Studies Review*, **6**, p. 25; and K. White, J. Barnett and M. Hill (1993), 'Religion, Medicine, and Deviance: Child Abuse and the Social Structure', *International Review of Sociology (New Series)*, (3), p. 144. The case is also briefly discussed in Richardson, 'Social Construction of Satanism', *op.cit.*

22   The full bench of the New Zealand Court of Appeal, in a second appeal (a rare occurrence), on 14 October 1999, declined to overturn Peter Ellis's conviction. A Commission of Inquiry into the Ellis affair may be the next step: see 'Upset Ellis Consoled by Inquiry Suggestion', *Sunday Star-Times*, 17 October 1999, A4.

23   This is reminiscent of research demonstrating impacts of 'death-qualifying' of jurors in American jurisdictions which have the death penalty. Death-qualifying refers to the process of inquiring of all potential jurors if they could render penalty of death if the defendant is found guilty. Research shows that the very process of death-qualifying itself increases conviction-proneness. See discussions of this research in *Grigsby* v.

Mabry, 569 F.Supp. 1273 (US Dist. Ct., E Dist. of Arkansas, 1983) and *Lockhart* v. *McCree*, 106 S.Ct. 1758 (1986).

24 One district court Judge in my county dared to challenge the evidence in one important case by first having the videotapes of the testimony developed by a therapist independently assessed and then throwing out the entire case on the grounds of tainted and insufficient evidence. His decision was eventually upheld by the Nevada Supreme Court, but he lost the next election after an opponent charged that the judge was 'soft on child sex abuse'.

25 See *Felix and Ontiverous* v. *Nevada*, 849 P.2d 220 (Nev. 1993).

26 This girl was a party in the case even though her family had moved away to another state. Local authorities sent a therapist to interview her, along with a local detective from the new area of residence. The sessions sometimes included her younger siblings who also had spent some time at the centre. The first session included denials by the young woman that anything had happened, but the therapist 'thought she seemed a little nervous', so the visits continued until the girl eventually agreed that she had been touched on her private parts.

27 See D. Goleman (1993), 'Studies Reveal Suggestibility of Very Young Children as Witnesses', *New York Times*, 11 June, p. A1.

28 See S. Ceci and M. Bruck (1993), 'Suggestibility of the Child Witness: A Historical Review and Synthesis', *Psychological Bulletin*, **113**, p. 403, which is the research referred to in the *New York Times* story in note 27.

29 See ibid. Another version of this research had the pediatrician, who did not carry out a genital examination, do some other things, such as use a ribbon to measure the diameter of a child's wrist, and tickle a child's tummy. One child reported that the doctor had wrapped something around her neck and pulled it very tight, as she did this to herself with a cord. Also, she stuck a stick in the doll's vagina, saying that the doctor had done this to her. Then she picked up a block and hammered the stick further into the doll's vagina, stating that the doctor had also done that to her!

30 There is a considerable scholarly literature on media effects in the area of new and minority religions. See Tim Anderson's book on his experiences in Australia with the Hilton bombing case (*Take Two, op. cit.*). See also other work by Richardson, such as 'Journalistic Bias', *op. cit.* Also see J. Richardson and B. van Dreil (1997), 'Journalistic Attitudes Toward New Religious Movements', *Review of Religious Research*, **39**, p. 116; B. van Dreil and J. Richardson (1988), 'Print Media Coverage of New Religious Movements: A Longitudinal Study', *Journal of Communications*, **38**, p. 37; and idem (1988), 'Categorization of New Religious Movements in American Print Media', *Sociological Analysis*, **49**, p. 171; D. Selway (1989), 'Religion in the Print Media: A Study of the Portrayal of Religion in the *Sydney Morning Herald* 1978–1988', unpublished Honours thesis, University of Queensland; J. Richardson (1995), 'Manufacturing Consent: The Role of the Media in the Waco Tragedy', in S. Wright (ed.), *Armageddon in Waco*, (Chicago: University of Chicago Press), pp. 153–76; J. Beckford (1994), 'The Media and New Religious Movements', in J. Lewis (ed.) 1994, *From the Ashes: Making Sense of Waco*, (Lanham, MD: Rowan and Littlefield), pp. 143–48.

31 Sometimes testimony, even though apparently clearly relevant, is precluded because of other policies of the court. For instance, some relevant testimony may simply be deemed too prejudicial to be admitted, or the testimony may violate other evidence rules, such as the rule against hearsay evidence (which, as we have shown, can have some important exceptions). In the United States there is a rule against the admission of information about settlement offers, even though such information would clearly be relevant to the case since it might indicate liability being admitted by a defendant in a

civil action. However, such evidence is not admitted as a matter of policy because to do so would, of course, discourage efforts to settle cases.

32   See, for instance, DeWitt *et al.*, 'Novel Scientific Evidence', *op. cit.*

33   The experience in school desegregation cases in the United States demonstrates that those who testified against desegregation often suffered professionally, and that it was sometimes quite difficult to get any professionals to testify on that side of such cases. See M. Chester, J. Sanders and D. Kalmuss, (1988), *Social Science in Court*, (Madison, WI: University of Wisconsin Press).

34   Again, see DeWitt *et al.*, 'Novel Scientific Evidence', *op. cit.*, note 3 above, for a discussion of such research.

35   *Daubert* v. *Merrell Dow Pharmaceuticals Inc*, 509 US 579 (1993).

36   *Frye* v. *United States*, 54 App.DC 46 (1923).

37   See J. Richardson (1994), 'Dramatic Changes in American Expert Evidence Law: From Frye to Daubert', *The Judicial Review: Journal of the Judicial Commission of New South Wales*, **2**, p. 13. This article discusses limits on applicability of *Frye's* general acceptance and examines the implications of the *Daubert* decision, particularly in the social and behavioral sciences.

38   See S. Gatowski, S. Dobbin, J. Richardson, C. Nowlin and G. Ginsburg (1996), 'Diffusion of Expert Evidence: A Comparative Analysis of Admissibility Standards in Australia, Canada, England, and the United States, and their Impact on the Social and Behavioral Sciences', *Expert Evidence,* **4**, p. 86; P. Roberts (1996), 'The Admissibility of Expert Evidence: Lessons from America', *Expert Evidence*, **4**, p. 93, and I. Freckelton (1989), 'Novel Psychological Evidence', in I. Freckelton and H. Selby (eds), *Expert Evidence*, (Sydney: Law Book Company), pp. 3331–454 for discussions of international standards of scientific evidence among Western societies.

39   See Richardson *et al.*, 'Problems Applying *Daubert*', *op. cit.*, note 19 above, for a discussion of the application of *Daubert* to child sexual abuse evidence. See also G. Ginsburg and J. Richardson (1998), '"Brainwashing" evidence in light of *Daubert*', in H. Reece (ed.), *Law and Science: Current Legal Studies 1998*, Vol. 1, (Oxford: Oxford University Press), pp. 265–88 which, after thoroughly applying the *Daubert* guidelines to 'brainwashing' claims, finds those claims sorely lacking.

7 From Toleration to Pluralism: Religious Liberty and Religious Establishment under the United Kingdom's Human Rights Act[1]

Julian Rivers

Introduction

The relationship between law and religion in any modern society is highly complex. This complexity is compounded in the case of the UK by the absence of any codified Constitution that might set out the basic principles governing the relationship between Church and state. As a result, the UK legal systems reflect a history of conflict and accommodation between various religious groups, rather than a system of principled resolution.[2] The religious positions that came into conflict during the seventeenth century for the most part did not challenge the unity of Church and state; the issues turned on which conception of Christianity was to be the governing one. The English Toleration Act 1689 marked the first substantial shift from this essentially medieval understanding, by removing the criminal penalties attaching to nonconformist worship. Tolerance was, in this case, limited to Protestant Christianity, but to the extent that one can generalize about religious liberty in the UK, its history thereafter is one of gradually expanding toleration, without ever attempting to move beyond toleration as a model of Church–state relations. Thus Christianity, either in its Anglican Episcopalian or Scottish Presbyterian manifestation, retained social and legal pre-eminence, but the social and legal consequences of dissent were gradually dismantled. In this way, religious establishment came to be reconciled with religious liberty.

Notable milestones in the process of expanding toleration were the removal of civil disabilities from Unitarians in 1813,[3] Roman Catholics in 1829[4] and Jews in 1846.[5] The Universities Tests Act 1871 abolished religious tests for access to university and the Oaths Act 1888 permitted witnesses to affirm rather than swear a religious oath. In 1917 the House of Lords upheld the validity of a testamentary gift to promote secular humanism as within the policy of the law.[6] The only general statutory provision against religious discrimination relates to Northern Ireland,[7] although from 1965 the Race Relations Acts have outlawed discrimination for those religions that are, in the main, racially distinctive. Recently, the government approved two state-funded Islamic primary schools. The UK is party to the major international human rights instruments that protect religious liberty such as the European Convention on Human Rights and Fundamental Freedoms 1950 (ECHR) and the International Covenant on Civil and Political Rights 1966.

However, despite what is now a broad civic equality between adherents of different religions, Christianity still retains a central position, both legally and socially. The sovereign must be a Protestant Christian in communion with the Church of England,[8] and in law appoints that Church's senior clergy. Although the Churches of Ireland and Wales have been disestablished,[9] the Churches of Scotland and England retain certain privileges and responsibilities. The coronation and some other civic functions are arranged in conjunction with the established Churches. Twenty-six bishops of the Church of England sit in the upper house of the legislature as Lords Spiritual;[10] parishioners may attend their local Anglican church and receive baptism, marriage and burial by right.[11] Schools – insofar as they are not independent or have a distinct religious ethos – are to be broadly Christian in character. Clergy of the established Churches have special rights of access to prisons and hospitals.[12] Sunday is still socially a day of rest, and, in England, legally subject to some trading restrictions.[13]

The consequence of this residual centrality of a Christian ethic and Christian forms of religion is that minority faiths – particularly those which are new or have arisen with immigration since the Second World War – experience some discrimination.[14] At times it is difficult to disentangle the causes of such discrimination, and it may be that the social causes are more significant than the legal ones. It is also hard to know, in the abstract, if it is possible for any human society to be fully non-discriminatory between a range of religions that have divergent ethical commitments. However, this is no reason for the process of negotiated and expanding toleration to cease. Into this variegated and complex process is enacted the Human Rights Act 1998 which incorporates into domestic law the European Convention on Human Rights with its guarantees of religious liberty, non-discrimination and pluralism.[15] As a result of the debates which took place during its parliamentary passage, the Act contains a section highlighting the significance of collective religious liberty. The purpose of this chapter is to assess the impact of the Human Rights Act 1998, particularly s. 13 (with its enhanced protection of religious liberty) on the law of religious liberty and religious establishment in the UK.

The Human Rights Act 1998

Although the UK was among the first to ratify the ECHR freedoms in 1951,[16] and granted the right of individual petition in 1966, both the principal political parties were long resistant to the introduction of a domestic Bill of Rights. However, as the toll of adverse decisions from Strasbourg mounted, and as influential members of the Commonwealth began to incorporate international human rights obligations into domestic law, the pressure for change increased. Consistent with the 'new' Labour Party's shift from socialism in the direction of liberal democracy, the 1995 election manifesto contained a pledge to 'bring rights home' by incorporating the European Convention into domestic law. Quite what form the incorporation would take remained obscure until the Human Rights Bill appeared for its first reading, without prior consultation, in the House of Lords on 23 October 1997. It passed all stages, more or less intact, and received Royal Assent on 9 November 1998. The bulk of the Act will come into force on 2 October 2000.[17]

The structure of the Act is complex, adding an additional layer of uncertainty to that inherent in the broad statements of substantive principle characteristic of all human rights documents.[18] 'Convention rights', defined as the rights protected by Articles 2 to 12 and 14 of the ECHR, together with those in the First and Sixth Protocols, are not recognized as domestic rights in themselves but enter the system by two indirect routes. First, all legislation is to be interpreted, 'so far as it is possible to do so' in a way compatible with Convention rights.[19] Second, it is unlawful for a public body to act in a way incompatible with Convention rights.[20] Victims of public acts in breach of Convention rights may bring proceedings to vindicate their rights.[21] The ultimate supremacy of parliament is preserved, in that where primary legislation cannot be interpreted in a way that is compatible with Convention rights, its validity is unaffected, but the higher courts may make a 'declaration of incompatibility'.[22] Such a declaration, along with any adverse decision of the European Court of Human Rights, empowers a government minister to amend the offending legislation by Order in Council[23] in what has become known as the 'fast-track' procedure. As regards the content of

Convention rights, the courts are bound to have regard to the jurisprudence of the Strasbourg enforcement organs, but are not bound to follow it.[24] Given that one key purpose of the Act is to avoid defeats abroad, it is to be assumed that the judiciary will develop an interpretation of the Convention that is at least as extensive as that developed by the Court of Human Rights.

A full review of the issues surrounding the impact of the Human Rights Act cannot be undertaken here, but a few of the more significant problems which relate to the subject matter of this chapter can be noted. First, it is not clear how creative the courts will be in interpreting the substance of Convention rights. The practice of the European Court is fairly conservative, tending only to find breaches of rights where there would be a broad European consensus against the state action in question, and allowing states a margin of appreciation in interpreting the Convention rights.[25] The British judiciary may, but need not, adhere closely to this jurisprudence. One fundamental issue will need to be resolved at an early stage. It could be argued that Convention rights are only relevant in the state–individual relationship, having no effect on the relationship between private individuals. Being an international treaty, the ECHR is ambiguous on the point, but the tendency of the Court has been to interpret Convention rights as important interests which the state is obliged by Article 1 of the ECHR to respect. This respect is expressed in the international context by both negative duties on state bodies to refrain from infringing the rights, and occasionally positive duties to protect individuals from the acts of private third parties.[26] Once the Convention is transposed into domestic law, it could have a direct impact on private relationships.[27] Many – although not all – commentators seem to assume that Convention rights, being universal human interests, are relevant in principle, but that the Human Rights Act limits the procedures by which they may be pleaded.[28] Thus, it is assumed that a statute which regulates a private relationship will need to be interpreted in line with the Convention under s. 3, and that the common law should continue to develop under the influence of Convention rights by virtue of s. 6.

Second, it is unclear how the Act will affect the interpretive practice of British courts. The courts have already decided that, where a statute is ambiguous, it is appropriate to have regard to the UK's international obligations to resolve the ambiguity.[29] The new interpretive duty seems to be stronger, requiring readings that are strained and unusual, if not impossible, in order to satisfy Convention rights. This approach is entirely plausible in dealing with a concrete decision of the European Court of Human Rights as against a statute that might be inconsistent, but could be read consistently with the decision without too much creativity. In many cases, however, the statute in question will be more precise than the Convention standards. Instead of deciding what the Convention requires in the abstract before turning to the statute, the judiciary may find it easier, in most cases, to see the statute as an acceptable way of balancing the competing interests expressed in the Convention. This avoids the political conflict consequent on declaring a statute incompatible, and it rightly allows parliament a role in constructing the meaning of the Convention for the UK. A clear example of this feature of interpretive practice is likely to be found in the context of schools with a religious character, discussed below.

Third, the impact of Convention rights on the common law is thoroughly unclear. There are a number of possibilities. It could be that the common law remains unaffected, save to the extent that public authorities exercise common law powers, when those powers would be limited by the need to respect Convention rights. However, it is odd for statute law to be subject to interpretation, but the common law not. In addition, courts are expressly included in the definition of public authorities required to act compatibly with the Convention. Where possible, the common law must therefore be reworked in line with Convention rights. The limits of possibility are controversial, and it may be that the courts will issue statements of incompatibility with respect to settled case law as well as statutes in an attempt to force the legislator to act. Finally, the s. 6 duty on the courts could be read as a strong duty not to apply the common law whenever it is inconsistent with Convention rights.

As regards issues of religious liberty and establishment, the debate in parliament was dominated by a concern that religious bodies might be considered public authorities, and the broad response of the government was to insist that religious bodies do not, in the main, exercise public functions. The Bill left the House of Lords with a number of amendments relating to religious liberty and establishment, all of which were subsequently removed, at the government's request, by the House of Commons.[30] These amendments, and the concerns which provoked them, will be discussed below. For the moment, it is worth noting that the government sought to allay all the fears expressed by religious bodies by a single 'soft' provision. S. 13 of the Act reads:

> If a court's determination of any question arising under this Act might affect the exercise by a religious organisation (itself or its members collectively) of the Convention right to freedom of thought, conscience and religion, it must have particular regard to the importance of that right.

Some have suggested that s. 13 is meaningless – a political statement to placate opponents of the Act.[31] It is argued that the section contains nothing beyond the Strasbourg jurisprudence on Article 9, and this thesis is supported by the fact that the government insisted throughout that the concerns raised by religious bodies were groundless. However, this view ignores the nature of the Human Rights Act, which is to increase the interpretive discretion of the judiciary. The government recognized that, while its opinions on the impact of the Human Rights Act might be significant, they are not determinative:[32] although the government might want the Act to have no effect in this respect, that is ultimately a matter for the judiciary. Detailed provisions were inappropriate, so the best that the government could do was to send a strong signal to the judiciary of the value of collective religious liberty, in the hope that this would discourage vexatious litigation which religious organizations can ill afford.[33] The Home Secretary emphasized the government's view that the purpose of s. 13 was to give special protection to the religious beliefs and practices[34] of both individuals and organizations, and that this protection was not to be limited to churches and their equivalent, but would extend to other organizations with a religious ethos.[35] Moreover, it was not to be limited to the principal religious traditions in the UK.[36]

It should be noted that, on its terms, s. 13 only covers collective, and not individual, religious liberty, although the boundaries between the two are not always obvious. Nonetheless, s. 13 is significant, because it addresses the root concern of the Churches in a broader way than would have been achieved by the amendments that were made to the Bill in the House of Lords. Although the debate was largely concerned with the public nature of religious bodies, the churches' basic fear was that the law might be affected in a way that forced them to conform to a uniform and incompatible conception of justice. This is as likely to occur in a reworking of private law, as in public law. S. 13 applies whenever the Human Rights Act is relevant, quite independently of the public–private divide.

The Church of Scotland and the Scope of Spiritual Jurisdiction

Religious liberty relies on the identification of types of religious activity, such as belief and worship, that are to be immune from legal control. Collective religious liberty likewise must identify a sphere of action within which religious bodies can act without challenge from secular, governmental or other religious bodies. The concerns of the Church of Scotland thus lie at the heart of the debate about the religious aspects of the Human Rights Act, since they are concerns about the scope of spiritual jurisdiction.

The Church of Scotland enjoys an autonomy greater than any other religious body in the UK.[37] The basic constitutional position is secured in the Church of Scotland Act 1921 which paved the way for a reconciliation between the Church of Scotland and the United Free Church of Scotland in 1929.[38] It draws a clear distinction between 'matters spiritual' in which the constitution of the Church of Scotland, as expressed in the Declaratory Articles of the General Assembly, shall be supreme, and matters affecting the civil courts and civil jurisdiction which remain unaffected by the Act. The Declaratory Articles appended to the 1921 Act protect the Church's 'right and power subject to no civil authority to legislate and to adjudicate finally, in all matters of doctrine, worship, government and discipline in the Church...'.[39]

Furthermore, under the Church of Scotland (Property and Endowments) Act 1925 and subsequent legislation, the General Trustees of the Church of Scotland have the power to administer the properties and endowments of the Church with a very broad discretion, subject only to the terms of the 1925 Act and the directions of the General Assembly.[40] The secular courts will not review their decisions. In short, the Church of Scotland has complete immunity from control by secular courts in matters relating to the rights of members and ministers and the administration of Church property and finance. It was the loss of this jurisdictional autonomy that caused the great Disruption of 1843, which led to the formation of the Free Presbyterian Church of Scotland, and it was the recovery of jurisdictional autonomy under the 1921 settlement that was the condition of reunification.

It was feared that the constitutional settlement brought about by the Church of Scotland Act 1921 and related legislation would be unravelled by the Human Rights Act by exposing decisions of the Church of Scotland to scrutiny by the ordinary courts according to human rights standards. It must be emphasized that the issue here was jurisdictional, not substantive. The principal worry was that it would be up to the ordinary courts, not the ecclesiastical courts, to determine the meaning of Convention rights in the context of religious matters. The jurisdictional nature of the complaint was clearly evidenced by the Church of Scotland's willingness to be subject to review in matters which it considered to be non-spiritual, such as the running of children's homes and hostels for drug addicts, coupled with its willingness to consider *for itself* how it might apply the European Convention within its own jurisdiction.[41]

The amendments proposed to preserve the 1921 settlement were hampered by the general lack of clarity as to how the Act would work. The Government's response was similarly equivocal. At times, very clear statements were given that the constitutional position of the Church of Scotland remained unaffected by the Act,[42] but this was often coupled with an insistence that, if the Church breached Convention rights, there should be a remedy before the secular courts. The jurisdictional issue was never squarely faced. One proposed amendment sought to preserve the 1921 settlement explicitly by exempting its provisions from the interpretive rule of s. 3.[43] Of course, this would not have addressed the possibility that the Church might be seen, for certain purposes, as exercising a public function under s. 6. In addition, the most obvious route by which the Act might have undone the settlement would be if the 'courts' stated to be bound to uphold Convention rights were to be construed as including Scottish ecclesiastical courts. For this reason, the Bill finally left the House of Lords with the additional subclauses in clause 6:

> (5) In subs. (3) 'court or tribunal' does not include any court or tribunal when it is exercising a jurisdiction, recognised but not created by Parliament, in matters spiritual.
> (6) In relation to a particular act, a person is not a public authority by virtue only of subs. (3)(b) if the act is done by or on behalf of a religious body exercising a jurisdiction, recognised but not created by Parliament, in matters spiritual.

Although phrased in general terms, these statements referred primarily to the Church of Scotland: it is a moot point whether courts of other religious denominations could have been brought within the term 'recognised, but not created'. However, the government insisted that the clauses were unnecessary and should therefore be removed. The Scottish ecclesiastical courts – indeed, all religious courts – were not courts for the purposes of the Act, since they were concerned with purely religious matters, and the acts referred to in subclause (6) would undoubtedly be held to be private acts not subject to review by secular courts. As indicated above, s. 13 was designed to strengthen this interpretation of the Act.

Two basic assumptions underlie many of the contributions to the debate, including those of the government. The first assumption was that Convention rights have a fixed content and are universally applicable. The idea that there might be competing conceptions of rights and different ways of balancing interests was hardly ever considered,[44] although it lies at the heart of the concerns of religious bodies. The second assumption was that there is a clear division in law between secular matters heard by civil courts and spiritual matters dealt with by religious bodies according to their own procedures. This implies that the legal position of the Church of Scotland is not exceptional but in line with the general law. This assumption is also incorrect, as the case law on the 1921 Act demonstrates.

In *Ballantyne* v. *Wigtown Presbytery*,[45] the Court of Session ruled that the effect of the Act was to deny the petitioning congregation their prior statutory right to appoint a new minister in opposition to the wishes of their local presbytery, which was acting within its powers, according to the government of the Church of Scotland. More recently, in *Logan* v. *Presbytery of Dumbarton*,[46] the Court of Session again refused to entertain an allegation of procedural unfairness made by a minister against the Church. The court had the jurisdiction to determine the meaning and effect of the 1921 Act, but not to review the exercise of powers by the Church of Scotland within its spiritual jurisdiction.

This must be contrasted with the general legal position of other religious bodies. Judicial review is not available for their decisions,[47] except possibly when they act outside the scope of their constitution or charter,[48] because such bodies do not perform a governmental function.[49] Nevertheless, they are regulated by private law. The rules of the religious body form a contract of association between the members, which the courts will intervene to uphold if necessary, and property is likely to be held on charitable trusts, the terms of which may be clarified and enforced before secular courts.[50] The leading authority on the relationship between ministers and the religious body is *Davies* v. *Presbyterian Church of Wales*.[51] In this case, the House of Lords insisted that there was no contract of employment between a non-conformist minister and his Church, and thus an industrial tribunal had no jurisdiction to consider whether a reasonable Church would sever the link between minister and congregation.[52] Nevertheless, the law imposed a duty on such Churches not to deprive a minister of an office carrying a stipend save in accordance with the procedures set forth in the 'book of rules'. In short, the secular courts had the jurisdiction to enforce the terms of association between members of a religious body to the extent that they affected financial and property interests of the members.

Davies was not considered by Simon Brown J in the frequently cited *Wachman* case in which a rabbi, who had been declared no longer religiously and morally fit to occupy his position, sought review of the Chief Rabbi's declaration on the grounds of procedural unfairness. The court denied that judicial review was available on the grounds that there was no public interest – in the sense of a governmental interest – in seeing that the functions of a Chief Rabbi were fulfilled. This part of the judgment is obviously correct. However, one of the grounds identified by the court for denying jurisdiction was that it was contrary to public policy to interfere in what was essentially a religious function. It would not be easy to separate out procedural complaints based on common law notions of natural justice from substantive requirements of Jewish law. The assumption made by the judge was that it would be wrong for him to consider whether or not requirements of Jewish procedural law had been satisfied. But this is precisely what the judgment in *Davies* does require, assuming that the rabbi in question had a financial or proprietary interest in the outcome. Under the law as stated in *Davies*, the rabbi had a private law right not to be deprived of the benefits of his office, save in accordance with Jewish law.

The legal position was, it is suggested, correctly stated in the recent (unreported) case of *R* v. *Provincial Court of the Church in Wales ex parte Williams*.[53] This was an attempt to challenge the removal of a minister for gross moral misconduct on the grounds of incorrect standard of proof, disproportionality of punishment and bias. Latham J held that he had no jurisdiction to consider the matter by way of judicial review, but that the case could proceed as if commenced by writ. The plaintiff lost on the facts, but the judge had to consider whether the normal procedures of the Church had been followed. The case turned on the *implication* of contractual terms into the canon law of the Church, and although the judge was cautious about this exercise, it was not ruled out entirely. *Ex parte Williams* demonstrates the key issue in this debate. Who is to be the authoritative interpreter of internal religious law? In the case of the Church of Scotland it is the Church itself but, in the case of all other religious bodies, it is in the last instance – however much deference they pay to religious authorities – the ordinary courts. All this may not matter very much where the 'rules' are clear, but cases are litigated when they are not clear. There is, then, no general jurisdictional autonomy for religious bodies.

The position of the Church of Scotland could potentially be undermined, either by a creative interpretation of the 1921 settlement according to s. 3 of the Human Rights Act, or by a broad reading of the s. 6 obligation on courts not to act in breach of Convention rights. If the courts take this expansive approach, the government's intention not to undermine the 1921 settlement is nonetheless clear, and s. 13 must be taken to express this intention. The right of collective religious liberty is a right of jurisdictional autonomy. In this way, s. 13 becomes potentially highly significant for all religious bodies. Particular regard for the collective right of religious liberty means that the religious body must, in principle, be granted jurisdiction to determine for itself whether its own internal law has been followed, and to determine for itself how those internal procedures are affected by Convention rights. This applies not only in respect of the appointment to, and dismissal from, official posts within the religion, whether remunerated or not, but also in respect of the use of property granted to the organization. It is not open to the courts to imply into the rules and values of religious bodies standards taken from the general common law or the European Convention. If the Human Rights Act has any impact at all in this field, it must be to assimilate the position of all religious bodies to that of the Church of Scotland.

This consequence might be considered objectionable, in that it removes from the ordinary courts the power to protect individuals who find themselves at odds with their religious communities. Of course, the right to collective religious liberty is not absolute, but limited in two ways. First, it presupposes an internal structure for the resolution of disputes. Second, the courts may need to intervene in cases of gross departure from the internal law of the religion in question. But individual liberty is protected by the ability to join and leave such communities, not by the right to undermine their distinct identity and values with the assistance of the ordinary courts. In principle, the question of whether a religious body has acted in accordance with its own 'book of rules' is a matter for the existing authority structure of that religion.

The Religious Liberty of the Church of England

Jurisdictional issues also concerned the Church of England which has not hitherto achieved the same degree of autonomy in spiritual matters as the Church of Scotland. Under the Church of England Assembly (Powers) Act 1919, the General Synod[54] may pass legislation in any matter concerning the Church of England which is then submitted to parliament for approval.[55] Parliament may accept or reject such proposed measures, but not amend them. If accepted, they become Measures with the status of primary legislation. The 'fast track' procedure of the Human Rights Act, as originally drafted, allowed a government minister to amend any primary legislation declared by the courts to be incompatible with Convention rights.[56] This would have included Measures of the Church of England and thus, in the event of a breach being found, would have given government ministers the power to legislate for the Church of England. The government accepted an amendment exempting Measures from the fast track procedure,[57] so, in the unlikely event of a court declaring a Measure of the Church of England incompatible with the Convention, it will be up to the General Synod of the Church of England to propose appropriate changes. No remedy is provided should the Church fail to act, since a failure to introduce into parliament a proposal for legislation is not reviewable.[58]

In view of the 1919 Enabling Act procedure and the Church of England (Worship and Doctrine) Measure 1974, which delegates to the General Synod a wide, if not complete, power to make provision with respect to worship and doctrine, the Church of England now enjoys a considerable degree of autonomy in matters spiritual. However, the possibility of parliamentary veto is always present and has occasionally been used, most notoriously in respect of the Prayer Book revision of 1928 and more recently in 1984 and 1989.[59] Conservative members of the Church are perhaps not overly worried by this additional obstacle to change, but given Synodical approval it represents a limitation of the Church's corporate liberty. To resist the conclusion that such opposition is a breach of Article 9 of the ECHR, it would have to be argued that parliament is still part of the governing structure of the Church of England. However, a future failure of parliament to approve a draft Measure could not be challenged under the Human Rights Act, since parliament is expressly not a public authority for the purposes of the Act.[60]

Nevertheless, it is arguable that the religious liberty of the Church of England has been enhanced in other respects. In law senior Church appointments are made by the sovereign,[61] but, in exercising the power of appointment, the sovereign acts by convention on the advice of others and has no independent role. Archbishops and diocesan bishops are appointed on the advice of the prime minister who since 1977 has been assisted by the Crown Appointments Commission, a Church body.[62] This body puts forward two names, and although there is an expectation that the prime minister will select the first, he or she may select the second,[63] or even reject both candidates.[64] The justification sometimes given for this involvement is that archbishops and diocesan bishops may sit in the House of Lords. This does not apply in the case of suffragan bishops, and there appears to be a convention that the prime minster will select the first of two names suggested by the relevant diocesan bishop.[65] Other senior Church appointments are made on the advice of the prime minister, following a variety of standard consultation procedures that have the status of usage, if not constitutional convention. A few appointments are made by the Lord Chancellor *ex officio*.

Statutory provision is made for the Lord Chancellor's powers of appointment to be exercised by the prime minister or another minister in the case that he is a Roman Catholic, and, despite the terms of the Lord Chancellor (Tenure of Office and Discharge of Ecclesiastical Functions) Act 1974, doubt has been expressed whether he may profess a faith other than Christianity.[66] But there is certainly no restriction on the office of prime minister, so it is entirely possible that, under the present system, a significant element of power over senior appointments in the Church of England could be exercised by a non-member of that Church.

The prime minster is a public authority for the purposes of s. 6 of the Human Rights Act. In advising the sovereign whom to appoint he must act compatibly with Convention rights – rights which include the right to corporate religious liberty of the Church of England. It is at least arguable that, under the Act, he must respect the wishes of the Church and select one of the names presented by the Crown Appointments Commission. Furthermore, should the Church wish to reduce the number of names it proposes, or even to 'leapfrog' the prime minister and advise the sovereign directly,[67] an insistence of real involvement by the prime minister sits uncomfortably with s. 13 of the Act. At the very least, the existing informal consultation processes and expectations of respect for the Church's own view as to whom it wishes to see appointed to senior posts must have been given legal status by the Act.

Religious Pluralism in the Education System

The state education system in England and Wales contains elements both of Christian toleration and religious pluralism.[68] The reforms brought about by the Education Act 1944 broadly divided schools into 'county schools' (now, 'community schools'), which were established and maintained by the state and which were to be Christian, but non-denominational, in ethos, and 'voluntary schools' which had been previously established and funded by Churches and religious bodies, but which were henceforth to be state-maintained. Voluntary schools provided predominantly primary education. The majority of such schools were Church of England or Roman Catholic, although there were also a few Methodist and Jewish schools. Most recently, two Islamic schools were finally successful in their application for voluntary-aided status.[69] The system in Northern Ireland is broadly similar, although 'non-denominational' state schools tend to be Protestant, and voluntary-aided schools Catholic.[70] The Scottish education system is less similar, although once again there is a comparable divide between non-denominational schools and Roman Catholic schools. The Scottish non-denominational schools seem to be more truly accommodating to diverse faiths than their Northern Irish equivalents.[71]

One of the principal concerns expressed during the passage of the Human Rights Act was that the Act might undermine the right of faith-specific schools to select and discipline staff by reference to religious criteria.[72] A teacher who converts to a faith inconsistent with that promoted by the school, or who engages in a lifestyle incompatible with the moral teaching of the religion in question, might complain of discrimination, a breach of privacy or a breach of freedom of expression if the relevant authority wished to dismiss him. To the extent that such rules are inherent in the concept of a school system that contains a plurality of religious schools, they are probably not in breach of the Convention. Once again, the government initially refused to accept the validity of the concern,[73] which led to the success of the following 'preserving amendment':

In relation to –
(a) a church school;
(b) a school or college with a religious foundation or trust deed or, as the case may be, memorandum or articles of association,
nothing in this Act shall be used to affect its ability to select for the position of headteacher, deputy headteacher or other senior post people whose beliefs and manner of life are appropriate to the basic ethos of the school and to dispense with the services of a person in the position of headteacher, deputy headteacher or other senior post whose beliefs and manner of life are not appropriate to the basic ethos of the school.

By subsequently promising to address the issue in the School Standards and Framework Bill[74] (also progressing through parliament at the time), the government implicitly accepted that an interpretation of the Convention making schools with a distinct religious character difficult to operate was at least plausible.

Strictly speaking, the introduction of a new statutory scheme for the regulation of schools with a religious character ought to be irrelevant. If the status quo is changed by the Human Rights Act, a new (and more restrictive) statutory regime ought to be of no avail, since to the extent that the regime is contrary to the Convention, it may be declared incompatible by the courts. But as has already been indicated, strict legal arguments based on a hierarchy of norms do not function when the higher norm is less precise. By developing a precise statutory regime, the government and parliament are indicating to the courts how the interests of teachers, parents and pupils are to be balanced – in short, how the Convention is to be interpreted. This is reinforced by the interpretive provision of s. 13. The rights of individual teachers are to give way to the collective religious interest in having schools that consistently reflect a specific religious ethos. The School Standards and Framework Act 1998, along with subsequent Regulations, creates a new procedure whereby state-maintained schools can be officially designated as having a particular religious character.[75] The designation simply declares what is already true as a matter of fact, but it is a condition for the subjection of the school to different rules as regards the religious education and collective worship provided, staffing issues, the criteria for admission of pupils, potential disposition of assets and statements of the school's ethos.

Christian toleration can be seen in the requirements that apply to schools which are not designated as having a religious character. Every school must include religious education in its basic curriculum,[76] which must 'reflect the fact that the religious traditions in Great Britain are in the main Christian whilst taking account of the teaching and practices of the other principal religions represented in Great Britain'.[77] Furthermore, every pupil is obliged to participate in a daily act of collective worship which must be 'wholly or mainly of a broadly Christian character'.[78] The provision of religious education and religious worship may be modified to take account of local variations in the religious composition of an area on the advice of a standing advisory council on religious education.[79] The appropriately named SACREs contain representatives of local government, schools, Christian and other principal religious traditions of the area, and the Church of England. SACREs have the power to dispense with the requirement that collective worship be broadly Christian.[80] Furthermore, parents may request that pupils be wholly or partly excused from receiving the religious education or attending the worship provided by the school. There is no obligation to provide alternative education (or worship) but, if there is no appropriate and reasonably convenient alternative at another school, parents have the right to withdraw their child from the school for a reasonable time during school hours to attend appropriate education.[81] The right to be excused attendance at religious worship and education applies to all schools.

In the case of schools with a religious character, religious education and worship is provided in accordance with its trust deed or, in the absence of such a deed, in accordance with the denomination or religion specified by the order made under the designation procedure.[82] The list of possible denominations currently provided for includes the Anglican, the Church in Wales, Roman Catholic, Methodist, United Reformed, Seventh Day Adventist, Jewish and Islamic. Whereas in schools without a religious character there is to be no discrimination on the basis of religious belief or practice,[83] in the case of schools with a religious character, in appointing a headteacher their ability and fitness to preserve and develop the religious character of the school may be taken into account and, in the case of teachers, preference may be given to those who share and practise the school's faith.[84] Regard may be had in terminating employment to any conduct incompatible with the tenets of the specified religion. The denominational affiliation of parents is also relevant in the selection of pupils.[85]

Although the judiciary are unlikely to find the entire statutory regime for religious schools incompatible with the Human Rights Act, a few issues might still arise.[86] First, it is questionable whether enough is done for objecting pupils at 'non-religious' schools. Articles 9 and 14 together require non-discrimination in the treatment of such pupils and, although practicality imposes limits, it could be argued that because schools choose to provide religious education and worship, the principle of non-discrimination obliges them to provide separate religious education and worship for significantly sized groups of children adhering to a minority faith.[87] Second, the duty to heed parental wishes in allocating pupils to schools may be strengthened where those wishes have a religious motivation. Third, the ability of private religious schools to transfer into voluntary-aided status may have been strengthened. The School Standards and Framework Act 1998 shifts the power to approve such changes from the secretary of state to the local education authority under central government guidelines.[88] In the past, requests have been turned down on the grounds that surplus places at non-religious schools are available, such that there is 'no need' for the new school.[89] This is inadequate as a reason, since it is the function of the state to provide sufficient school places, thus effectively preventing any reorganization of schools that might shift the balance between 'non-religious' community schools and faith-specific maintained schools. Arguably, under the Human Rights Act, the correct question to ask is whether the proposed religious school can attract sufficient pupils to be economically viable, not whether other 'non-religious' schools might become economically unsustainable as a result.

The area of religion within education is complicated by the fact that the government entered a reservation with respect to Article 2 of the First Protocol.[90] It remains to be seen whether, in this area, the courts will accept arguments based directly on the more general provision of Articles 9 and 14, which may well give more extensive rights to pupils and parents.

The Law of Marriage

The fear that Churches, and in particular the Church of England, might be legally obliged to marry homosexuals and divorcees was perhaps the least plausible concern expressed by religious bodies in the course of the parliamentary proceedings surrounding the Human Rights Act.[91]

Once it was realized that the public function test embraced certain Church activities, of which marriage was the most obvious candidate, it was argued that the right to marry (Article 12 of the ECHR) might in the future be interpreted to include a right of homosexual 'marriage'.[92] Any religious body simultaneously fulfilling the public function of regulating civil marriage would be obliged to respect this right, contrary to the religious convictions of its members. Thus it was that the Bill left the House of Lords containing the words:

> Nothing in this Act shall be used to compel any minister, official or other person acting on behalf of a Christian or other principal religious tradition represented in Great Britain to administer a marriage contrary to his religious doctrines or convictions.

The fear provides interesting evidence of some of the assumptions surrounding the impact of the Human Rights Act. First, it was assumed that the right to marry could, in the foreseeable future, be interpreted to cover homosexual 'marriage'. Second, it was assumed that the religious liberty protected by Article 9 of the Convention was not relevant, perhaps only applying to individual, not collective, behaviour. Third, it was assumed that any right to marry was equally enforceable against any body exercising the public function of regulating marriage. Each of these assumptions is questionable.

As regards the scope of the right to marry, common law,[93] statute law[94] and the jurisprudence of the European Commission of Human Rights[95] are all clear in presupposing a conventional heterosexual conception of marriage. The right to marry under the ECHR contains neither a right to divorce,[96] nor a right to select the ceremony of one's choice. Given the composition of the European Court, with judges representative of many countries in which Roman Catholicism is socially dominant, it is difficult to see this conception of marriage being abandoned in the foreseeable future. Of course, the British judiciary are not prevented from interpreting the Convention in the future to grant more extensive rights, but the thought that parliament could also do the same, introducing homosexual 'marriage' by statutory amendment, seems not to have figured in the debates. When one takes into account the spread of political opinion in both the judiciary and parliament, coupled with the judicial commitment to precedent and the desire to avoid public controversy, the idea that the judiciary are more likely than parliament to use the Human Rights Act to create a conception of homosexual marriage was unrealistic.

Even if Article 12 did embrace homosexual partnerships, any consideration of its scope would have to take into account the freedom of religion protected by Article 9, in both its individual and collective aspects. The collective implications of Article 9, now highlighted in s. 13 of the Act, are that entire organizations may have a religious ethos that it is important to preserve.[97] Forcing a religious organization to participate in an activity that is contrary to its teachings is not only a breach of the individual participant's freedom of conscience, but also a breach of the organization's collective liberty.[98] It can only be justified if 'necessary in a democratic society in the interests of public safety, for the protection of public order, health or morals, or for the protection of the rights and freedoms of others' (Article 9 II). Since a marriage can be celebrated by civil ceremony, the infringement of the religious organization's collective liberty is not necessary. Exactly the same argument applies in the case of religious bodies who might wish to use Article 9 to broaden the scope of marriage law in line with their own conceptions – perhaps to include polygamous marriages or marriage by proxy. Any change to the statutory regime of marriage can only be achieved by way of a declaration of incompatibility, and the easiest way of achieving that will be to challenge the refusal of a superintendent registrar to celebrate a civil marriage that is currently illegal, rather than confuse the issue by wishing both to challenge the current legal conception of marriage and the right of a religious body to refuse to recognize the new conception.

The broader assumption underlying this debate was that all public functions must be carried out in conformity to the same ethical principles – either there is a right to homosexual 'marriage' or there is not. But the consequence of accepting both that religious organizations undertake public functions and that the collective religious ethos of such organizations is to be protected is that religious liberty requires religious pluralism. Different public bodies perform similar functions according to different criteria. As we have seen, the model is familiar in the case of schools, where an entire state school may have an ethos that is Christian, Jewish or Islamic.

There is no need to structure the law of marriage in a pluralistic fashion. One could have a uniform civil process that is legally necessary and quite independent of any religious ceremony, which then could be undertaken or not at the discretion of the parties.[99] In the UK, however, the marriage ceremony is pluralistic, with religious ministers functioning simultaneously as public officials. This has been the case for the Church of England, the Society of Friends (Quakers)[100] and Jews[101] since Lord Hardwicke's Act of 1753.[102] Other religious groups may perform marriages if they are held at registered places of worship and conducted by an authorized person.[103] No one has the right to get married according to a particular religious ceremony, but must comply with the requirements of the religion in question. The Church of England is in a different position, in that it is legally obliged to marry couples entitled to marry and resident in the parish,[104] although even here an element of pluralism has crept in concerning the marriage of persons too closely related by canon law[105] and the remarriage of divorcees.[106] The civil ceremony of marriage before a registrar is an option for anyone entitled to marry, but who cannot or will not be married by a registered minister of religion. Scotland has a similar, if more uniform, system, whereby the registrar issues a marriage schedule which is simultaneously a licence authorizing the celebrant of any registered religion to proceed with the marriage. After the ceremony, the schedule is signed and returned to the registrar.[107]

It is interesting to speculate on how far religious pluralism in marriage could be extended. At present, it is limited to the formalities of the legally binding ceremony, but it could be extended to questions of the capacity and consequences of marriage as well. As conceptions of sexual morality diversify, we need not assume that the law should enforce only the highest common factor among the competing ethical positions. Instead, the law could lend its support to the ethical conception of marriage freely entered into by the parties, making (for example) divorce and remarriage easier or more difficult as appropriate.[108]

Employment

In principle, employment law does not prevent employers from incorporating religious tests into their selection and disciplinary procedures.[109] Where employees have been dismissed for failing to perform contractual duties, the courts have tended to ignore the religious motivation for doing so and have upheld the dismissal.[110] In the most well known case, *Ahmad* v. *ILEA*, the Court of Appeal upheld the dismissal of a Muslim teacher who wished to have 45 minutes' leave of absence during Friday afternoons to pray at a mosque. A majority of the Court refused to give the statutory requirement of non-discrimination on grounds of religious belief within education[111] a broad interpretation to cover attendance at religious worship outside the school. The Court of Appeal's decision's was upheld by the European Human Rights Commission[112] on the grounds that he had freedom to contract or not as he pleased, and that the alternative offer of part-time employment for four days a week was not unreasonable. More recently, the Commission rejected a complaint simply by referring to freedom of contract.[113]

The first question is thus whether the Human Rights Act enhances the individual freedom of religion of employees, by giving them rights to prac-tise their beliefs, even when inconvenient for their employers. By contrast, the Churches seeking amendments in the House of Lords were concerned with the opposite problem. They assumed that the Human Rights Act would prevent employers from discriminating on grounds of religion and wished to preserve the collective right of religious organizations and charities with a distinct religious ethos to continue doing so. The Bill left the House of Lords with an amendment designed to meet the core of these concerns:

> In relation to a charity which has as one of its aims the advancement of religion, nothing in this Act shall be used to affect its ability to select for the position of chief executive, deputy chief executive or other senior post people whose beliefs and manner of life are appropriate to the basic ethos of the charity and to dispense with the services of a person in the position of chief executive, deputy chief executive or other senior post whose beliefs and manner of life are not appropriate to the basic ethos of the charity.

In many ways the clause was too narrow in referring only to a charity and to senior appointments. The government's catch-all response was deliberately couched in wider terms; by referring to religious organizations, it covered both Churches and their equivalents – that is, religious charities and non-charitable companies that have a distinctive religious ethos.[114] S. 13 implies that it is primarily up to such an organization to decide whether it requires only senior posts, all posts or even no posts to be filled by people committed to the values of the organization.

The government's initial view that the Convention has nothing to do with employment law is unsustainable.[115] Once it is accepted (as the vast major-ity of commentators do) that Convention rights are individual interests capable of infringement by both public and private bodies, the key issue concerns the procedural route by which a Convention argument can be made.[116] Certainly, 'pure' public authorities are bound by the Convention in all their actions, so Ahmad would have a direct cause of action to vindicate his Convention rights.[117] In addition, the court will now be obliged to read the employment provisions of the education legislation in the light of Convention rights. It has also been argued that, despite s. 6(5) of the Human Rights Act, private bodies exercising public functions are bound by Convention rights in employing people to fulfil those functions.[118] Where one is dealing with a purely private body, there is scope for developing the common law in the case of unfair dismissal, but not in the case of discriminatory appointment practices.[119] There is also some scope for interpreting employment protection legislation to give enhanced protection to religious rights.[120]

It is not sufficient to show that Convention rights are relevant to the dispute, it has to be shown that they swing the balance of interests in favour of the employee. While the case law of the Strasbourg organs has so far taken refuge in freedom of contract as sufficient protection for freedom of religion, it is to be hoped that British courts will give the interest in religious liberty higher priority as against commercial and business considerations than hitherto. It is difficult to accept that dismissal is a proportionate response to, for example, the refusal of a doctor's secretary to type a letter in connection with an abortion.[121] It is not clear whether s. 13 is relevant in disputes between individuals and their employers.[122] However, in the case of employers with a religious ethos, this section is clearly relevant, and serves to strengthen their position under existing employment law. Employees of organizations that seek to preserve a distinct religious ethos will not be able to use their Convention rights to renegotiate or breach their employment contracts and thus undermine that ethos.

Blasphemy and Religious Hatred

It was thought that the English common law offences of blasphemy and blasphemous libel were obsolete, until Mary Whitehouse succeeded in persuading the House of Lords to declare the offences very much alive.[123] Although there has been no successful prosecution since the *Gay News* case, the law is still relevant in guiding the decisions of the British Board of Film Classification as to certification of films and videos and as a general restraint on publication.[124]

The case law makes it clear that only the religion established by law in England is explicitly covered, with other faiths benefiting to the extent that they share common ground with Anglican Christianity. The existence of the offences can thus only be justified as part of a broader defence of religious establishment. Such a defence would require two main elements: a defence of the principle that a state may identify with a particular religion, and then a further debate internal to that religion that it is an appropriate use of state power to prevent individuals from offering gratuitous insult to God (as conceived by the established faith).[125] That internal debate may conclude that, despite the truth of the established religion, the particular use of state power represented by blasphemy laws is illegitimate.[126] In practice, public debate has rarely sought to defend the law in this way, preferring the more neutral justification that the law of blasphemy serves to protect the religious feelings of believers.[127] In short, the English law of blasphemy is almost always conceived as a law against Christian religious hatred.

Once that move has been made, the offence becomes obviously unsatisfactory, in that the religious discrimination ceases to be objectively justified – unless one wishes to maintain the implausible thesis that the religious feelings of Christians are stronger than those of other religions. Broadly speaking, commentators are split between those who would prefer to abolish the law as an unacceptable limitation on free expression[128] and those who would prefer to expand the law to cover other faiths.[129] The Law Commission was, unusually, split on precisely this issue.[130] It is not unfair to suggest that blasphemy has survived its renaissance by dividing the opposition.

The same divergence can be found in the interpretation of the ECHR. Abolitionists rely on Article 10 and suggest that the restriction on freedom of expression is not necessary in a democratic society to protect the interests of others. This argument has been rejected by a majority of the European Court which has permitted states to limit free expression to protect the religious feelings of its citizens.[131] Thus the English law of blasphemy has survived challenge.[132] Expansionists can either attempt to bring religious feelings within the scope of Article 9, arguing that states have a positive duty under that article to protect the religious feelings of others,[133] or they can point to Article 14 which requires states not to discriminate in the protection of rights. Whatever one's views on the scope of Article 9, the Article 14 argument is hard to resist. The Court has expressly held that Article 14 prevents a state from discriminating in the otherwise justifiable limitations it places on substantive rights.[134] Thus, while Article 10 may permit a state to criminalize religious hate speech, Article 14 requires the state to criminalize such speech with an even hand. The European Commission rejected Choudhury's attempt to expand the law of blasphemy to include Muslim religious feelings,[135] on the narrow ground that the Convention gave him no right to bring a specific form of proceedings (here criminal) to vindicate any putative right.[136] But, as a matter of objective law, his case was surely sound.

It is a subtle question whether future plaintiffs will be able to negotiate the procedural complexities of the Human Rights Act to persuade an

English court to rework the common law of blasphemy. Attention has already been drawn to the uncertainties surrounding the relationship between the Act and the common law. One could argue that because magistrates and the director of public prosecutions are public authorities bound by s. 6, if the law of blasphemy is an unjustifiable restriction on freedom of speech it would be illegal for them to take any proceedings. The same argument can be made *mutatis mutandis* with respect to the British Board of Film Classification. But note what a curious state of affairs this would be: a statute would prevent law enforcement agencies from enforcing otherwise valid law. Furthermore, if the heart of the objection is based on discrimination, it is not clear which way the discrimination should be removed – the situation can be equalized by levelling down (no blasphemy law) or levelling up (offences of incitement to religious hatred across a variety of faiths). Given the settled nature of the common law and the uncertainty as to which way it should be changed, the judiciary may be limited to making a statement of incompatibility, leaving it up to parliament to sort out the policy arguments either way.

Should the judiciary consider that the Act gives them implicit authority to change settled case law to bring it into line with the Convention – and it is bizarre that the most intrusive form of state intervention should not be subject to the Convention – the dilemma on the substantive question of consistency is heightened without being resolved. While s. 13 of the Human Rights Act would seem to point in the direction of a multifaith 'blasphemy' law, s. 12 also requires the court to have 'particular regard' to the importance of freedom of expression. This is perhaps another reason to decline jurisdiction and hand the problem back to the legislator, who will no doubt wish to continue avoiding such a contentious issue.

Conclusions

No one can be sure of the precise impact of the Human Rights Act 1998. Not only is the Act vague as a matter of substance, but it is also vague as to the relevance of Convention rights at all in many areas of law. This necessarily speculative chapter has focused primarily on the areas of law raised in the parliamentary debates, but there are several other areas on which the religious rights contained in the Act may have a significant impact, such as planning law, medical law and child law. In broad perspective, the Act refuses to see religion as purely a matter of private and individual belief, but rightly recognizes that it is membership of a religio-ethical community that matters to most adherents. The unavoidably public nature of aspects of religious commitment results in areas of overlap between public and religious functions, and the distinctive nature of religious ethics may create conflict with substantive principles of law. Far from being irrelevant, s. 13 of the Human Rights Act 1998 indicates the general strategy by which such areas of overlap and conflict are to be regulated. The interest in preserving a collective religious ethos prevails, since religious liberty lies extensively in the freedom of the individual to participate in a variety of institutions that fulfil similar social functions, but in accordance with divergent ethical and doctrinal commitments.

In general, then, the Human Rights Act would appear to be shifting the nature of religious liberty in the UK from a model of Christian toleration to one of religious pluralism. The non-coercive establishment of a single faith, and a single organization expressive of that faith, is being replaced with a series of 'mini-establishments' in which religious bodies are granted a degree of protected autonomy and authority over those who choose to belong to them. Individuals may decide which of a series of ethically and religiously distinct institutions they adhere to. It remains to be seen how far this process of religious pluralism can continue and whether it will not, in time, topple the symbolic commitment to Christianity still implicit in the UK's constitutional arrangements.

Notes

1   I am grateful to Malcolm Evans, Steven Greer, Francis Lyall and Michael Nazir-Ali for their comments on an earlier draft. This does not imply that they necessarily agree with the views propounded.
2   General accounts of the relationship of law and religion in the UK can be found in St J.A. Robilliard (1984), *Religion and the Law*, (Manchester: Manchester University Press); *Stair Memorial Encyclopaedia* (1987), Vol. 10: 'Constitutional Law', (Edinburgh: Butterworths), paras 679–704; A. Bradney (1993), *Religions, Rights and Laws*, (Leicester: Leicester University Press); *Stair Memorial Encyclopaedia* (1994), Vol. 3: 'Churches and other Religious Bodies'; C. Hamilton (1995), *Family, Law and Religion*, (London: Sweet and Maxwell); S.H. Bailey, D.J. Harris and B.L. Jones (1995), *Civil Liberties: Cases and Materials*, 4th edn, (London: Butterworths), ch. 9; P. Cumper (1995), 'Freedom of Thought, Conscience and Religion', in D. Harris and S. Joseph (eds), *The International Covenant on Civil and Political Rights and United Kingdom Law*, (Oxford: Clarendon Press); P. Cumper (1996), 'Religious Liberty in the United Kingdom', in J.D. van der Vywer and J. Witte, jr (eds), *Religious Human Rights in Global Perspective – Legal Perspectives*, (The Hague: Martinus Nijhoff); K. Boyle and J. Sheen (1997), *Freedom of Religion and Belief: A World Report*, (London: Routledge), pp. 314–329.
3   The Act 53 Geo III c. 160 extended the benefit of the Toleration Act 1689 to persons denying the doctrine of the Trinity.
4   Roman Catholic Relief Act 1829.
5   Religious Disabilities Act 1846.
6   *Bowman* v. *Secular Society* [1917] AC 406.

7   Government of Ireland Act 1920 s. 5(1), Northern Ireland Constitution Act 1975, ss 17 and 19. On Northern Ireland, see S. Livingstone (1997), 'Religious Discrimination' in B. Dickson (ed.), *Civil Liberties in Northern Ireland*, 3rd edn, (Belfast: CAJ).

8   Act of Settlement 1700, s. 3.

9   By the Irish Church Act 1869 and the Welsh Church Act 1914 respectively.

10   *Halsbury's Laws of England*, (4th edn), Vol. 34, 'Parliament', para. 528. The position is unaffected by the House of Lords Act 1999, but may change when the composition of the second chamber is finally settled.

11   *Halsbury's Laws of England*, (4th edn), Vol. 14, 'Ecclesiastical Law', paras 993, 1004, 1041 respectively. The position with respect to marriage has been disputed: N. Doe (1996), *The Legal Framework of the Church of England*, (Oxford: Clarendon Press), pp. 358–362.

12   See Robilliard, *Religion and the Law*, *op. cit.*, ch. 8.

13   Sunday Trading Act 1994.

14   See, in particular, J. Montgomery (1992), 'Legislating for a Multi-faith Society: Some Problems of Special Treatment', in B. Hepple and E.M. Szyszczak (eds), *Discrimination: The Limits of Law*, (London: Mansell); S. Poulter (1998), *Ethnicity, Law and Human Rights*, (Oxford: Clarendon Press), especially ch. 2.

15   Article 9 of the ECHR provides:

> (1) Everyone has the right to freedom of thought, conscience and religion; this right includes freedom to change his religion or belief, and freedom, either alone or in community with others and in public or private, to manifest his religion or belief, in worship, teaching, practice and observance.
>
> (2) Freedom to manifest one's religion or beliefs shall be subject only to such limitations as are prescribed by law and are necessary in a democratic society in the interests of public safety, for the protection of public order, health or morals, or for the protection of the rights and freedoms of others.

Article 14 of the ECHR provides:

> The enjoyment of the rights and freedoms set forth in this Convention shall be secured without discrimination on any ground such as sex, race, colour, language, religion, political or other opinion, national or social origin, association with a national minority, property, birth or other status.

Article 2 of the First Protocol to ECHR provides:

> No person shall be denied the right to education. In the exercise of any functions which it assumes in relation to education and to teaching, the State shall respect the right of parents to ensure such education and teaching in conformity with their own religious and philosophical convictions.

16   Cmnd. 8969.

17   Home Secretary, HC Deb, 18 May 1999, col. 293 (written answer).

18   For an overview of the Act, see Steven Greer (1999), 'A Guide to the Human Rights Act 1998', *European Law Review*, **24**, p. 3.

19   S. 3(1).

20   S. 6(1).

21   S. 7.

22   S. 4.

23   S. 10.

24   S. 2(1). .

25   For a useful evaluation, see C.A. Gearty (1993), 'The European Court of Human Rights and the Protection of Civil Liberties: An Overview', *Cambridge Law Journal*, **52,** p. 89.

26   D.J. Harris, M. O'Boyle, C. Warbrick (1995), *Law of the European Convention on Human Rights*, (London: Butterworths), pp. 19–22.

27   For a general account of the problem, see A. Clapham (1993), *Human Rights in the Private Sphere*, (Oxford: Clarendon Press). As regards the Human Rights Act in particular, see M. Hunt (1998), 'The "Horizontal Effect" of the Human Rights Act', *Public Law*, p. 423.

28   See, for example, the contributions of B. Hepple and M. Hunt (1998) in B.S. Markesinis (ed.), *The Impact of the Human Rights Bill on English Law*, (Oxford: Clarendon Press). The divergence of views on this point is notable in C. Baker (ed.) (1998), *The Human Rights Act 1998: A Practitioner's Guide*, (London: Sweet & Maxwell), between the more conservative approach of the editor and the more expansive assumptions of his contributors.

29   *Morris* v. *Beardmore* [1980] 2 All ER 753; *R* v. *Secretary of State for the Home Dept. ex p. Brind* [1991] 1 AC 696.

30   The government accepted one amendment with respect to the legislative procedure of the Church of England, discussed below.

31   J. Wadham and H. Mountfield (1998), *Blackstone's Guide to the Human Rights Act 1998*, (London: Blackstone Press), p. 55.

32   It is unclear whether the decision in *Pepper* v. *Hart* [1993] AC 593, which permits judges to have recourse to *Hansard* for statements of legislative intent to resolve statutory ambiguities, extends to the interpretation of broad legislative provisions. The general assumption during the debate and by commentators is that official government statements will be relevant. See F. Klug (1999), 'The Human Rights Act 1998, Pepper v Hart and All That', *Public Law*, p. 246.

33   HC Deb, 20 May 1998, cols 1019–20 (Home Secretary, Jack Straw MP).

34   Ibid., col. 1021.

35   Ibid., col. 1022.

36   Ibid., col. 1026.

37   This causes dispute as to whether the Church is 'established' or not. While the Church of Scotland was (arguably) not created by the authority of the state, it certainly enjoys a special pre-eminence and is for that reason to be regarded as established. See C.R. Munro (1997), 'Does Scotland have an Established Church?', *Ecclesiastical Law Journal*, **4,** p. 639.

38   See generally *Stair Memorial Encyclopaedia* (1994), Vol. 3: 'The Laws of Scotland', (Edinburgh: Butterworths).

39   Article IV.

40   *Stair, op. cit.*, Vol. 3, paras 1574–1577; The Church of Scotland General Trustees 1931 SC 704.

41   HL Deb, 19 January 1998, cols 1272–75 (Lord Mackay of Drumadoon).

42   HL Deb, 19 January 1998, col. 1288 (Lord Hardie, Lord Advocate); HL Deb, 5 February 1998, col. 794 (Lord Hardie, Lord Advocate); HC Deb, 20 May 1998, col. 1064 (Donald Dewar MP, Secretary of State for Scotland).

43   Amendments tabled by Lord Mackay of Drumadoon at Report Stage and Third Reading to this effect were unsuccessful.

44   Lord Peston was among the few to draw attention to this: 'If I were a religious or spiritual person, I should feel very threatened': HL Deb, 19 January 1998, col. 1287.
45   1936 SC 625, 1936 SLT 436.
46   1995 SLT 1228.
47   *R* v. *Chief Rabbi of the United Hebrew Congregations of Great Britain and the Commonwealth, ex parte Wachman* [1992] 1 WLR 1036; *R* v. *Imam of Bury Park ex p. Sulaiman Ali* [1992] COD 132; upheld by CA in *R* v. *Imam of Bury Park ex p. Sulaiman Ali* [1994] COD 142; *R* v. *London Beth Din ex p. Bloom* [1998] COD 131.
48   *Ex p. Bloom* per Lightman J, p. 133.
49   *R* v. *Jockey Club ex p. Aga Khan* [1993] 1 WLR 909, 932 (per Hoffmann LJ) and subsequent cases *passim*.
50   *Free Church of Scotland General Assembly* v. *Lord Overtoun* [1904] AC 515.
51   [1986] 1 WLR 323.
52   See also *Santokh Singh* v. *Guru Nanak Gurdwara* [1990] ICR 309.
53   CO 2880/98 (Lexis Transcript 23 October 1998). In respect of Scottish law, see the decision in *Brentnall* v. *Free Presbyterian Church of Scotland* 1986 SLT 471.
54   Under the Synodical Government Measure 1969, the Church Assembly was reconstituted as the General Synod of the Church of England.
55   N. Doe (1996), *The Legal Framework of the Church of England*, (Oxford: Clarendon Press), ch. 3.
56   Clauses 10(2) and 21 as originally drafted.
57   HL Deb, 19 January 1998, cols 1346–47 (Lord Chancellor) and Human Rights Act 1998, s. 10(6).
58   S. 6(6).
59   Appointment of Bishops Measure and Clergy (Ordination) Measure. For a critical account of such incidents, see C. Buchanan (1994), *Cut the Connection*, (London: Darton Longman and Todd).
60   S. 6(3).
61   Appointment of Bishops Act 1533 (archbishops and diocesan bishops); Suffragan Bishops Acts 1534–1898. See, generally, *Senior Church Appointments* (1992), (London: Church House Publishing).
62   Announcement of James Callaghan, Prime Minister, HC Deb, 8 June 1976.
63   As did Margaret Thatcher in connection with the bishopric of London: *The Times*, 31 March 1981.
64   As did Tony Blair in connection with the bishopric of Liverpool: *The Times*, 16 September 1997.
65   *Senior Church Appointments*, *op. cit.*, para. 5.4.
66   P. O'Higgins (1980), *Cases and Materials on Civil Liberties*, cited in Robilliard, *Religion and the Law*, *op. cit.*, p. 203.
67   As was proposed in respect of senior Church appointments other than archbishops and diocesan bishops by the Working Party chaired by Sir William van Straubenzee: *Senior Church Appointments*, *op. cit.*, paras 5.29–5.32.
68   As well as the literature at note 2 above, see J.D.C. Harte (1998), 'Influences of Church and State in the English School System' in Eibe Riedel (ed.), *Öffentliches Schulwesen im Spannungsfeld von Staat und Kirche*, (Baden-Baden: Nomos).
69   *Daily Telegraph*, 10 January 1998.
70   C. Moffat (1997), 'Education Rights' in Dickson, *Civil Liberties in Northern Ireland*, *op. cit.*
71   For an overview, see Cumper, 'Freedom of Thought', *op. cit.*
72   The Christian Institute, *Hammering Rights Home*, p. 3; Baroness Young, HL Deb, 24

November 1997, cols 790, 791; HL Deb, 19 January 1998, col. 1322; Edward Leigh MP, HC Deb, 16 February 1998, col. 849.

73 HL Deb, 19 January 1998, col. 1345 (Lord Chancellor).
74 HC Deb, 20 May 1998, col. 1016 (Home Secretary).
75 School Standards and Framework Act 1998, s. 69(3); The Religious Character of Schools (Designation Procedure) Regulations 1998 SI 1998, 2535.
76 Education Act 1996, s. 352(1)(a).
77 Education Act 1996, s. 375(3).
78 Education Act 1996, ss 385(1) and 386(2); School Standards and Framework Act 1998, s. 70 and Schedule 20, s. 3.
79 Education Act 1996, ss 390–393.
80 Education Act 1996, ss 394–396.
81 Education Act 1996, s. 389; School Standards and Framework Act 1998, s. 71.
82 School Standards and Framework Act 1998 s. 69 and Schedule 19 (education), s. 70 and Schedule 20 (worship), respectively.
83 School Standards and Framework Act 1998, s. 59.
84 School Standards and Framework Act 1998, s. 60.
85 School Standards and Framework Act 1998, s. 91. The legitimacy of this practice had already been upheld by the courts: *Choudhury* v. *Governors of Bishop Challoner Roman Catholic Comprehensive School* [1992] 3 All ER 277.
86 S. Fredman (1998), 'Equality Issues' in B.S. Markesinis (ed.), *The Impact of the Human Rights Bill on English Law*, (Oxford: Clarendon Press), pp. 124–125.
87 Cf., for example, the implication of strict neutrality drawn out of rights to religious liberty and non-discrimination by the German Federal Constitutional Court: BVerfGE 41, 29 etc. (Christian community schools), BVerfGE 52, 223 (school prayers), BVerfG NJW 1995, 2477 (crucifixes in classrooms).
88 School Standards and Framework Act 1998, s. 28 and Schedule 6.
89 See, for one round in a long battle to get approval for an Islamic primary school in London, *R* v. *Secretary of State for Education ex parte Yusaf Islam, The Times,* 22 May 1992.
90 The government considers itself bound to 'respect the right of parents to ensure such education and teaching in conformity with their own religious and philosophical convictions' (Article 2 First Protocol) 'only so far as it is compatible with the provision of efficient instruction and training and the avoidance of unreasonable public expenditure'. Reservations are common with respect to this article: see J.E.S. Fawcett (1987), *The Application of the European Convention on Human Rights*, 2nd edn, (Oxford: Clarendon Press), p. 413.
91 The Christian Institute (1997), *Hammering Rights Home*, p. 3.
92 See, for example, Baroness Young, *Hansard* HL, 24 November 1997, col. 791, the Lord Bishop of Ripon, *Hansard* HL, 19 January 1998 cols 1325–6, Lord Alton, ibid. at col. 1338, Ann Widdecombe MP, *Hansard* HC, 16 February 1998 col. 800; Sir Brian Mawhinny MP, *Hansard* HC, 20 May 1998, col. 1034.
93 *Hyde* v. *Hyde* (1866) LR 1 P & D 130; *Corbett* v. *Corbett* [1970] 2 WLR 1306. For the position in Scotland, see *Stair Memorial Encyclopaedia* (1990), 'Family Law', Vol. 10, para. 818.
94 Matrimonial Causes Act 1973, s. 11.
95 *S* v. *UK*, 47 DR 274 (1986). The case actually concerned the question of whether homosexual relationships constitute 'family life' for the purposes of Article 8. *A fortiori*, there is no right to marry. Note that this view is not without dissent. See Harris *et al.*, *Law of the European Convention, op. cit.*, p. 439.

96   *Johnston* v. *Ireland* A112 (1986).
97   Implicit in the Home Secretary's discussion of the marriage issue: HC Deb, 20 May 1998, cols 1015–17: 'The right of any Church, which we intend to strengthen, to refuse to marry divorced people remains protected by the Convention.'
98   See also the Lord Chancellor, HL Deb, 19 January 1998, col. 1348.
99   This was proposed as early as 1836 in the Marriage Bill, and recommended again by the Law Commission in 1973 (Law Com. No. 53). See Hamilton, *Family, Law and Religion, op. cit.*, pp. 50–51.
100 See now Marriage Act 1949, s. 47.
101 See now Marriage Act 1949, s. 26(1)(d).
102 26 Geo. II c. 33.
103 See Bradney, *Religious Rights and Laws, op. cit.*, pp. 39–43 for a discussion of why some ethnic minority religious groupings seem not to take advantage of this possibility. Hamilton, *Family, Law and Religion, op. cit.*, p. 50 suggests that the relaxed registration requirements of the Marriage (Registration of Buildings) Act 1990 may have a beneficial effect in this respect.
104 This is the general opinion (M. Hill (1995), *Ecclesiastical Law*, (London: Butterworths), p. 305) but for a contrary view, see N. Doe (1996), *The Legal Framework of the Church of England*, (Oxford: Clarendon Press), pp. 358–62.
105 Marriage Act 1949, s. 5A, as inserted by the Marriage (Prohibited Degrees of Relationship) Act 1986, s. 3.
106 Marriage Act 1949, s. 8(2).
107 *Stair Memorial Encyclopaedia* (1990), Family Law, **10**, paras 807, 809.
108 It is reported that the concept of a 'covenant marriage' is being tested in Louisiana: *The Sunday Telegraph,* 29 June 1997. For recent accounts and critique see K.S. Spaht (1998), 'Louisiana's Covenant Marriage: Social Analysis and Legal Implications', *Louisiana Law Review* **59**, p. 63; K.S. Spaht (1998), 'For the Sake of the Children: Recapturing the Meaning of Marriage', *Notre Dame Law Review* **77**, 1547; S. Hager (1998), 'Nostalgic Attempts to Recapture What Never Was: Louisiana's Covenant Marriage Act', *Nebraska Law Review*, **77**, p. 567.
109 *Jones* v. *Lee* [1980] ICR 310.
110 *Ahmad* v. *Inner London Education Authority* [1978] QB 36; *Esson* v. *United Transport Executive* [1975] IRLR 48; *Storey* v. *Allied Breweries* (1976) 84 IRLIB 9; *Janaway* v. *Salford Health Authority* [1989] AC 537.
111 Education Act 1944, s. 30; see now School Standards and Framework Act 1998, s. 59.
112 *Ahmad* v. *United Kingdom* (1982) 4 EHRR 126.
113 *Stedman* v. *United Kingdom* (1997) 23 EHRR CD 168.
114 HC Deb, 20 May 1998, col. 1022 (Home Secretary, Jack Straw MP).
115 HL Deb, 19 Jan 1998, col. 1344: '[It] is absolutely correct to say that the convention rights have nothing whatever to do with employment rights' (Lord Chancellor, Lord Irvine of Lairg). See also HL Deb, 5 Feb 1998, col. 757.
116 See K.D. Ewing (1998) 'The Human Rights Act and Labour Law', *Industrial Law Journal*, **27**, p. 275. D. Carter (1998), 'Employment and Labour Relations Law' in C. Baker (ed.), *The Human Rights Act 1998: A Practitioner's Guide*, (London: Sweet & Maxwell), assumes without debate that Convention rights will be relevant.
117 Ewing, 'The Human Rights Act', *op. cit.*, at p. 285 n. 52.
118 G.S. Morris (1998), 'The Human Rights Act and the Public/Private Divide in Employment Law', *Industrial Law Journal*, **27**, p. 293.
119 Ewing, 'The Human Rights Act', *op. cit.*, p. 287.
120 Ibid., p. 289.

121 See *Janaway* v. *Salford Health Authority* [1989] AC 537. S.H. Bailey, D.J. Harris and B.L. Jones (1995), *Civil Liberties: Cases and Materials*, (London: Butterworths), p. 606, note one case in which the Industrial Tribunal awarded £3000 compensation to a Muslim who was dropped from a sales representatives training course after being refused an hour's leave to attend a mosque. This represents an extremely generous reading of the Race Relations Act 1976, but demonstrates the potential of s. 3 of the Human Rights Act 1998.

122 S. 13 gives enhanced protection to a collective right. Often, the individual in dispute with his employer seeks an opportunity to join with others in some religious exercise, which arguably activates the enhanced protection. The European Commission in *Ahmad* rejected an overly individualistic characterization of his dispute. See 4 EHRR 126 at 132–133.

123 *R* v. *Lemon* [1979] AC 617. For a general account, see Robilliard, *Religion and the Law, op. cit.*, ch. 2; D. Feldman (1993), *Civil Liberties and Human Rights*, (Oxford: Clarendon Press), pp. 685–98.

124 G. Robertson and A. Nicol (1992), *Media Law*, 2nd rev. edn, (London: Penguin), pp. 124–127, 460.

125 J. Rivers (2000), 'Blasphemy Law in the Secular State' in Michael Schluter *et al.*, *Christianity in a Changing World*, (Marshall Pickering).

126 I. Leigh (1998), 'Towards a Christian Approach to Religious Liberty', in P.R. Beaumont (ed.), *Christian Perspectives on Human Rights and Legal Philosophy*, (Carlisle: Paternoster Press), pp. 52–59.

127 Law Commission Report no. 145, pp. 20–23.

128 J. R. Spencer (1981), 'Blasphemy: The Law Commission's Working Paper', *Criminal Law Review*, p. 810.

129 S. Poulter (1991), 'Towards Legislative Reform of the Blasphemy and Racial Hatred Laws', *Public Law*, p. 371; D. Edwards (1985), 'Toleration and the English Blasphemy Law', in P. Horton and S. Mendus (eds), *Aspects of Toleration*, (London: Methuen).

130 The Law Commission divided 3–2, and a similar division can be observed among the judges of the European Court of Human Rights.

131 *X & Y* v. *UK, DR* 28, 77; *Otto-Preminger Institut* v. *Austria*, A–295 A; *Wingrove* v. *United Kingdom*, 24 EHRR 1.

132 The Court recognized the English situation as 'anomalous' (*Wingrove* v. *UK*, para. 50) but was prepared to approve an enforcement policy of the Austrian 'neutral' religious hatred law that follows the interests of the dominant Roman Catholic population (*Otto-Preminger* v. *Austria*, para. 56).

133 The Court made a suggestion along these lines in *Otto-Preminger*. In a separate opinion in *Wingrove*, Judge Pettiti made his dissent on this point explicit, while the majority of the Court simply dealt with the matter under the limitations to Article 10. Since then, the Commission has insisted that Article 9 imposes positive obligations on the state to ensure respect for religious feelings, which can be violated by provocative portrayals of objects of veneration. See *Dubrowska & Skup* v. *Poland*, Appl. no. 33490/96, 24 EHRR CD75, 78.

134 Belgian Linguistic case, B3 para. 400.

135 *R* v. *Chief Metropolitan Stipendiary Magistrate, ex parte Choudhury* [1991] 1 All ER 306.

136 *Choudhury* v. *UK*, 12 HRLJ 172 (1991).

8 Religion, International Law and Policy in the Wider European Arena: New Dimensions and Developments

Sophie C. van Bijsterveld

Introduction

Religious liberty is well established in international fundamental rights texts. Following the Universal Declaration on Human Rights 1948 (UDHR), religious liberty was guaranteed by the European Convention on Human Rights 1950 (ECHR) and the International Covenant on Civil and Political Rights 1966 (ICCPR). Religious liberty also features in many other international treaties and documents and is implied in guarantees of equal treatment or non-discrimination. In these texts, the predominant model is that of individual rights backed by the courts.[1]

International fora are increasingly being discovered by individuals pleading their cases and, whatever the domestic reception of international law, international decision-making is bound to have effects at the national level. It is interesting to see how the case law develops and how issues related to religious liberty are treated. In this respect, the decisions of the European Court of Human Rights are fascinating in their attempt to build a common European human rights understanding and develop concrete human rights standards. By overemphasizing case law, however, one risks overlooking broader developments in law and policy with regard to religion. This is true at the national as well as the international level.

163

My purpose is to explore and analyse the attitude towards, and *understanding of*, religion in the international domain. To this end, I will review the broader attitudes and developments relating to religion in the European arena.[2] I shall focus on the Council of Europe, the United Nations, the Organization for Security and Cooperation in Europe and the European Union. Following a short historical survey of international attempts to protect religious freedom, I will then turn to the social and political context in which the classic religious liberty guarantees operate. The chapter concludes with an evaluation.

From the International Level to the National Level and Back[3]

International protection of freedom of religion and belief has a long history.[4] Since the sixteenth century and the spectre cast by the Reformation, there has been a need for international arrangements concerning religion and belief in Western Europe. Initially, legal settlements on religion did not focus on the private individual[5] but concentrated on the way in which public authorities dealt with the various Christian denominations, taking the form of institutional settlements regulating 'Church and state' relations. The Peace of Augsburg 1555 and the Treaty of Westphalia 1648 are examples. The latter was particularly progressive, both in terms of the religious denominations covered and the nature of the freedoms it guaranteed. In addition, it broke away from the principle of *cuius regio, eius religio*, according to which the ruler determined the official religion to be exercised within his territory. The seventeenth- and eighteenth-century cession treaties decisively abandoned this principle, an example of a special institutional arrangement enduring to the present day can still be found. In the three French departments of Haut-Rin, Bas-Rin and Moselle – in the Elzas and Lotharingen – the regime of Church and state is based on principles quite different from the rest of France. Upon their return to the French Republic, these territories, which were under German authority from 1871–1918, stipulated the Church and state regime of the 1801 Napoleonic Concordat. This was formalized by an Act of Parliament in 1924. The arrangement has far-reaching consequences, especially financial ones, for the relationship between Church and state.

After the French Revolution, when fundamental freedoms were recognized as rights of private individuals, the institutional dimension of freedom of religion remained an important feature of international arrangements. The Congress of Vienna (1815) is consistent with this tradition. Within the scope determined by these international agreements, early nineteenth-century national constitutions devised their own particular Church and state arrangements. In shaping such arrangements, the international element played a key role.[6]

During the nineteenth century, religion continued to play a role in international relations in that the recognition of freedom of religion was a criterion for being regarded as a civilized nation. In due course, Islamic and other faiths also qualified for this recognition. Breaches of the code justified international intervention. By that time, however, the diverse national structures of religion and law in Western Europe were firmly established. Following unsuccessful attempts to incorporate a provision on religion in the Covenant of the League of Nations, the United Nations succeeded in formulating, among other things, the right to freedom of religion and belief. Soon after the Universal Declaration of Human Rights 1948, a UN treaty on fundamental rights was prepared (the International Covenant on Civil and Political Rights (ICCPR)) and, prior to its adoption, the European Convention on Human Rights (ECHR) was signed. Both treaties include similarly worded guarantees on religious freedom. Neither is primarily concerned with the 'broader' aspects of religion and law, concentrating instead on the rights of the private individual.[7]

The Social and Political Context of Religious Liberty

To fully comprehend the *locus* of religion in law and to assess the legal developments relating to religion, both at the national and international level, one needs to understand the prevailing social and political perceptions of religion. These are hardly ever made explicit; instead, they consist mainly of implicit and tacit assumptions.

In assessing the social and political context of religious liberty in Western Europe over the last few decades, I offer the following observations. Although these do not directly relate to religion, they do nevertheless influence the intellectual 'environment' in which religion is understood. Together they contribute to a 'mindset' that affects the way in which religion, as a phenomenon, is perceived in law and politics. In fact, the manner in which religion is understood seems to be determined by a variety of philosophical, constitutional and social presuppositions and schemes. At least three of these deserve mention.

First, there is the liberal paradigm whereby a distinction is drawn between the realm of the 'public' and the 'private'. This distinction has profoundly influenced the law as well as political life. Second, there is the dichotomy between the state and the individual. Although reality is much more complex, constitutional law is shaped by this dichotomy. This model oversimplifies social reality with the latter's range of intermediate structures.

Third, there is the classic conception of fundamental freedoms: civil liberties belong to private individuals and such liberties deserve corresponding duties of non-interference by the public authority. Within this set of presuppositions and schemes religion firmly belongs in the private sphere. Seen through such a lens, religion is a matter for the individual and not a policy issue for the state. Religious liberty, therefore, is a right of the individual citizen to non-interference from the public authority. In its purest sense, this model echoes the American Jeffersonian notion of the 'wall of separation' between Church and state.

Of course, in current Western philosophical and political thought there are nuances and countercurrents. Furthermore, legal realities are much more varied and complex, differing from country to country, and changing and developing over time. In fact, religion is firmly enmeshed in the constitutional structures of practically all Western European countries,[8] characterized by established churches, systems of cooperation and systems of separation of Church and state. However inadequate these approaches have become in defining Church and state relationships today,[9] they demonstrate that religion is more than a purely private phenomenon. Despite this, the popular perception remains that religion is a personal concern functioning in the private sphere – a view that is, of course, congruent with the classic liberty approach.

There is, however, also a social dimension to religion. Sociologists have long argued that Western society is characterized by differentiation and segmentation. Religion, then, is just one segment, distinct and separate from others such as politics, culture, labour, health care, education and so on. Processes of secularization and atomization – whatever meaning these concepts have – only tend to reinforce this. Legal atomization is a way of dealing with increasing religious pluralism. The views of traditional religious denominations tend to run in parallel to those of mainstream society; their practices are well inculturated. There are strong theoretical challenges to the idea of the liberal paradigm, but these have had little impact in most Western states. Only in the emerging discussions on 'public values' and 'public morality' is the religious challenge to the liberal paradigm felt.

The privatized model of religion has been adopted by, and incorporated in, international guarantees of religious liberty, and it is all too tempting to approach international religious liberty clauses exclusively from this perspective. Recently, however, a sensitivity to a 'broader' conception of religion has emerged – one which reaches beyond the strict boundaries of the liberal paradigm and takes into account the societal significance of religion and the both problemactic and benign forces it can unleash, whilst recognizing the inadequacy of 'relegating' it to the purely private sphere.[10] A leading proponent of this perspective is Samuel Huntington who, in 'The Clash of Civilizations?',[11] argued that, in the modern world, ideological and economic divisions are not the key threat to world peace. Instead, he claims, cultural contrasts – clashing civilizations – will be the most important source of tension. And one of the most important cultural determinants is religion. It is not surprising that such a renewed awareness becomes more clear when one looks across borders of national states and adopts a regional and world-wide perspective – instead of focusing on what happens merely as incidents in a particular country. Huntington focused on the potentially problematic side of public religion. This, too, is one-sided in that it ignores the (non-problematic) institutional, social and communicative dimensions of religion, to name a few. It will be interesting to see how, at the international level, the challenges of a more inclusive conception of religion are met.

The Council of Europe

The focal point for religion within the Council of Europe is the European Convention on Human Rights (ECHR). Under the ECHR the individual liberty approach dominates. Article 9 of the European Convention guarantees religious liberty in a traditional way,[12] defining it as a right to exercise one's religion either individually or in community with others and providing a non-exhaustive enumeration of the various ways in which religious expression is protected. The article emphasizes the private individual and guarantees a right of non-interference from public authorities and thus seems to have no direct bearing on the 'structural' links between religion and the law. Before turning to religion-oriented initiatives within the Council of Europe, I wish to make three further comments on Article 9. The first concerns the meaning of the article for national systems of Church and state. The second relates to the institutional aspect of religion, and clarifies the significance of Article 9 for organizational freedom of religion. The third deals with positive action by states.

First, the European Convention presupposes existing national arrangements concerning religion and the law and contains no preference to any particular model of Church–state relationship. Nonetheless, Article 9 exercises a critical function with respect to existing national laws. If national legal arrangements do not comply with the guarantee they cannot be upheld. The article provides a minimal safeguard. Indirectly, therefore, Article 9 can modify Church and state arrangements.[13]

Second, Article 9 may have an influence on institutional aspects of religious liberty. The European Commission of Human Rights has respected existing national institutional arrangements, and the Churches themselves, by rejecting individual claims that challenge these structures. A complaint by a Danish church minister, disciplined following a refusal to baptize (in contravention of the Church rules) is a case in point. Once voluntarily in the service of the Church, he had to comply with its internal rules and disciplines. Another example is the rejection of a claim by a Swiss couple against the payment of Church tax: the couple were free to leave the Church and thus avoid the tax. A complaint from a dismissed medical assistant who publicly took a position contrary to Roman Catholic doctrine on abortion was also rejected. These examples[14] show that institutional liberty is protected as well. Furthermore, the right of appeal for religious bodies has been accepted. In a 1979 ruling, the Commission held that Churches, when filing a complaint, do so as a representative of their members.[15] This device was, admittedly, somewhat artificial.[16] The right of religious organizations to institute proceedings in their own name is now undisputed.[17]

Third, we have noted that Article 9 guarantees the right to non-interference with religion. However, there is evidence of a more refined model being developed too. This model recognizes, for both classic individual and social human rights, a need for a degree of *state responsibility* with respect to fundamental rights: a responsibility to respect, protect, ensure and promote rights. Each corresponds with different modes of state activity, ranging from a 'hands-off' strategy to a long-term policy of active implementation.[18] In several cases (notably in the context of Article 8 of the ECHR) the Court has pointed out that the difference between interference and non-interference is hard to distinguish. In certain instances, a positive state obligation with respect to religion has been acknowledged: some form of positive action in order to help ensure that religion can actually be practised. In horizontal relationships – that is, those between citizens – Article 9 guarantees at least a minimum of freedom. In cases where the religious intolerance of certain citizens interferes with the freedom of others, and the state tolerates it, there are grounds for arguing that Article 9 has been violated.[19]

In special legal settings, such as in penal institutions, the positive obligation of public authorities has also been recognized. Obviously there are limits to what can be expected of public authorities in such cases. Nevertheless, the principle is accepted that, in such legal relations, there should be room for the free exercise of religion in such matters as worship, pastoral care and diets.[20]

Thus, Article 9 serves not only to guarantee individual religious liberty, but also has implications for the legal infrastructure of religion.[21] However, we must realize that, in the instances above, we are dealing with a *judicial* approach towards religion. Courts depend on litigation and are hardly in a position to actually develop a 'policy' with respect to religion. In interpreting Article 9, moreover, the Court's constitutional position cannot be over-looked. This body does not function as a true constitutional court of Europe, but rather grants a measure of deference toward states. This is illustrated by the doctrine of the 'margin of appreciation' whereby the member states have some latitude in judging whether or not a particular measure violates the Convention. For a more inclusive approach, we must therefore look outside the realm of the judiciary.

Within the Council of Europe there are various initiatives which relate to religion in some way or other. The Convention for the Protection of Individuals with regard to Automatic Processing of Data (1981), for instance, designates religious affiliation as 'sensitive data' and thus brings religion into a stricter regime of personal privacy protection. The European Convention for the Protection of Animals for Slaughter (1979), to take a completely different example, governs legislation on ritual slaughtering.

However, what is even more interesting is the Council's active interest in matters religious – something seen as part of its wider cultural mission. These initiatives take a variety of forms. There is, for instance, the Redundant Religious Buildings project, aimed at preserving redundant religious buildings as part of our cultural heritage.[22] Then there is the attention paid to the effective realization of religious freedom in the workplace – an initiative especially tailored to the position of religious minorities.[23] The Council of Europe has also focused on the question of religion and the settlement of immigrants, and religious considerations are incorporated into strategies for integration and community-building.

The Council is also concerned with issues that have strong ethical over-tones which, although not overtly religious, are nevertheless linked to conceptions of humanity, the world and liberty – matters that are, of course, at the core of religion. I cannot give an exhaustive account of the activities of the Council in this field here. These initiatives – carefully approached, long-term in their development, and embedded in wider policy initiatives for the promotion of human rights – represent a way of dealing with religion beyond the strict individual–liberty scheme and reveal an awareness of the institutional, social and communicative facets of religion.

The United Nations

With their global reach, UN guarantees[24] are no less relevant for European religious liberty. Article 18 of the UDHR and Article 18 of the ICCPR guarantee religious liberty, as well as the freedom of conscience and thought and belief. Article 18 of the ICCPR is similar to Article 9 of the ECHR.[25] (One should also not forget the UN Declaration on the Elimination of All

Forms of Intolerance and of Discrimination Based on Religion or Belief 1981).[26]

The ICCPR has no judicial supervisory mechanism as such. Instead, the Committee on Human Rights deals with individual complaints through a reporting system.[27] Individual complaints concerning religious liberty cover a variety of issues. Supervision also takes place through a system of country reports. Two elements in the UN system of protection of religious liberty deserve further brief discussion. The first is the 'General Comment' on Article 18 issued by the Committee on Human Rights in 1980. The second is the Committee's stance on structural aspects of religion and law in the wake of the country reports.

Like Article 9 of the ECHR, Article 18 of the ICCPR is not primarily concerned with existing Church–state relationships. Nevertheless, such relationships have – more overtly than in the context of the ECHR – been a topic of discussion under the ICCPR. The General Comment of the Committee on Human Rights dedicates paragraph 9 to this:

> The fact that a religion is recognized as a State religion or that it is established as official or traditional or that its followers comprise the majority of the population shall not result in any impairment of the enjoyment of any of the rights under the Covenant, including Articles 18 and 27 [guaranteeing freedom of religion and minority protection respectively], nor in any discrimination against adherents of other religions or non-believers. In particular, certain measures discriminating against the latter ... are not in accordance with the prohibition of discrimination based on religion or belief and the guarantee of equal protection under Article 26 ... . The Committee wishes to be informed of measures taken by States Parties concerned to protect the practices of all religions or beliefs from infringement and to protect their followers from discrimination. Similarly, information as to respect for the rights of religious minorities under Article 27 is necessary for the Committee to assess the extent to which the freedom of thought, conscience, religion and belief has been implemented by States Parties. States Parties concerned should also include in their reports information relating to practices considered by their laws and jurisprudence to be punishable as blasphemous.[28]

Paragraph 10 continues:

> If a set of beliefs is treated as official ideology in constitutions, statutes, proclamations of the ruling parties, etc, or in actual practice, this shall not result in any impairment of the freedoms under Article 18 or any other rights recognized under the Covenant nor in any discrimination against persons who do not accept the official ideology or who oppose it.

These passages indicate that the Committee acknowledges the persistence of various types of Church–state relationship and their historical, social, and religious derivation. While accepting these realities, certain minimal conditions are established to safeguard religious liberty for all. Importantly, the starting point is the prevailing *social and legal reality*, instead of some abstract *a priori* legal scheme.

Furthermore, pursuant to the reporting procedure of the ICCPR, various 'structural' religious concerns have also been addressed by the Committee on Human Rights. This is done through discussions with representatives of states. One recent analysis of these discussions revealed various themes.[29]

One theme was the question of the registration of religions. The purpose of, criteria for and legal consequences of registration were reviewed. A second theme was state support for religion, both financial and non-financial. The Committee was sensitive to possible discrimination between religions in this respect. Taxation systems benefiting a particular religion should be voluntary for the individual. Yet another issue was the status of established religions. The Committee was anxious to be informed on the full range of legal consequences for such organizations and the differences, if any, between established and non-established churches. It appears that the Committee also expects action on the part of the states, possibly through legislation. States also have a duty to counter discrimination and unequal treatment, to promote tolerance and review potentially obsolete legislation.

The ICCPR seems to be superior to the European Convention in developing mechanisms for the effectual realization of religious freedom. It achieves a balance between the relative positions of specific faiths by taking active measures to safeguard the freedom of all religions. Clearly, states bear the responsibility of not only passively, but also actively, safeguarding religious liberty.

ICCPR standards stress non-discrimination and equal treatment of religions – matters not to be interpreted as simply meaning identical treatment. With changing circumstances and the passing of time, as we have seen, existing structures should be subjected to scrutiny. It is clear that religion is seen in a broader context than through that of individual–liberty alone. Throughout, promoting tolerance and combating discrimination play a substantial role. These themes indeed unify the initiatives and ideas within the UN generally. Emphasis has been repeatedly placed on the importance of education and interreligious dialogue – in short, on non-legal approaches.[30]

The Organization for Security and Cooperation in Europe (OSCE)

The positive stance towards religion in general is also reflected in the OSCE Vienna Concluding Document of 1989. It expressly encourages positive action:

16. In order to ensure the freedom of the individual to profess and practise religion or belief the participating States will, *inter alia*

16a. take effective measures to prevent and eliminate discrimination against individuals or communities, on the grounds of religion or belief in the recognition, exercise and enjoyment of human rights and fundamental freedoms in all fields of civil, political, economic, social and cultural life, and ensure the effective equality between believers and non-believers; ...

16c. grant upon their request to communities of believers, practising or prepared to practise their faith within the constitutional framework of their states, recognition of the status provided for them in their respective countries; ...

16e. engage in consultations with religious faiths, institutions and organizations in order to achieve a better understanding of the requirements of religious freedom; ...

They will ensure in their laws and regulations and in their application the full and effective implementation of the freedom of thought, conscience, religion or belief.

These are not legally binding treaty provisions but, as commitments, they have a strong political significance. First, they oblige the participating states to take *effective* measures. By explicitly indicating what is generally tacitly assumed in human rights guarantees, Articles 16a and 16e reflect the social reality. Second, and perhaps most striking, is Article 16e which is revolutionary in its approach to religious liberty. The opening words of Article 16 emphasize that the guiding motif is very much the freedom of the individual – he or she is the end point of fundamental guarantees. Nevertheless, the wording of Article 16e stretches beyond the confines of the private individual, for it provides for *consultations* between states and 'religious faiths, institutions and organizations'. Such an explicit exhortation to direct communication, dialogue and exchange of views and ideas between states and religious traditions is a significant step forward.

Since 1996 religion and religious liberty have been of special interest to the OSCE. In that year its Office of Democratic Institutions and Human Rights (ODIHR) organized a seminar on the topic 'Constitutional, Legal and Administrative Aspects of the Freedom of Religion', the scope of which extended beyond the classic individual–liberty approach. Besides reviewing constitutional and legal structures, the practical functioning of national legal mechanisms, the attitude towards religious minorities, and the social effects of changes in the religious 'map' of countries were discussed. This initiative accords with the organization's role in promoting and protecting 'Security and Cooperation in Europe'.

The OSCE works in a diplomatic and political, rather than a strictly legal, setting. It also functions, to a large extent, by means of consultation and dialogue. Its human rights texts are not legally binding conventions: there is no judicial supervisory mechanism. The organization's strength, therefore, lies in its unique approach. Preventing conflict, creating and supporting a stable balance between adherents to various religious denominations (whether in majority or minority situations) are often delicate tasks. The goal of the OSCE is enduring results, so building understanding, dialogue and education are therefore appropriate long-term tools. Religion is recognized as a social phenomenon, one interwoven into the very fabric of society, culture and citizens' worldviews. The OSCE's concern is focused on eliminating any tensions that may be associated with this situation. The view of some that the OSCE has 'downgraded' religion in terms of a security threat[31] is thus one that I do not support.

The European Union

At first sight, the connection between the EU and religion may seem somewhat remote. The link is an inevitable one, however, and, with the expansion of EU authority, the relationship between religion and EU law and policy will be of increasing practical significance. Over the last few years, a slight change in attitude towards religion has developed. A tangible sign of this is the adoption of a Declaration to the Final Act of the Treaty of Amsterdam which states:

> The European Union respects and does not prejudice the status under national law of churches and religious associations or communities in the Member States. The European Union equally respects the status of philosophical and non-confessional organizations.[32]

This statement marks an important step for legal development and policy. To understand the significance of this so-called 'Church Clause', it is necessary to see how religious liberty is guaranteed within the EU and how, in fact, EC–EU activity and religion overlap.

Through a long and cautious development process, the status of fundamental rights within the EU has been clarified. However, debate on the best way to protect fundamental rights within the EU continues, and their ultimate legal form is still some distance away.[33] The systematic protection of fundamental rights was not foreseen at the time the communities that now form the EU were founded, since the activities of the European institutions simply did not seem to pose a threat to liberty at that time. It was the European Court of Justice that actually developed fundamental rights' protection in the EC framework. The E(E)C Treaty states that the European Court of Justice shall ensure that, in the interpretation and application of the

Treaty 'the law' is observed (Article 164 of the EC Treaty (new: Article 220 EC)). The Court has interpreted this to include fundamental rights, and later invoked 'the constitutional traditions common to the Member States' as a source of inspiration for such protection. The Court went on to refer explicitly to the European Convention on Human Rights and, subsequently, to other international treaties guaranteeing fundamental rights.

The Maastricht Treaty consolidated the development in Article F(2) of the Treaty of European Union (new: Article 6(2) EU) which provides that 'The Union shall respect fundamental rights, as guaranteed by the European Convention on Human Rights and Fundamental Freedoms', and the Treaty of Amsterdam brought Article 6(2) within the review competence of the Court of Justice. Article 6(1) restates that the Union is founded on respect for human rights and fundamental freedoms.[34] Thus, there is no doubt that Article 9 of the ECHR is part of Community law. At the same time, it is not adequate, by itself, to deal exhaustively with the issue of religion. Within the EU, as in other Western societies, threats or impediments to the Church or to religious liberty are usually not found in wilful restrictions,[35] but are often a side-effect of other general policy measures not aimed at religion. Both by acting and by not acting, EC institutions influence the legal position of Churches and religion – with or without additional activity of Member States acting to implement EC law. This makes it necessary to reflect upon religious liberty at EC/EU level. The adoption of the new Article 13 EC (which is concerned, inter alia, with religious discrimination) simply reinforces this.

The kind of issues dealt with by the EC/EU therefore do not primarily relate to the religious liberty of the individual, but touch upon more collective and structural matters. EC activity stretches, for example, to: labour law (including legislation on working hours), privacy legislation, mass media law, taxation and the law relating to legal persons. Here, indirect burdens on religious exercise are considered. One example is taxation, where religious purposes and organizations are mentioned in the conditional exceptions, along with charitable and social institutions. Other instances are more symbolic in nature. The Council Directive relating to trade marks, for example, allows refusal of registrations should offence be given to religion.

The erratic character of EC provisions that take religion into account does not in itself reflect the importance of such provisions. The erratic nature of the provisions was unsatisfactory.[36] With the adoption of the Declaration, it is recognized that, when designing law, EU institutions also need to take religious institutions and structures into account. They need to be aware of, and develop, a relationship with religious bodies themselves, so that the former can evolve a legal framework which reflects religion's social and institutional aspects.[37]

The adoption of the Declaration is not just a matter of legal significance. It is a public recognition of the presence and role of Churches in society. This is critical, for the EU has also acknowledged other institutions – political parties, both sides of industry, voluntary associations and so on – as relevant social actors under the European legal framework.

The relevance of religion has been underlined by the formation of a *dialogue structure* between the EU and Churches. Impetus for this came from an appeal by the former president of the Commission for a 'soul for Europe'. As a consequence, a programme with the same name has also been established to encourage activities in multireligious settings. A 'soul' cannot, of course, be realized through a clause in a Declaration; it requires a vibrant social matrix.[38] Nevertheless, the Declaration opens doors. It acknowledges that religious traditions can, and do, offer ethical approaches and insights on values-oriented policy matters and play an active role in discussions on the future of Europe and its legal development.[39] Religion provides a natural integrative framework.

Reviewing recent EU developments with respect to religion (first and foremost embodied in the 'Church Clause') we see that the focus is not purely on the private individual. Not only is the strict legal protection of religious liberty of importance, but there is also an awareness of the insights of religious traditions and their contribution to society. The ethical import and the integrative function of religion are acknowledged. These developments are still quite modest, but the important point is that they reveal an emerging consciousness of the positive role of religion within the EU.

Evaluation

The implementation of religious liberty requires a domain of freedom for individuals to adhere to a set of beliefs and a corresponding duty on the part of public authorities not to curtail this freedom. However, religion also has social, institutional and communicative dimensions which should be taken into account by the law: structural or institutional arrangements transcending the individual–liberty approach are necessary. In devising these legal arrangements, a careful balance is required to ensure adequate freedom for all.

Here, we are dealing with complex issues which are difficult to isolate. I have not, I concede, dealt specifically with the pressing issue of the protection of minorities as such, for my goal was to point out a changing general awareness of religion in law and public policy. Earlier, I sketched the predominant intellectual 'atmosphere' against which issues of religion (and law) tend to be set. This is naturally more an impression of the prevailing intellectual mood than a precise linear analysis of the actual situation in the various Western European countries. Nonetheless, I suggest that this mood might be changing.

In the international arena there are signs of change as well. Religion is always a sensitive issue, so it is not surprising that the primary approach to religion in international law accords with what I have called the liberal–individual scheme.

The change of mood can be substantiated by various developments at the international level. Just as the individual–liberty scheme runs parallel to certain philosophical, political and legal presuppositions, the wider law and policy scheme which seems to be emerging runs parallel to a certain broader understanding of religion. Three aspects, which all recognize the public nature of religion, are noteworthy. The first is the potentially problematic tendencies of religion. The second is religion's positive aspect – namely, the contribution of religion to ethical understanding and its part in the construction of civil society. Third, there is the awareness that, given the social character of religion, the protection of fundamental rights requires more than simple abstention by public authorities.

The public nature of religion is more visible at the international and cross-border levels than at the national level. While at the national level in Western Europe, religion's social and communicative dimensions often seem to be neglected, on the international plane religion is seen less as a private phenomenon with its own segregated place but increasingly as a complex reality that influences opinions, actions and culture, and thus also entails a vision of society and a concept of freedom itself.

In this global age, the shaping of the international community and support for international decision-making are recurring and fundamental themes. It is in this area that interest in so-called (international) 'civil society' and the role of intermediary institutions (NGOs) has become so important. This is a fascinating development for the idea of civil society, and the role of intermediary institutions reaches far beyond the dichotomy of the private individual and state within which national policy issues are still often set. It is also here that the positive aspect of religion – its integrative functions and community-building propensities – can play an important role. The potential contribution of religion to 'value' discussions and contemporary legal and ethical problems is obvious. In this perspective, religious communities can become co-builders of a 'soul of Europe'.

Finally, we have seen that the protection of religion requires not only a policy of non-interference, but also positive action. This flows from a deeper grasp of religion as something beyond mere liturgical practices and opinions of private individuals. This broader positive concept of religious liberty needs to be taken into account. While it is fascinating to see a growing awareness of this dimension at the international level, certain nations continue to merit criticism for confining their understanding of religious liberty to the individual–liberty, non-interference model. However, the broader approaches do not, in fact, conflict with the individual liberty scheme, which will always remain important. The difference is that an approach that recognizes the public and potentially positive nature of religion is far more inclusive, realistic and forward-looking.

The developments at the international level are not only interesting for the reasons stated above, but also because they often involve the 'soft' approach – promotion, consultation, dialogue and education. The traditional 'hard law' approach will always be important, but innovative approaches can be refreshing, and have their advantages. Each international organization obviously deals with the relevant issues within the framework of its mission. This enriches the ways in which religion is dealt with overall. The EU, in its processes of European integration, has taken up dialogue as a strategy for general policy-making (the ethical dimension). The Council of Europe with its cultural and educational mission and its role in protecting fundamental rights has its own approach. The OSCE takes an interest in religion pursuant to its goal of promoting security and cooperation in Europe. The same can be said with respect to the UN, with its worldwide mission of promoting peace and respect for human rights. All these various approaches are necessary to do justice to such a complex phenomenon as religion and to realize religious liberty in its fullest sense as a human right.

Complex processes are often slow, and this is certainly true at the international level. Within the full gamut of various international organizations' concerns and activities religion tends not to loom large. Complexity and lack of speed are a disadvantage, but perhaps they can be an advantage too. Care should be taken to avoid simply making religion a tool of overt policy, and changes in this field require vision and wisdom. Thus, the state abstentionist approach to religious liberty will always remain important.

Religion is a social reality which cannot be ignored. Law and politics find it difficult, or experience a certain embarassment towards religion and do not know how to relate to it. We must not cling to the past, but choose an approach which is realistic and forward-looking. Practical recommendations are not the objective of this chapter: my approach has been to concentrate on attitudes, perceptions and understandings of religion as a phenomenon. We must not exaggerate the changing attitude towards religion but, equally, we must not ignore it. We are dealing with colossal, very diffuse, organizations, which often work in quite an abstract and long-term fashion. Nevertheless, in my view, there are hints of real change and, as such, they are welcome.

Notes

1 Even when there is actually no court system *stricto sensu*, this is often the model referred to.

2 This chapter is by no means exhaustive in its treatment. Its purpose is merely to point out those broader developments.

3 This section draws from S.C. van Bijsterveld (1998), *Godsdienstvrijheid in Europees Perspectief*, (Deventer: W.E.J Tjeenk Willink), pp. 151 ff. For a more detailed history, see Theo C. van Boven (1967), *De Volkenrechtelijke Bescherming van de Godsdienstvrijheid*, (Assen: Van Gorcum); Malcolm D. Evans (1997), *Religious Liberty and International Law in Europe*, (Cambridge: Cambridge University Press), pp. 42 ff. See also Martin Heckel, *Gesammelte Schriften, Staat, Kirche, Recht, Geschichte*, Jus Ecclesiasticum, Bd 38, ed. A. von Campenhausen *et. al.* Tübingen: J.C.B. Mohr (Paul Siebeck), p. 1–82; 'Zur Entwicklung des Deutschen Staatskirchenrechts von der Reformation bis zur Schwelle der Weimarer Berfassung', in ibid., Vol. I, pp. 366–401; 'Itio in Partes', in ibid., Vol. II, pp. 636–736; 'Säkularisierung', in ibid., Vol. II, pp. 773–911.

4 See also Mark W. Janis (ed.) (1991), *The Influence of Religion on the Development of International Law*, (Dordrecht: Nijhoff).

5 Although naturally they would affect the individual's position.

6 Obviously, in some European countries this international element was less pronounced than in others.

7 Regarding minority protection and treaties with the specific aim of protecting minorities, religion is clearly relevant. In this chapter, I shall not deal with minority protection as such. See Eduardo Ruiz Vieytez (1999), *The History of Legal Protection of Minorities in Europe*, (Derby: University of Derby); and Evans, *Religious Liberty, op. cit.*, pp. 104 ff.

8 For discussion of the systems of Church–state relationships within the European Union countries, see Gerhard Robbers (ed.) (1995), *State and Church in the European Union*, (Baden-Baden: Nomos Verlagsgesellschaft).

9 See Van Bijsterveld, *Godsdienstrvrijheid in Europees Perspectief, op. cit.*

10 See, for example, M. Juergensmeyer (1992), *Violence and the Sacred in the Modern World*, (London: Frank Cass); M. Juergensmeyer (1993), *The New Cold War? Religious Nationalism Confronts the Secular State*, (Berkeley, CA: University of California Press); G. Kepel (1994), *The Revenge of God: The Resurgence of Islam, Christianity and Judaism in the Modern World*, (Cambridge: Polity Press); R. Wuthnow (1992), *Rediscovering the Sacred: Perspectives on Religion in Contemporary Society*, (Grand Rapids, Mich: Eerdmans); G. Aijmer (ed.) (1992), *A Conciliation of Powers: The Force of Religion in Society*, (Gothenburg: University of Gothenburg). See also Rat der Europäischen Bischofskonferenzen (Rom 1996) (1997), *Religion als Privatsache und als Offentliche Angelegenheit. Kirche in Pluralistischen Gesellschaften*, Köln.

11 Samuel P. Huntington (1993), 'The Clash of Civilizations?', *Foreign Affairs*, **72**, pp. 22–49.

12 On Article 9 of the ECHR, see Van Boven, *De Volkenrechtelijke Bescherming, op. cit.* See also Jean Duffar (1994), 'La liberté religieuse dans les textes internationaux',

Revue du Droit Public et de la Science Politique en France et à l'Étranger, pp. 939–67; and Evans, *Religious Liberty, op. cit.*, ch. 10 *et seq.*

13   For examples, see S.C. van Bijsterveld (1998), 'Religion and the Law: Legal Structures in an International and Comparative Context', in *Church and State Consultation*, (Geneva: Conference of European Churches), pp. 22–36, at p. 25.

14   Eur. Comm. HR, 8 March 1976, no. 7374/76, DR 5, 157; Eur. Comm. HR, 4 December 1984, no. 10616/83, DR 40, 284; Eur. Comm. HR, 6 September 1989, no. 12242/86, DR 62, 151, respectively.

15   Eur. Comm. HR, 5 May 1979, App. 7805/77, DR16, 68.

16   Nikolaus Blum (1990), *Die Gedanken-, Gewissens- und Religionsfreiheit nach Art. 9 der Europäischen Menschenrechtkonvention*, (Berlin: Duncker & Humblot), p. 175.

17   See Evans, *Religious Liberty, op. cit.*, pp. 286 ff.

18   G.J.H. van Hoof (1984), 'The Legal Nature of Economic, Social and Cultural Rights: A Rebuttal of Some Traditional Views', in P. Alston and K. Tomasevksi (eds.), *The Right to Food*, ('s-Gravenhage: Nijhoff), pp. 97–110.

19   Eur. Comm. HR, 14 July 1980, no. 8282/78, DR21, 109.

20   Eur. Comm. HR, 16 December 1966, no. 2413/65, col. 23, 1; Eur. Comm. HR, 20 December 1974, no. 5442/72, DR 1, 41; Eur. Comm. HR, 5 March 1976, no. 5947/72, DR 4, 8.

21   The interpretation of Article 9 is often restricted to the more traditional and liturgical aspects of religion. Furthermore, the Commission tends to deny the fact that 'neutral' legislation, which is not aimed at religion *per se*, can constitute a restriction on religious liberty. I cannot explore these aspects of the interpretation of Article 9 here. For analysis of this issue, see Evans, *Religious Liberty, op. cit.*, pp. 281 ff; Van Bijsterveld, *Godsdiensrvrijheid in Europees Perspectief, op. cit.*, pp. 156 ff.

22   *Redundant Religious Buildings* (1989), Report of the Committee on Culture and Education (Rapporteur: Mr Pino Rauri), (Doc. 6031, Strasbourg: Council of Europe, Parliamentary Assembly).

23   See *The Integration of Immigrants: Towards Equal Opportunities*, a study drawn up by the Group of Consultants chaired by Mr Jörgen Nielsen, Strasbourg, 22 August 1996, MG-S-Rel (96) 2.

24   For a comprehensive study on religious liberty in the UN context, see B.G. Tahzib (1996), *Freedom of Religion or Belief: Ensuring Effective International Legal Protection*, ('s-Gravenhage: Nijhoff). See also Bruce Dickson (1995), 'The United Nations and Freedom of Religion', *International and Comparative Law Quarterly*, **44**, pp. 327–357. Elements of this section also appear in Van Bijsterveld, 'Religion and the Law', *op. cit.*

25   See Van Boven, *De Volkenrechtelijke Bescherming, op. cit.*; Duffar,'La liberté religieuse', *op. cit.*

26   G. A. Res. 36/55, 25 November 1981.

27   See, generally, Malcolm Evans, Chapter 3 of this volume.

28   See Tahzib, *Freedom of Religion or Belief, op. cit.*, pp. 260–262.

29   Ibid., pp. 33 ff.

30   In Articles 18 and 19 of the Declaration, special attention is given to minorities and the active role states should adopt in order to ensure the effective realization of their rights.

31   Evans, *Religious Liberty, op. cit.*, pp. 369–70. Similarly, see negative judgements at pp. 363–66, which cannot be supported from the line of approach adopted in this essay.

32   Declaration on the Status of Churches and Non-confessional Organizations (Declaration no. 11).

33   See S.C. van Bijsterveld (1999), 'Grundrechte in der EU: Über Ideale und

Wertvorstellungen', in Karl-Hermann Kästner, Knut Wolfgang Nörr and Klaus Schlaich (eds.), *Festschrift für Martin Heckel zum siebzigsten Geburtstag*, (Tübingen: Mohr Siebeck), pp. 707–724.

34   In other ways, the Treaty of Amsterdam also represents a positive step in the protection of fundamental rights. See Van Bijsterveld, 'Grundrechte in der EU', *op. cit.*

35   EU institutions can be directly confronted with questions concerning religious freedom as well. Thus the Court of Justice has heard cases dealing with individual religious freedom, as well as with more structural aspects. The European Parliament has shown some interest in religion, both within the EU and outside of the EU. See Gerhard Robbers (1994), 'Europarecht und die Kirchen', in J. Listl and D. Pirson (eds.), *Handbuch des Staatskirchenrechts*, Vol. I, (Berlin: Duncker & Humblot), pp. 315–32; and van Bijsterveld, *Godsdiesnstvrijheid in Europees Perspectief*, *op. cit.*, pp. 162 ff.

36   For further analysis of the relationship between religion and the EU, see the contributions contained in European Consortium for Church and State Research (1998), *Religions in European Law*, Proceedings of the Colloquium, Luxembourg/Trier, November 1996, (Milan: Nomos Verlagsgesellschaft, Bruylant, Giuffrè) and the contributions in Hans-Joachim Kiderlen, Heidrun Tempel, Rik Torfs (eds) (1995), *Which Relationships between Churches and the European Union? Thoughts for the Future*, (Leuven: Peeters).

37   For more on the Church Clause (including its legal status), see G. Robbers (1997), 'Partner für die Einigung. Die Kirchenerklärung der Europäischen Union', *Herderkorrespondenz*, **51**, pp. 622–25; G. Robbers (1998), 'Europa und die Kirchen. Die Kirchenerklärung von Amsterdam', in *Stimmen der Zeit*, pp. 147–57 and S.C. van Bijsterveld, *Godsdienstvrijheid in Europees Perspectief*, *op. cit.*, pp. 161 ff.

38   The Churches themselves supported a slightly different version of the Declaration – one that emphasized the dynamic character of their role in and contribution to society.

39   Thomas Jansen (1998), 'Kirchen und Europa', *EU Magazin*, December, pp. 12–13.

Art, Expression and the Offended Believer

Reid Mortensen

Serrano and *A History of Sex*: The National Gallery of Victoria, 1997

Isobel Crombie, senior curator of photography at the National Gallery of Victoria in Melbourne, described Andres Serrano's photograph of the crucifix as 'an extremely beautiful work'.[1] It could well be. The right side of the cross-beam tilts toward the photographer, so that the top of Christ's bowed head faces him directly. The crucifix itself is a luminous gold, and glows through an inconstant, profound red fog. The whole image creates a mood that, without more, could inspire thought, reflection or even devotion from a believing Christian. However, there *is* more – *much* more.

Far from inspiring devotion, Serrano's photograph shocks. And it is not the shock that Christian clergy often call us to confront, through an appreciation that the Son of God suffered extended torture and execution as a criminal. It is the way in which Serrano has handled a sacred symbol of Christianity – Catholic Christianity in particular – that generates disgust and the most extreme responses from believers. US Senator Al D'Amato tore up a copy of the photograph on the steps of the Capitol in 1989, sparking the so-called 'culture wars' of the 1990s that led to large cuts in the public funding of galleries. In Melbourne, the Catholic Archbishop, Dr George Pell, lobbied the National Gallery of Victoria (NGV) not to display the photograph as part of an exhibition of Serrano's work called *A History of Andres Serrano: a History of Sex* during the Melbourne Festival in October 1997. That failed. He then approached State Premier, Jeff Kennett, asking that the photograph not be displayed in a public institution like the NGV but that it be incorporated into a parallel exhibition of Serrano's work at the private Kirkcaldy Davies Gallery. The Premier refused to intervene and instead offered his support for the NGV's decision to display the photograph. The Archbishop finally resorted to litigation on Wednesday 8 October 1997, asking the Supreme Court of Victoria for an injunction to restrain the display of an indecent, obscene and blasphemous figure. That also failed.[2] However, the NGV's curators decided to cancel the whole exhibition of *A History of Sex* when, on the following Friday, a man tried forcibly to remove the photograph from the gallery and, on the Saturday, a teenager attacked the photograph and a security guard with a hammer.[3]

Serrano never displays the photograph without expounding how it was produced. The crucifix was immersed in Serrano's own urine, mixed also with samples of his semen and blood. It is that combination of Serrano's bodily fluids that provides the red mist surrounding the crucified Christ. For that reason and the symbolism of a crucifix plunged into his own body's excretions, Serrano called the photograph *Piss Christ*. As one art historian offered, *Piss Christ* can be understood as a macabre inversion of the sacrament of baptism. The crucifix is immersed in the least holy of waters.[4] That naturally does not mean that the only possible interpretation of the photograph is that is it blasphemous. The same historian argued that, as the crucifix can be taken to represent the institutions of clerical authority, the photograph symbolizes the humiliation of the institutional Church and invites the viewer to empathize with the crucified Christ himself.[5] However the meaning of *Piss Christ* is subjectively received, it is the story surrounding the taking of the photograph that sends a message that offends believing Christians. Furthermore, the NGV's exhibition, *A History of Sex*, provided an even broader setting for the photograph that was bound to cause even deeper offence to believers. *Piss Christ* was the most prominent of the works advertised in the exhibition. There were 58 others; including a man fellating himself, a woman urinating into a man's mouth, a woman masturbating a horse, a priest bound and gagged, and so on. *Piss Christ* was plainly in the company of serious sinners.

The issues raised by *Piss Christ* and the enraged response to it were paralleled across the Tasman Sea soon afterwards. At its opening in March 1998, the Museum of New Zealand (also known as 'Te Papa') in Wellington mounted an exhibition called *Pictura Brittanica* which included two works that caused equal offence to Christians in New Zealand. Tania Kovats' *Virgin Mary in a Condom* is a statuette in which Kovats professed to demonstrate her respect for the Virgin, but wished to locate this in the midst of her concerns about the Catholic Church's teaching on sexuality, abortion and contraception. She did so by enveloping the statue of the Virgin in a condom. Sam Taylor-Woods' painting *Wrecked* followed the pattern of Michelangelo's *Last Supper* but with contemporary figures, male and female. Where Michelangelo had centred the figure of Christ, Taylor-Wood placed a bare-breasted woman with arms outstretched in crucifix form.

However, she was no figure dying and exhausted of life, but instead seemed sexually aroused. *Pictura Brittanica* provoked outrage that included the making of personal threats against Te Papa staff. The glass case holding *Virgin Mary in a Condom* was smashed, and a curator was assaulted. The damage to property and the assault were dealt with in the criminal courts in mid-March of that year,[6] but the Solicitor-General, John McGrath, refused to prosecute Te Papa for displaying *Virgin Mary in a Condom* and *Wrecked* and also refused permission for private prosecutions for indecency and blasphemous libel to be brought.[7]

A feature of the public responses to the exhibits of *Piss Christ*, *Virgin Mary in a Condom* and *Wrecked* is the appeal that Christians in Victoria and New Zealand consistently made to the common law misdemeanour of blasphemous libel. As Dr Pell's litigation brought the question of blasphemy to the civil courts, *Piss Christ*, in particular, allows us to revisit the merits of the misdemeanour of blasphemous libel and its potential use as a tool for censoring the display of visual art. Although the discussion in this chapter undoubtedly has a decidedly antipodean – and specifically Australian – accent, the law in Australia and New Zealand does have direct relevance to other parts of the common law world. Furthermore, the different approaches taken by various Australian states to the question of blasphemous libel also make possible a more focused appraisal of the social significance of the continued operation of the misdemeanour in other parts of the common law world.

Remedying Offence: The Law of Blasphemous Libel

Dr Pell's efforts to persuade the NGV not to exhibit *Piss Christ* having failed, legal proceedings were brought in the Supreme Court of Victoria. The other large Churches baulked at litigation. Dr Keith Rayner, the Anglican Archbishop, would only give moral support: 'on the matter of the principle involved we stand together'.[8] The Uniting Church doubted that there was any value at all in litigating.[9] The moderator of the Victorian Synod, the Reverend Pam Kerr, said: 'If there were to be any good to come out of this it might be that it reminds us Christians that the cross was a highly offensive event and that Christ himself was treated brutally. ...'[10] Dr Salaheddin Bendak of the Islamic Council of Victoria had already complained to the NGV and the Premier that *Piss Christ* mocked a prophet of Islam. That was as much support as the Muslim community could give.[11] Consequently, Dr Pell alone, representing the Catholic Church, sought an injunction from the Supreme Court to restrain the exhibition of *Piss Christ*.

The novel feature of this application was the legal right that Dr Pell claimed that the showing of *Piss Christ* would violate. The Archbishop alleged that the public display of the photograph would be indecent and obscene, and would constitute:

> ... the common law misdemeanour of publishing a blasphemous libel by reason of the fact that the photograph is so offensive, scurrilous and insulting to the Christian religion that it is beyond the decent limits of legitimate difference of opinion and is calculated to outrage the feelings of sympathisers with or believers in the Christian religion.[12]

Justice Harper eventually resolved the questions of indecency, obscenity and blasphemy under the same principle. The Archbishop's central point was that exhibiting the photograph would constitute the commission of two separate criminal offences: the publication of an indecent and obscene representation[13] and blasphemous libel. However, rather than bringing a prosecution the Archbishop was asking for a civil remedy: an injunction. And the courts are extremely reluctant to order an injunction to restrain a breach of the criminal law.[14] So the application was refused.

The *Piss Christ* litigation nevertheless offered, for Australian courts, a rare opportunity to explore the law of blasphemous libel. The offence is, for much of the Commonwealth and the United States, an English inheritance. In England, blasphemy has been an offence in one form or another since the consolidation of the medieval canon law – although it assumed greater importance after the Reformation. The modern offence dates from 1677[15] – the middle of the period of Anglican monopoly which followed the Restoration of Charles II. However, from that time the offence has undergone considerable transformation and laicization. Three periods in particular have punctuated its development. From the 1790s to the 1820s, prosecutions for blasphemous libel frequently accompanied prosecutions for sedition as liberals and Chartists often professed radical agnosticism or deism.[16] In the 1880s the English courts confirmed that the offence was no longer committed merely by sober denial of Christian doctrine: the *manner* in which a person denied Christian doctrine became the centrepiece of the offence, Lord Chief Justice Coleridge demanding that there be 'licentious and contumelious abuse' or 'wilful misrepresentations or artful sophistry' before the offence was committed.[17] Finally, in the 1970s the appellate courts reiterated that blasphemous libel was a misdemeanour under English law but, instead of resting on an abusive denial of Christian doctrine, it required that there be something that shocked or offended a believing Christian.[18] This latest form of the law of blasphemous libel was stated by the Judicial Committee of the House of Lords in the *Gay News* case, a prosecution for the publication of *The Love that Dares to Speak its Name* – an erotic poem in which a Roman centurion had sexual fantasies about the body of Jesus after its removal from the cross. The newspaper, *Gay News*, and its editor, Denis Lemon, were prosecuted privately for blasphemous libel by morals campaigner Mary Whitehouse. Both accused were convicted, and were unable to shake the convictions through two appeals in England and a complaint to the European Commission of Human Rights.[19]

The *Gay News* appeals did not resolve a question that had been left in suspension since the early eighteenth century: did the prosecution have to show that the publication would lead to a breach of the peace – that is, a threat of injury or damage to property?[20] Lord Scarman hinted 'no': the question of any requirement for a breach of the peace was only 'a minor contribution to the discussion'.[21] Accordingly, what could be distilled from the *Gay News* appeals was that the offence of blasphemous libel only prohibited expression that was likely to arouse resentment amongst believing Christians for criticisms of their beliefs. Probably the one constant in the evolution of the offence from 1677 is that those beliefs should be the beliefs of the Church of England.[22] The offended believer does not need to be Anglican, but the beliefs that are attacked at least have to be shared with Anglicans.

In England there is therefore a close association between the blasphemy law and the political status of the established Church. The best assumption that can be made is that the misdemeanour was also exported to those British colonies which received the common law of England, even though the reception of the common law was always subject to its being considered appropriate for local conditions, and even though none of those former colonies have had an established Church since the 1830s. The offence has certainly surfaced sporadically in Canada, New Zealand and the United States.[23] Until the *Piss Christ* litigation no court in Australia had ever expressly decided that the offence *tout court* was received in the Australian colonies, although colonial parliaments had assumed that reception did take place.[24] Indeed, the first occasion that offered an opportunity for the judicial clarification of the question whether the misdemeanour was received was the *Piss Christ* litigation itself. Unfortunately, Justice Harper's judgment on this point demonstrates some well executed fence-sitting. He began:

The law of England does not necessarily coincide with the law of Victoria[25]

only to add:

Not only may there be a place in a multicultural society for the offence of blasphemous libel of any recognised faith, but the ancient misdemeanour of that name may have survived transportation to the colonies.[26]

Having stated both logical possibilities, Justice Harper gave no stronger indication as to which he thought was the position in Victoria. He did, however, assume that *if* blasphemous libel was a misdemeanour in Victoria then it probably demanded that there be evidence that the publication tended to cause a breach of the peace.[27] Of course, this was before the photograph that was eventually exhibited in the NGV and a security officer designated to protect it were attacked with a hammer. On 8 October the Archbishop had no evidence of a threat to person or property and so, even on a civil standard of proof, there could be no finding against the NGV.

Abolishing the Blasphemy Law

The arguments for abolishing the offence of blasphemous libel have been well rehearsed since the *Gay News* appeals showed that it was still alive and, as Denis Lemon learned, still kicking. The Law Commission of England and Wales recommended the abolition of the blasphemy laws in 1985.[28] The Australian Law Reform Commission did the same in 1992.[29] The New South Wales Law Reform Commission followed suit in 1994.[30] All have been ignored, but the reasons for the recommendation remain compelling. The circumstances of the *Piss Christ* litigation enable a review of these arguments from a different angle, and identify another problem with the offence that is unique to the display of visual art.

   At the core of these three Commissions' arguments for the abolition of the blasphemy law is an account of freedom and equality that individualizes the citizen's religious experience and, consequently, disconnects it from public life and social relationships. The *Gay News* appeals themselves recognized how personal religious life had become by identifying the injury caused by blasphemous communication in the feeling of resentment experienced by the Christian believer. However, in recommending the abolition of the blasphemy laws the Commissions particularly emphasized the precepts of equality which inform secular government: a person's religion should be regarded as irrelevant to her enjoyment of first class citizenship.[31] The persistence of a misdemeanour that only treats a Christian's resentment as an injury is nigh impossible to reconcile with this ideal. While the established status of the Church of England might offer a formal justification for the offence in England itself, that is not the case elsewhere in the common law world.[32] Indeed, one of the reasons that Justice Harper mustered for the possibility that the offence may not now be law in Victoria was that the Australian federal Constitution forbids the establishment of a *national* religion.[33] Although the Victorian Constitution has no similar ban on the establishing of a *state* religion, there has been no established Church in Victoria since the colony was proclaimed, and there is no serious proposal that there should be.

The *Piss Christ* litigation further illuminated the oddity of a blasphemy law in a secular state in that this was the first reported occasion in the Commonwealth in which a civil claim was founded on an allegation of blasphemous libel. Dr Pell's application was a suit for an injunction, but, while the misdemeanour dates from 1677, at no point has a court considered that there is a parallel civil wrong which, once proved, entitles the injured plaintiff to damages or an order restraining further wrongdoing. Justice Harper certainly did not contemplate any tort of blasphemous libel, nor the award of a civil remedy for the commission of a criminal offence if that could be established. At the least the NGV did not doubt that the photograph was 'offensive, scurrilous and insulting' to Christians – including Catholics – and had 'outraged their feelings'.[34] Furthermore, the gallery did not question that Dr Pell, as Catholic Archbishop, represented those who were injured in this way.[35] Even so, the law still did not recognize that this gave rise to a private legal right capable of vindication in a civil court. That begs a question. If the Archbishop of Melbourne has no interest recognized by law to protect Catholics from insult to their beliefs,[36] why then should a secular state be recognized as having such an interest? It shouldn't, but the law of blasphemous libel recognizes that the state has that very interest.

A more evenhanded treatment of citizens could be achieved by extending the blasphemy law to beliefs held by denominations other than the Anglican Church, and religions other than Christianity. Lord Macaulay sponsored a non-sectarian offence of blasphemous libel in the Indian Penal Code,[37] and the approach was again advanced by Lord Scarman in the *Gay News* appeal.[38] The publication of Salman Rushdie's *Satanic Verses* made this a much more serious proposition in the UK in the early 1990s. It is no libel to scandalize Islam in such a way as to shock practising Muslims,[39] and the Muslims who tried unsuccessfully to prosecute Rushdie for blasphemous libel can rightly resent a law that protects a citizen's private religious feelings only if he is a Christian. However, the Commissions' preferred response to this undervaluing of non-Christians has been the abolition of the offence:[40] its extension to non-Christian religions is regarded as a second-best option.[41] There are also practical drafting problems in defining the limits of an extended offence. How can the law define an offence that comprehends and protects all legitimate expressions of the religious life and that simultaneously provides the certainty needed in the criminal law?[42] Furthermore, the more general problem is that any law of blasphemous libel places the constraints of the criminal law on expression. Even the Australian and New South Wales Commissions, which have traditionally been uninterested in strengthening rights to freedom of expression, considered that the present form of the blasphemy law imposed an unreasonable burden on expression. Accordingly, an extension of the blasphemy law would just make an unreasonable burden worse.[43]

Even if the argument cannot be accepted on principle, there are also the questions of utility and effect. How does the blasphemy law assist in regulating human conduct and the organization of our common life? The law of blasphemous libel is essentially not enforced. The power to prosecute largely rests with the government, and governments have themselves long refused to enforce the blasphemy law.[44] Significantly, the latest attempts in the Commonwealth to enforce the blasphemy laws were not instigated by the Crown. *Gay News* was a private prosecution, *Satanic Verses* was an attempt to prosecute privately, and *Piss Christ* was a misconceived civil claim. The New Zealand Solicitor-General refused to allow a private prosecution for Te Papa's display of *Wrecked* on the ground that it would be an improper burden on the freedom of expression.[45] The effective nullification of offences by prosecutors who decide that the trial of the offenders is not going to advance the public interest could be considered a legitimate means of minimizing the effect of harsh idiosyncratic laws, or of simply disregarding laws that have long lost social relevance.[46] In most places the nullification of the blasphemy law probably just occurs through prosecutor's indifference to the law, or sheer ignorance of it. The consequence is that enforcement of the law is left more haphazardly to those who feel personally aggrieved – a Mary Whitehouse or a George Pell. However, where government consent is required to undertake a prosecution – in New Zealand and Tasmania for example[47] – prosecutorial nullification of the offence is effectively complete. The law of blasphemous libel simply has no operation in a substantive sense.

The fact that, in Australia, two states abolished the offence in the late nineteenth and early twentieth centuries is a further corrective for any claims that the blasphemy law serves a useful purpose. In 1897 Sir Samuel Griffith, then Chief Justice of Queensland, pronounced that the English law of blasphemous libel 'represented the sentiments of two hundred years ago' and was 'manifestly obsolete or inapplicable to Australia'.[48] Sir Samuel did not include the misdemeanour of blasphemous libel in his draft Criminal Code for Queensland and, as it turned out, the Code that the colonial parliament eventually enacted did not prohibit any communication that might hold religious faith up to derision or contempt.[49] There has therefore been no offence of blasphemous libel in Queensland since 1900 and, as it also adopted the Griffith Code, in Western Australia since 1913.[50] However, few would be prepared to suggest that the tone of public debate and expression is significantly more irreligious in those states than it is in the rest of the country. If anything, national stereotypes would probably suggest a more restrained and conservative strain of religious discourse in Queensland and Western Australia.

The *Piss Christ* litigation did reveal a structural weakness in the existing offence that makes it an extremely inappropriate means of censoring visual art, and this reveals an additional problem with the law of blasphemous libel that the *Gay News* appeals and the *Satanic Verses* application could not have unearthed. As mentioned earlier, the photograph, without more, could be considered inspiring or enigmatic. Justice Harper thought so: 'Of itself, it is not only inoffensive, but might be thought to be a reverent treatment of a sacred symbol of the Christian Church....'[51] It is the context in which the viewer places the image that creates the insult. The name *Piss Christ*, and Serrano's own account of how he created the image have caused controversy in most places where it has been shown. In the NGV exhibition of *A History of Sex*, the display of the photograph alongside the most explicit, lurid sexual images that would appall any Christian compounded the affront. However, in bringing his application for an injunction, Dr Pell was asking the Supreme Court to consider how the conduct of the NGV measured against the law of blasphemous libel. What then were the bounds of the communication to be considered? Is the court only to consider the photograph, the visual image that records one moment and arrangement of colours, shapes and finishing chemicals? Or is it to consider the photograph and the context in which it is presented? If so, how broad and deep is that context to be? Is it to include the name, the story of its creation, and the presentation of the photograph with other unambiguously pornographic material? Justice Harper was aware of the problem in the *Piss Christ* litigation, although he discussed it in relation to the offences of indecency and obscenity.[52] There was no answer but, given the judge's approach to the application, there didn't have to be. However, it is enough to fuel additional concern that any prosecutor might have about the likelihood of a conviction.

While, with *Piss Christ*, it might seem artificial to limit the communication that is to be measured against the standards of the blasphemy law to the photographic image itself, in obscenity cases American courts *have* directed juries to disregard any consideration of the context in which the photograph was presented.[53] So, with *Piss Christ*, it could make all the difference between the extremes of desecration and iconography whether the context of the exhibition of the photograph could be considered. But the present form of the law of blasphemy simply does not enable us to be able to state the precise bounds of the communication that is to be scrutinized by the jury.

The nullification of the blasphemy law by prosecutors undeniably reduces the pressure for further reform in those places where it is still an offence. During the twentieth century scarcely anyone has been punished as a result of a conviction for blasphemy in the Commonwealth, with the result that parliaments see little mischief that needs immediate correction by legally abolishing the offence. This means that the common sense of public prosecutors who refuse to pursue blasphemers itself indirectly perpetuates the life of the offence. Accordingly, despite longstanding recommendations in both England and New South Wales to abolish the blasphemy law, the parliaments have still refused to take the step. In practice, this would not matter if prosecutorial nullification of the offence were complete. However, it hasn't been where private prosecutions are still possible: after all, Mary Whitehouse was able to secure the conviction of Denis Lemon for publishing *The Love that Dares to Speak its Name* in 1979.[54] The unevenness of enforcement probably makes the offence even more dangerous. The blasphemy law is not applied frequently enough to make it a significant factor in the regulation and modelling of social behaviour, and so when it does succeed it does so by ambush and caprice.

The Ethical Judgements of Art Galleries

The anachronism of the law of blasphemous libel does not suggest that, in displaying *Piss Christ* during the Melbourne Festival in 1997, the NGV was meeting the ethical standards that the citizenry can expect of a public institution which appreciates that its actions could cause serious disquiet amongst the general public. All too frequently public officers underestimated the depth of the resentment felt in some Christian communities, and that this resentment could spill into violence. In the *Piss Christ* litigation, Justice Harper lamented the need for any law protecting a person from suffering offence:

> ... a plural society such as contemporary Australia operates best where the law need not bother with blasphemous libel because respect across religions and cultures is such that, coupled with an appropriate capacity to absorb the criticisms or even the jibes of others, deep offence is neither intended nor taken.[55]

The ethic of mutual respect must be central to the life of a liberal democracy. However, the judge's assessment that religionists should not feel wounded by degrading representations of their sacred symbols envisions a rational, passionless Utopia that has no parallel in any human society. Similarly, the discussion from Melbourne arts circles about the impact of *Piss Christ* generally made the same detached assumptions. The NGV was certainly aware that *A History of Sex* would offend. The advertising before the exhibition laboured the pornographic dimension of Serrano's other work, and the hostility *Piss Christ* generated in the American 'culture wars'. Certainly, there were some that denied any offensive or pornographic quality to the exhibition,[56] but Isobel Crombie admitted, 'All Serrano's work deals with taboos, so it's never going to be safe or easy. He uses pornography but presents it differently. It's edgy.'[57] Tony Kirkcaldy, Director of the Kirkcaldy Davies Gallery, made a similar distinction between pornography and Serrano's reflection on pornography,[58] placing artistic significance on the offence that *Piss Christ* and the other photographs caused. It was not only the right of Christians to be offended by the photograph; he regarded 'a strong reaction as an integral function of Serrano's images'.[59] It was therefore well understood that Christians could be offended by *Piss Christ*. However, these comments also reveal that people in the arts community understood terms such as 'offence' and 'pornography' in a more rarefied, flippant sense than is generally the case.[60] There was little appreciation that a person's suffering 'offence' can represent his or her genuine anger, frustration and rage. That not only meant that the NGV management was unprepared for the real violence done to its exhibit of *Piss Christ* and to its staff,[61] it failed to consider ethical issues that should have been addressed once it became apparent that there was a significant degree of public concern about the photograph.

First, as a public institution, the NGV was bound by principles of accountability to the broader Victorian community that a private institution could disregard. Dr Pell's submission to State Premier, Jeff Kennett, recognized this; the Archbishop suggested that *Piss Christ* be relocated to the private Kirkcaldy Davies Gallery in order to deny the work the official imprimatur of a publicly funded gallery.[62] As in the American 'culture wars', the debates in both Australia and New Zealand squarely raised the question 'Why should I have to fund it if I find it so offensive?'.[63] Thus, as mentioned earlier, the NGV's exhibition of Serrano's works was undertaken in collaboration with the Kirkcaldy Davies Gallery in Melbourne. This gallery had Serrano's images that it intended to exhibit classified by the Office of Film and Literature Classification, notified entrants that the material being exhibited could be considered offensive, and restricted entry to those aged over 18.[64] Even if the artistic judgement of the gallery directors in deciding to exhibit Serrano's work is questionable, the making of these arrangements demonstrates impeccable institutional ethics for a *private* organization in a liberal society.[65] However, that is not sufficient for a *public* institution, which is not limited in the ethics of its decision-making to ensuring that it manages its doorkeeping properly. Accountability is a longstanding principle of good public sector administration, even if the Victorian parliament only articulated that belatedly in legislation in 1998.[66] At the least, it requires that real and serious consideration be given to the interests of the whole public and that the institution consult more thoroughly when it is aware that its actions will scandalize parts of the citizenry. This even includes those who never actually consume the services that the institution provides: after all, they are ultimately providing the service. At no time did the NGV do this. Te Papa did consult with interested religious groups, but only after the *Pictura Brittanica* exhibition had been displayed and the museum had been publicly embarrassed.[67]

The public debates about *Piss Christ*, *Virgin Mary in a Condom* and *Wrecked* raised claims that the galleries did have self-imposed ethical constraints on the exhibition of artworks, albeit that these constraints are only revealed by positing hypothetical circumstances. Questions about the NGV's and Te Papa's possible responses to the exhibition of art that would denigrate non-Christian religions were posed repeatedly. As one objector to *Piss Christ* asked:

> … what will the gallery exhibit next? Photographs of a person defecating on the Koran, vomiting on the Star of David or masturbating Buddha? I find these possibilities as vile and repugnant as the filth you defend as art.[68]

Even more frequently asked, was whether the NGV would have exhibited a photograph of Aboriginal totems immersed in the photographer's bodily fluids.[69] The same points were made about *Virgin Mary in a Condom*: 'It's the same as putting a pig's head on a copy of the *Koran*, which would arouse terrible anguish from the Muslim society.'[70] It was also noted that the Te Papa administration allowed Maori prayers and observed strict protocols to avoid causing offence to Maori.[71] In present social circumstances in Australia and New Zealand, it is inconceivable that the NGV and Te Papa would exhibit any images of that kind. That would not stem from any greater sympathy the curators would have with Islam, Judaism, Buddhism or indigenous religious traditions, but because there is a more readily understood public ethic that it is unacceptable to malign indigenous peoples, ethnic minorities and the beliefs that help to define them as coherent groups. It can be objected that this is hypothesizing: there was *no* proposal before the galleries to exhibit a pig's head or a person defecating on the Koran. However, the analogical argument does reveal some assumptions, underlying the refusal in Melbourne and Wellington to heed the Churches' voice, that raise the relevance of a second ethical consideration for public institutions: respect for all citizens. The galleries were willing to intentionally offend Christians when they would be most reluctant to offend other religionists in similar ways. Almost perversely, that arises precisely because of the dominance of Christianity in Australia and New Zealand and the ambiguous place the Christian tradition now occupies in modern Western culture. The explanation that reflects best on the galleries is that they might consider that the Christian predominance gives it a cultural strength that enables Christian belief to absorb shocks that would be more damaging to, say, the smaller Muslim community.[72] That may be so, but the resilience of the particular religious group is irrelevant once we focus on the ethics of a public institution that is obliged to treat all citizens impartially and with respect.[73] If there is any accuracy to this account of the galleries' decision-making about exhibiting artworks that offend believers from different religious traditions, then (like the law of blasphemous libel) it fails to fulfil the precepts of equality that should moderate government action in a liberal democracy. This is not to conclude that the NGV or Te Papa should have categorically refused to display *Piss Christ*, *Virgin Mary in a Condom* or *Wrecked*. However, it is to conclude that, once the galleries predicted that they would cause affront by doing so, they should not have so lightly dismissed the concerns of offended believers. That response rests on policies that are almost the exact opposite of those underlying the blasphemy law, but they are no less impoverished for it.

Notes

1 R. Gill (1997), 'Art that's Hard to Swallow', *The Age*, 26 September 1997, p. C3.
2 *Pell* v. *The Council of the Trustees of the National Gallery of Victoria* [1998] 2 VR 391 (Harper J).
3 E. Yaman (1997), 'Second Attack Closes Christ Photo Exhibit', *The Australian*, 13 October 1997, p. 1.
4 R. Nelson (1997), 'Blasphemy or Just Bad Taste, It's All in the Eye of the Beholder', *The Age*, 10 October 1997, p. A19.
5 Ibid.
6 'Virgin Statue on Show Despite Attack', *Sunday Star-Times*, 8 March 1998, p. A2; 'Museum Refuses to Remove Exhibit', *Otago Daily Times*, 8 March 1998, p. 2; 'Violent and Personal Threats to Museum Staff over "Virgin"', *Otago Daily Times*, 9 March 1998, p. 2; 'Man Charged with Assault at Museum', *Otago Daily Times*, 13 March 1998, p. 2; S. Catherall (1998), 'Te Papa's Fingers Burnt in Outrage over Condom Art', *Sunday Star-Times*, 15 March 1998, p. A5.
7 'No prosecution over exhibits', *Otago Daily Times*, 28 March 1998, p. 35.
8 T. Pegler and R. Usher (1997), 'Row on Crucifix Art Heads for Court', *The Age*, 8 October 1997, p. A2.
9 To clarify Church structures unique to Australia, the Uniting Church was formed in 1977 as the organic union of the former Congregational, Methodist and Presbyterian Churches in Australia. It is therefore the principal institutional representative of liberal mainstream Protestantism in Australia, although the Church is doctrinally pluralized and also includes evangelical, charismatic and more liturgically oriented Protestants: R. Humphreys and R. Ward (1988), *Religious Bodies in Australia*, (Melbourne: Humphreys and Ward), pp. 46–49.
10 Indeed, the Reverend Kerr seemed to accept some of Serrano's own arguments about

Piss Christ: 'In a way this portrayal reminds us very sharply of that and stops us from seeing the cross in a sanitised sort of way': Pegler and Usher, 'Row on Cruxifix Art', *op. cit.*

11   J. Koutsoukis, G. Boreham and R. Gibson (1997), 'Police Refer Serrano Work to Censors', *The Age*, 9 October 1997, p. A4.

12   *Pell* v. *The Council of the Trustees of the National Gallery of Victoria* [1998] 2 VR 391, 392.

13   Summary Offences Act 1966 (Vic.), s 17(1)(b).

14   *Pell* v. *The Council of the Trustees of the National Gallery of Victoria* [1998] 2 VR 391, 395–396. Ample authority exists for this principle: *Paton* v. *British Pregnancy Advisory Trustees* [1979] 1 QB 276; *Attorney-General (ex rel Kerr)* v. *T.* [1983] 1 Qd. R. 404; *cf. Gouriet* v. *Union of Post Office Workers* [1978] AC 435; *Commonwealth of Australia* v. *John Fairfax & Sons Ltd.* (1980) 147 CLR 39; and see, for example, *Peek* v. *New South Wales Egg Corporation* (1986) 6 NSWLR 1, 3. In *Peek*, the President of the Court of Appeal, Justice Kirby identified at least three reasons for the principle. First, it prevents the civil courts from meddling in matters which the law has entrusted to the criminal courts. Second, in the case of statutory offences, if parliament had thought it appropriate to make, say, an injunction available, it would have done so in the statute itself. Third, and most importantly, there are different procedural rules for civil and criminal trials. To obtain a permanent injunction a plaintiff need only prove his case to the balance of probabilities. In criminal procedure, the commission of an offence must be proved beyond reasonable doubt before a conviction can be entered. As Justice Kirby said, 'If matters which are in substance appropriate for criminal trials could too readily be brought into courts of equity, by a claim for injunctive relief, the careful precautions, developed over centuries, for the accused in a criminal trial could be put at nought (or at least seriously undermined) by the expedient of seeking an injunction to enforce compliance with the criminal law': ibid.

15   *R.* v. *Taylor* (1677) 1 Vent. 293.

16   *R.* v. *Williams* (1797) 26 St. Tr. 653; *R.* v. *Eaton* (1812) 31 St. Tr. 927; *R.* v. *Richard Carlile* (1819) 1 St. Tr. (NS) 1388; 3 B. & Ald. 161; *R.* v. *Mary Carlile* (1819) 3 B. & Ald. 167; *R.* v. *Wedderburn* (1820) 1 St Tr. (NS) 1370; *R.* v. *Davison* (1821) 4 B. & Ald. 329; *R.* v. *Boyle* (1822) 1 St. Tr. (NS) 1370; *R.* v. *Tunbridge* (1822) 1 St. Tr. (NS) 1368; *R.* v. *Wright* (1823) 1 St. Tr. (NS) 1370; *R.* v. *Waddington* (1823) 1 B. & C. 26.

17   *R.* v. *Bradlaugh* (1883) 15 Cox CC 217; *R.* v. *Ramsay & Foote* (1883) 15 Cox CC 231, 236.

18   *Whitehouse* v. *Lemon* [1979] AC 617, 632, 656–57. For these developments in the law of blasphemous libel, see C. Kenny (1922), 'The Evolution of the Law of Blasphemy', *Cambridge Law Journal*, 1, p. 127; G.D. Nokes (1928), *A History of the Crime of Blasphemy*, (London: Sweet & Maxwell); R.G. Mortensen (1994), 'Blasphemy in a Secular State: A Pardonable Sin?', *University of New South Wales Law Journal*, 17, pp. 409–415.

19   *R.* v. *Lemon* [1979] 1 QB 10; *Whitehouse* v. *Lemon* [1979] AC 617; *Gay News Ltd. & Lemon* v. *United Kingdom* (1982) 5 EHRR 123.

20   In *R.* v. *Curl* (1727) 1 Str. 790, the Court of King's Bench held that offending religion was, *ipso facto*, a breach of the peace – an outcome that identifies religion as an essential ingredient of a civilized polity. However, in *Bowman* v. *Secular Society Ltd* [1917] AC 406, Lord Parker and Lord Sumner considered that a breach of the peace was required, at least in the sense that there was a threat to person or property: ibid., pp. 446, 467.

21   *Whitehouse* v. *Lemon* [1979] AC 617, 662.

22   See, for example, *R.* v. *Gathercole* (1838) 2 Lew. 237, 254; *R.* v. *Chief Metropolitan Stipendiary Magistrate; ex parte Choudhury* [1990] 3 WLR 986, 998–999.

23   Mortensen, 'Blasphemy in a Secular State', *op. cit.*, pp. 416–420.

24   Ibid., pp. 416–417.

25   *Pell* v. *The Council of the Trustees of the National Gallery of Victoria* [1998] 2 VR 391, 393.

26   Ibid., p. 394.

27   Ibid., p. 395.

28   Law Commission (UK) (1985), *Criminal Law – Offences Against Religion and Public Worship*, (London: Her Majesty's Stationery Office), pp. 28–29.

29   Law Reform Commission (Australia) (1992), *Multiculturalism and the Law*, (Sydney: Law Reform Commission), pp. 163–167.

30   New South Wales Law Reform Commission (1994), *Blasphemy*, (Sydney: New South Wales Law Reform Commission), pp. 57–58.

31   Law Commission, *Criminal Law, op. cit.*, pp. 28–29; Law Reform Commission, *Multiculturalism and the Law, op. cit.*, p. 166; New South Wales Law Reform Commission, *Blasphemy, op. cit.*, pp. 56–57.

32   Mortensen, 'Blasphemy in a Secular State', *op. cit.*, pp. 426–27.

33   Constitution (Cth.), s. 116; *Pell* v. *The Council of the Trustees of the National Gallery of Victoria* [1998] 2 VR 391, 394.

34   Ibid., p. 392.

35   Ibid.

36   It is not strictly true that the Archbishop has *no* interest capable of protection. In *Ogle* v. *Strickland* (1987) 71 ALR 41, the Full Court of the Federal Court of Australia held that Anglican and Catholic priests had standing to challenge a decision of the federal Censorship Board to allow the import of the film *Hail Mary*, as blasphemous material could not be legally imported into Australia. Justice Wilcox thought that any Christian would have standing to seek judicial review of the decision, an opinion he later attributed to his own belief in 'the priesthood of all believers': ibid., p. 59; see *Executive Council of Australian Jewry* v. *Scully* [1998] 66 FCA (13 February 1998).

37   Penal Code 1860 (India), s. 298.

38   *Whitehouse* v. *Lemon* [1979] AC 617, 658; *Pell* v. *The Council of the Trustees of the National Gallery of Victoria* [1998] 2 VR 391, 393.

39   *R.* v. *Chief Metropolitan Stipendiary Magistrate; ex parte Choudhury* [1990] 3 WLR 986; *Choudhury* v. *United Kingdom* (1991) HRLJ 172.

40   Law Commission, *Criminal Law, op. cit.*, pp. 28–29; Law Reform Commission, *Multiculturalism and the Law, op. cit.*, p. 166; New South Wales Law Reform Commission, *Blasphemy, op. cit.*, pp. 52–58.

41   Law Commission, *Criminal Law, op. cit.*, pp. 26–28; Law Reform Commission, *Multiculturalism and the Law, op. cit.*, p. 166; New South Wales Law Reform Commission, *Blasphemy, op. cit.*, pp. 48–52.

42   In *Church of the New Faith* v. *Commissioner of Pay-roll Tax (Vic.)* (1983) 154 CLR 120, the High Court of Australia has produced a broad, workable definition of 'religion' for the purposes of the civil law, but this might still be too vague to serve as a definition of an element of a serious criminal offence. The definition was considered by the English Court of Appeal in *Choudhury* [1990] 3 WLR 986, but not openly accepted as an adequate definition of religion for the purposes of the blasphemy law: ibid., p. 1000.

43   Law Reform Commission, *Multiculturalism and the Law, op. cit.*, note 29 above, p. 167; New South Wales Law Reform Commission, *Blasphemy, op. cit.*, pp. 55–57. In

Australia, the federal Human Rights Commissioner has recommended that the federal parliament introduce national religious vilification laws that could have an effect analogous to a non-sectarian blasphemy law. However, it is not recommended that these make religious vilification a criminal offence: Human Rights Commissioner (1998), *Article 18 – Freedom of Religion and Belief*, (Sydney: Human Rights and Equal Opportunity Commission), pp. 137–140.

44   The British government's defence before the European Commission of Human Rights of the convictions of *Gay News* and Denis Lemon in *Gay News Ltd. & Lemon* v. *United Kingdom* (1982) 5 EHRR 123 could be an exception. Conversely, in the specific circumstances of *Choudhury* v. *United Kingdom* (1991) HRLJ 172, the same government could be interpreted as preferring that Salman Rushdie *not* be prosecuted for blasphemous libel.

45   'No Prosecution over Exhibits', *Otago Daily Times*, 28 March 1998, p. 35.

46   W.H. Simon (1998), *The Practice of Justice*, (Cambridge, MA: Harvard University Press), pp. 84 and 90.

47   Crimes Act 1961 (N.Z.), s. 123; Criminal Code (Tas.), s. 119.

48   R.S. O'Regan (1992), 'Two Curiosities of Sir Samuel Griffith's Criminal Code', *Criminal Law Journal*, **16**, pp. 212–213.

49   Ibid., p. 212.

50   Criminal Code Act 1899 (Qld.), ss 3 and 5; Criminal Code Compilation Act 1913 (WA), s. 4.

51   *Pell* v. *The Council of the Trustees of the National Gallery of Victoria* [1998] 2 VR 391, 391.

52   Ibid., p. 395.

53   *Cincinnati* v *Contemporary Arts Center*, 566 NE 2d 214, 218 (1990). In this case, the jury's considering the presentation of the photograph alone worked against the defending Arts Center. The offending material comprised five photographs taken by Robert Mapplethorpe of sadomasochistic practices and naked children. These five photographs were to be exhibited with 170 others in an exhibition called *Robert Mapplethorpe: Perfect Moment*, and the Arts Center argued that the jury should be directed to consider the exhibition as a whole. That, undoubtedly, would have been harder to interpret as obscene. However, Judge Albanese said that 'when considering that each photograph is a whole image, the focus will be each picture "taken as a whole". Arranging photographs within an exhibition to claim a "privilege of acceptability" is not the test; the "whole" is a single picture, and no amount of manipulation can change its identity.' Despite this ruling, the Arts Center was acquitted. See also *Cincinnati* v. *Contemporary Arts Center*, 566 NE 2d 207 (1990), and J.H. Merryman and A.E. Elsen (1998), *Law, Ethics and the Visual Arts*, (London: Kluwer Law International), pp. 487–93.

54   *R.* v. *Lemon* [1979] 1 QB 10; *Whitehouse* v. *Lemon* [1979] AC 617; *Gay News Ltd. & Lemon* v. *United Kingdom* (1982) 5 EHRR 123.

55   *Pell* v. *The Council of the Trustees of the National Gallery of Victoria* [1988] 2 VR 391, 393.

56   Gill, 'Art that's Hard to Swallow', *op. cit.*

57   Ibid.

58   R. Gibson (1997), 'Treading the Line Between Art and Pornography', *The Age*, 9 October, p. A4.

59   Ibid.

60   Ellen Goodman noted this 'culture clash' between the arts community and the broader public, and argued that the fault lies primarily with the 'chic insularity' of the arts community. It 'speaks its private language to a circle so small, so cozy and so closed as

to be dangerously isolated': quoted in Merryman and Elsen, *Law, Ethics and the Visual Arts, op. cit.*, pp. 491–492.

61 D. Jones (1997), 'Director Made his own Cross', *The Australian*, 16 October, p. 17.
62 F. Devine (1997), 'Roll up, Roll up, for the Greatest Cock-and-Bull Show on Earth', *The Australian*, 13 October, p. 13.
63 Koutsoukis *et al.*, 'Police Refer Serrano Work', *op. cit.*; A. Sutherland (1998), 'Remove that Statue', *Sunday Star-Times*, 8 March, p. A10.
64 Gibson, 'Treading the Line', *op. cit.*
65 Police investigations in response to complaints of obscenity continued at the Kirkcaldy Davies Gallery after the exhibition was opened: S. McCulloch and C. Le Grand (1997), 'Artist Applauds Rejection of Ban on Christ Work', *The Australian*, 10 October, p. 5.
66 Public Sector Management and Employment Act 1998 (Vic.), s. 8.
67 S. Catherall (1998), 'Te Papa to Pay $3500 for Mediator', *Sunday Star-Times*, 29 March, p. A5.
68 A. Rollins (1997), 'Crucifix Artwork Prompts Complaint', *The Age*, 7 October, p. A3.
69 Jones, 'Director Made his own Cross', *op. cit.*; 'Viewing the Art of Offence', *The Age*, 10 October 1997, p. A18; B. Muelenberg (letter) (1997), *The Australian*, 13 October, p. 10; A. Burton (letter) (1997), *The Australian*, 14 October, p. 14.
70 'Museum Refuses to Remove Exhibit', *Otago Daily Times*, 9 March 1998, p. 2.
71 Ibid.; Catherall, 'Te Papa's Fingers Burnt', *op. cit.*
72 Jones, 'Director Made his own Cross', *op. cit.*
73 For example, see Public Sector Management and Employment Act 1998 (Vic.), s. 8.

10 'And was Jerusalem Builded Here?' Talmudic Territory and the Modernist Defensive[1]

Davina Cooper

Introduction

This chapter explores the conflict that arose in the early 1990s over attempts to install an eruv – a Talmudic, symbolic perimeter – in the borough of Barnet, in suburban north-west London. In particular, it seeks to explain why opposition proved so intense and fierce. My argument focuses on antagonists' investment in, and commitment to, modernist norms and values of rationality, the public–private divide, nation-state and legal centrism – values seemingly imperilled by the eruv's prospective installation.

On the Sabbath Jewish law forbids a range of labour. This includes, as well as formal work, travelling, spending money and carrying objects beyond the home. The eruv concerns this latter injunction. It enables objects to be carried or pushed within a non-domestic area through the creation of a bounded perimeter which notionally extends the private domain.

Eruvs have become common in large urban districts in Canada, the United States, Australia and Europe, as well as in Israel. Nevertheless, the requirement symbolically to enclose space, including, in many instances, miles of urban city, and the dwellings of gentiles as well as Jews, has subjected eruv proposals to intense hostility, particularly where enclosure requires the installation of new structures rather than exclusively using existing edifices such as railway lines, fences and walls. In Barnet, because the proposed boundary could not be fully completed through existing structures, an application had to be made for planning permission to erect a series of poles joined by thin, high wire to complete the perimeter. It was this application which provided the focal point for the fierce and prolonged battle which emerged.

On the surface, the Barnet conflict can be read as a utilitarian contest of cost and benefit. According to proponents, an eruv would help mobility-impaired people and parents of young children to attend synagogue, go to the park, or visit relatives. Since nobody would suffer from its installation, there was no good reason to refuse permission (as ascertained from interviews by author). Critics, however, disagreed. First, they claimed that the degree of benefit had been greatly exaggerated. The number of observant Jews who were disabled, or parents of young children, was minimal,[2] and most could get rabbinical dispensation (although the availability, status and extent of this was contested). Second, the extra street furniture – poles and wire – would cause extreme visual disfigurement to the landscape.

This utilitarian framing was, in part, the product of the legal discourse of development control within which the conflict occurred. Yet, the environmental and physical harm wrought by 80 additional poles and wire, in a borough with many thousand similar installations, cannot alone explain the concerns expressed. When reading press coverage and conducting interviews,[3] I was struck by the intensity of anxiety (at times close to panic), and by people's willingness to devote enormous time and energy to oppose the eruv's construction. This chapter attempts to explain why the eruv generated such powerful, hostile feelings. What social meanings underpinned the depiction of this planning application as an aggressive territorial initiative? Exploring this question highlights the wider resonance of the eruv conflict. While the struggle over Orthodox Jewish spatial boundaries is interesting in its own right, it also has a wider relevance in terms of its resonance with other struggles over religious identity, the spatialization of cultural expression and belonging, and the specific role of law and government.

At the centre of my analysis is the eruv's representation within modernist discourse. My focus is thus on opponents' arguments, rather than on the question of whether or not the eruv *does* threaten, challenge or negate modernity.[4] At the same time I do not assume that arguments reflect in any direct and unmediated way opponents' inner concerns. As I discuss, the formation of successful arguments is heavily contingent on prevailing, wider discourses as well as conceptions of which expressions are authoritative and legitimate. For instance, a major concern for many opponents may have been the unpredictable effects of the eruv on residential property prices. This argument, however, was largely downplayed, no doubt because it seemed to carry less weight and validity within public sphere debate than arguments about sustaining the 'secular' public status quo. At the same time, I treat opponents' arguments as bearing some relationship to real concerns and fears. The tenuous and problematic character of many opponents' arguments suggest that these concerns were their own. In addition, while some claims were undoubtedly exaggerated, this was done on the assumption that such claims would resonate with the pre-existing concerns of other residents.

In the main, eruv critics adopted a 'traditional', liberal perspective. They attacked the eruv for undermining universalism, evolutionism, the public–private divide, secularism and Enlightenment rationality.[5] To understand why opponents adopted this approach, we need to consider further who they were. Perhaps the most striking characteristic of the opposition was the high number of Jewish people involved[6] – largely over 45, European, and middle-class.[7] Their stance towards the eruv and commitment to Enlightenment norms replicates a common theme of modern Jewish history.[8] For European Jews who took advantage of nineteenth-century emancipation and assimilated, secularism, rationality and formal equality functioned as both means of integration as well as personal symbols of its achievement. The intense faith in modernist norms that this generated paralleled an equally powerful antagonism towards Orthodox Jews who remained visibly and 'anachronistically' Jewish,[9] thereby drawing attention to assimilated Jews' own roots, and precarious sense of belonging.

At the same time, I do not wish to suggest that liberal Jews simply passively absorbed a modernist discourse. How discourses are internalized and negotiated depends on history, social and personal context. Thus, in my analysis, I explore how the modernist terms in which opposition was framed were also inflected, extended and, in some cases, overridden by the context at hand. My interpretation focuses on three sites of tension: first, conceptions of space and demography; second, the public status of difference; and third, the problematic of governance and nation-building. I begin, however, with an account of the conflict, and tackle a preliminary question: what impact did legal process have on the discursive form the conflict took?

A Town Planning Issue?

Barnet's Eruv Proposal

'Eruv' literally means 'to mingle', and can take several forms.[10] The one relevant here is the eruv that creates a mingling of space, enabling a relaxation of Sabbath carrying restrictions. According to Jewish law, Jews are prohibited from transporting objects between the public and private domain during the Sabbath.[11] The creation of an eruv enables transportation to take place by turning the space between private domains into a single private arena.[12] However, the requirements for establishment are extremely complicated. They are also subject to rabbinical dispute over the kind of perimeter acceptable; how large a population an eruv can encompass; and how difficult structures such as busy roads and parkland should be treated. Disagreement has led many eruvs only to be recognized by certain rabbis. In Toronto, for instance, such a dispute led, in 1996, to the establishment of a new eruv in the hope it would prove more widely acceptable than its predecessor constructed in the 1930s (interview by author).

Although eruvs go back many hundreds of years, the modern eruv movement gained force in the 1960s. Interest in eruvs has been associated with growing orthodoxy amongst young people;[13] the women's liberation movement – particularly women's interest in participating more fully in religious life;[14] and, more recently, with demands for disability rights. Eruvs also function as a sign of increasing Jewish confidence and a readiness to make demands that refigure the cultural landscape.

In London the initiative to establish an eruv emerged out of an alliance that included Rabbi Kimche, an Orthodox rabbi with a young, observant congregation, and United Synagogue (US), the largest grouping of orthodox synagogues in Britain. In 1992, US submitted a planning proposal to Barnet Council. It encountered deep opposition. Protests came from residents' associations, local amenity groups and individuals, as well as the Barnet Eruv Objectors Group, formed to intensify and focus resistance.

In late February 1993 the application came before Barnet Town Planning and Research Committee. To understand what happened there, we need to consider the guidance provided by planning officers. While their report recognized the level of feeling on both sides, it nevertheless stated, 'many of the reasons cited have no direct relevance to planning and in reaching a decision on this application the Committee should only take into account material planning considerations'.[15] These were identified narrowly – the impact on trees, visual amenity of local residents, and acceptability in terms of the free flow of traffic and public safety along highways.[16] Officers then recommended approval.

The Planning Committee followed officer guidance in keeping debate within strict planning boundaries. While other issues were raised, the Committee chair 'strove to maintain that only relevant matters were debated'.[17] Indeed, the concept of the eruv was itself refused admittance as an irrelevant consideration. As one councillor stated when interviewed:

> I'm concerned with poles not an eruv. We dealt with it as a town planning issue. It's got nothing to do with religion. Some people worried about a ghetto but that's not a town planning issue.... You need to stick to the tramlines and be very blinkered. (Interview with objecting councillor)

Witnessed by several hundred supporters and opponents, the Committee rejected the application on the grounds that 'the proposed poles and wires would result in the introduction of additional street furniture which would be visually intrusive and detrimental to the character and appearance of the street scene....'[18]

United Synagogue appealed to the Secretary of State who, in accordance with standard planning procedures, authorized an inquiry which commenced on 30 November 1993. Two months later, the inspector's report was privately passed to the minister. For eight months no decision was released. Then in the autumn of 1994, the Secretary of State for the Environment's decision was published, upholding the inspector's recommendation that planning permission be granted.

According to the inspector's report, the central issue was poles and wire:

> In the inquiry I found many objectors and supporters directed most of their comments and arguments at the Eruv as a religious concept.... It seems to me that the appeal applications comprise pieces of street furniture in the form of small groups of cylindrical poles.... The Eruv itself does not require planning permission as most of it is not development in terms of the Act.[19]

Considering each site in turn, the inspector found the visual impact of poles and wire insufficient to justify refusal.[20] It was therefore unnecessary to consider other balancing factors such as planning need (which he did find existed).[21] A complicated question concerned whether there existed material considerations sufficient to amount to a planning objection[22] – in particular whether the opponents' claim that the eruv would damage social harmony could constitute such a consideration. Although the inspector held that human factors could be material considerations in special circumstances, he rejected these claims. The argument that the poles would remind people of the Holocaust and create a ghetto were too difficult to substantiate and too tenuously linked to land-use planning.[23]

The inspector's conclusion opened up the possibility of extending development control criteria; however the minister did not grasp the opportunity, confirming the decision on narrow planning grounds. In his rejection of the visual impact argument, the minister claimed that he had no cause to consider the issue of need.[24] He also avoided identifying the breadth of 'other material considerations' such as 'social harmony'.[25]

The Discursive Authority of the Law

I have set out in some detail the development control process, and arguments deployed, to reveal how the eruv was institutionally produced and examined within the limited, balancing structure of planning law.[26] Yet this is not the only juridical framework within which eruvs have been considered. In the United States conflicts over their establishment have revolved around constitutional questions concerning the relationship between Church and state. In particular, courts have addressed whether an eruv does, or does not, entail state promotion or endorsement of a particular faith.[27] Even in Barnet, other legal principles were raised. One couple, whose home fronted the perimeter, claimed that use of their property to manifest a religious belief deprived them of their civil rights, while the installation of poles beside their house was a trespass since they owned both soil and air.[28]

Yet, while planning law was not the only influence on protagonists' arguments, it did play a key structuring role. For some – principally councillors opposed to the eruv – this meant focusing exclusively on narrow environmental concerns (from interviews by author). For others – mainly eruv proponents – legitimate harm concerned the structure's possible impact on the physical environment (which they denied), while need was articulated more broadly to the eruv concept.[29] Only community opponents attempted to broaden planning objections to include the *harm* caused by the eruv *concept*. However, they did not see their attempt as successful.[30]

> The council and Eruv Committee said the issue was one of street furniture…and nothing else. Planning law allows any material consideration so it could have been wider…. We said what we thought but were ignored. Barnet's case concerned the physical environment. The real issue was people's feelings and identities…. (Objector, interview)

Yet, to see the planning process simply as obscuring more important concerns is too simple. By providing a procedure and set of institutional sites for conflict, development control also facilitated, albeit hierarchically, the expression of other issues, as one objector identified: 'The debate about poles and planning consent was a surrogate for debate about minorities and what is and isn't permissible behaviour' (objector, interview).

Symbolic Space and Territorial Agendas

The spatial dimension to conflict has received increasing academic attention in recent years.[31] In this section I explore how opponents portrayed the spatial aspect of the eruv's apparent threat.[32] Opponents' conception of space comprised several elements. First, space was seen as a domain in which symbols had a widespread effect; in other words, readings were not containable by the symbolic structure's host community. Second, the impact on the wider area was presumed to be an *intended* effect of symbolic activity. Third, ownership or control of space was zero-sum; thus activity which privatized space for one group simultaneously withdrew space from others. Fourth, ideal city spaces are well planned and ordered, offering an 'ethnically coherent' equilibrium.

Symbolically Staining Space

> Driving under the gateways… to enter the Barnet Ghetto would be like entering a concentration camp.[33]

> Public space is a place for competing symbols. (Eruv supporter, interview)

At the heart of the eruv struggle lay fundamentally different conceptions of the relationship between space, symbols and cultural meanings. While opponents' *normative* conception of space – that is, their view of how space should be ordered – generally expressed a modernist imagary (as I discuss below), their *interpretative* understanding of the relationship between space and symbol is more difficult to categorize. Let me explain what I mean by this categorical ambiguity. A central element of opponents' critique was a modernist belief in symbolic impact – that symbols do not exist in a vacuum but 'stain' the wider space or community within which they function.[34] At the same time, they adopted a more postmodern stance in strategically acknowledging the possibility of multiple readings.

> To A the Eruv symbolizes 'Sabbath limits', to B 'a desecration of the Sabbath'… to C 'a communal dividing line' to E [sic] 'the walls and gates of the ghetto', to F 'non functional street clutter'. To G 'a focus for antisemitism'.…[35]

While some opponents argued that the eruv was at heart a ghetto, or symbol of the *shtetl*, claims about the eruv's core and overriding meaning were generally avoided. Opponents simply demanded that eruv advocates respond to more negative meanings, and take responsibility for the offence such meanings would cause to many residents.

In contrast, eruv supporters relied on the multivalent capacity of space to hold discrete, separate symbols. Instead of seeing spaces as articulated according to dominant cultural meanings – meanings that would be shaped or affected by local symbols – supporters identified meaning as a voluntary, collective practice in which groups established and maintained interpretative authority over their own symbolic structures. Thus, they declared, the eruv existed symbolically only for users: 'It is of immense significance to those who can benefit, but of none to others' (eruv supporter, interview).

Territorial Claims

As I have said, opponents did not deny that Orthodox Jews might see the eruv as a carrying zone. Nevertheless, they argued, this interpretation could not prevail at the level of public policy given the eruv's other meanings and more concrete effects. Adopting a rationalist account of agency, opponents argued that these other consequences – which they declared would result from installing an eruv – must have been intended by eruv advocates. Thus, they dismissed the suggestion that the eruv was simply to facilitate synagogue attendance or Sabbath socializing. Indeed, some opponents went so far as to reject proponents' claims altogether: 'We see the wire as an ethnocentric demonstration, the religious side is just a ruse... They put up poles as a demonstration of their territoriality – they don't need poles' (objector, interview).

One Barnet rabbi partly confirmed this view when he said, in an interview, that the eruv was partly about developing a spatially identified community 'which has a boundary... that comes into play on the Sabbath'. However, his words were taken further by critics who identified (with varying degrees of explicitness) other, more covert, territorial agendas, aimed at expulsion and transformed terms of spatial belonging. These objectors' arguments subtly drew on existing discursive anxieties about religious fundamentalism in which symbols not only define territory, but also define appropriate practices within it. Thus, orthodoxizing territory does not impact only on religious community members; in religious neighbourhood space, opponents suggested, everyone else must also comply with ultra-Orthodox norms.[36] From the perspective of objectors, the liberal-sounding claims of eruv advocates for equal opportunities and disability rights were the serpent-tongued words that obscured the inevitable reality of religious territorialization: 'primitive' expressions of horror and repression such as, in Jerusalem, the stones and dirty nappies thrown by Orthodox residents at cars, driven through their neighbourhoods, on the Sabbath.[37]

In their assertions that spatial appropriation was taking place in the guise of the request for planning permission for an eruv, objectors drew for evidence on the Halakic principle that an eruv privatizes space. Objectors refused to accept that such privatizing existed only symbolically for Orthodox Jews. Conceptualizing ownership of space as a zero-sum relationship, they argued that attempts by Orthodox Jews to create a private or communal domain must be at the expense of other communities (and of the community in general):[38]

> People feel they've taken over. This isn't my area anymore... [The eruv] identifies a non-Jewish area as a Jewish area. The Jewish area is moving further out, away from Golders Green. (Objector, interview)[39]

While the eruv was seen as symbolically withdrawing space from existing residents – turning them into a new dispossessed – opponents also saw the eruv as a deliberate demographic strategy to increase the visibility, strength and numbers of ultra-Orthodox Jews:[40] 'They want to demographically alter the population of the area… to deliberately move Jewish people into the area to live together' (objector, interview). Interviewees described property advertisements in the local Jewish press that identified homes as within the proposed eruv. Thus, the eruv was seen as a political technique of desecularization – a symbol and starting point for a slippery slope that would eventually remake Barnet in the image of its ultra-orthodox, poorer, north-east London neighbour, Stamford Hill.[41]

Rational Space

It's a question of what you expect to see in a good quality neighbourhood. (Objecting councillor, interview)

So far I have discussed opponents' portrayal of the eruv as a 'rational' technique for achieving communalist objectives. However, coinciding with this instrumentalist image was another which depicted the eruv as fundamentally irrational in its expression of premodern norms.[42] Opponents emphasized both the importance of, and threat posed to, stable, planned neighbourhoods regulated according to rational, coherent norms.[43] Yet, opponents' desire for urban equilibrium was shot through with ethnic concerns. For instance, one opponent, drawing on a racialized discourse of geographical science, declared the area's historic stability 'would be harmed if the proportion of Jews increased… It is a matter of the right proportions and balance in the community'.[44]

Given opponents' conception of residential space as appropriately governed by quasi-scientific norms, even in its ethnic–racial aspect, it is perhaps unsurprising that some of the most vigorous opposition came from the affluent Barnet neighbourhood of Hampstead Garden Suburb (HGS), a prime example of the early twentieth-century garden suburb movement.[45] To this spatially, highly regulated community – where even minor architectural change is discouraged – and where identification with place is particularly strong,[46] the proposal to impose a new, external structure was anathema.[47] Not only was the eruv structure seen as arbitrary in terms of its terrain, but its purpose was perceived by many HGS residents as fundamentally antithetical to the foundational principles of their own community.[48] For residents, proud of their modern, highly acclaimed suburb, the notion that poles and wire might be installed so that people could engage in everyday 'shlepping' on the Sabbath seemed intellectually absurd. In this way, the eruv not only jeopardized a careful, racialized equilibrium but, just as importantly (and clearly the two are connected), HGS residents' conception of their neighbourhood's civilized character.

Difference, Majority Rights and Secularism

Opponents interpreted the eruv as a territorial act which appropriated space; yet, articulated to this rather exaggerated position, were other, more complex arguments concerning Britain's cultural identity and the legitimacy of minority expression. In this section I argue that these arguments reflected a modernist perspective on society, revolving around three principal themes. First, membership of the public sphere as universal citizens necessitates difference remaining within the private domain. Second, democracy and the imperatives of nation-state history require primacy to be given to majoritarian interests. Third, religion should not be privileged as a basis for action.

Privatizing Difference

> What they do in their own home is of no concern to anyone else. (Objector, interview)

Opponents' argument that difference should be expressed within the private sphere echoes a conventional tenet of liberal modernist discourse: that society is divided into separate spheres of activity organized according to their own distinct norms and values.[49] However, aside from the question of whether boundaries dividing social spheres of life can ever function effectively, the premise of 'walls' appears to clash with opponents' claims of symbolic impact and community permeability discussed above. For the concept of division into discrete spaces suggests meanings *can* be contained, if not by particular communities, then at least within particular, functionally defined arenas.

In discussing the eruv with interviewees, opponents stressed both the capacity to achieve, as well as the legitimacy of, *private* difference in order to distinguish the eruv from a synagogue or church. The latter's acceptability was owed to the fact that people go *into* a building to worship; with its doors closed, only attenders know what takes place. By contrast, creating a perimeter around a neighbourhood or district makes difference a 'public' matter. 'There's a distinction between an edifice and a more widely spread delineation of an area' (objecting councillor, interview).

Two criticisms are implicit in this argument. First, a 'delineation', through the installation of public boundary markers, soils the cultural landscape, attacking (and reconstituting) the prec(ar)ious relationship of land to identity, disfiguring the 'deep' national–racial identity of terrain. One instance where this fear was made particularly explicit concerned a Church of England school whose playground formed part of the eruv boundary.[50] Here, the prior, explicit racialization of the soil was seen to make the concept of a 'Jewish boundary line' particularly inappropriate.[51] The second criticism was that a delineation generates increased public visibility for Orthodox Jews. This is, however, a contradictory point. On the one hand, an eruv allows Orthodox Jews to more easily use public space on the Sabbath. While, at the same time, an eruv *normalizes* Orthodox Judaism by enabling observant Jews to come out as 'ordinary' citizens. Yet, even in the ordinariness of Sabbath 'pushing and carrying' activities, the essential otherness of the Orthodox Jew remains. What the eruv does is to give such 'otherness' public expression. Thus Orthodox congregants are able to express publicly aspects of their private identity in ways which opponents saw as antithetical to a modernist conception of personhood.[52]

Opponents articulated the public expression of (minority) difference to four concerns. First was the danger of precedent as other minorities might come to expect a similar entitlement: 'It would be a slippery slope of ethnic minorities asking for things, wanting special facilities' (objecting councillor, interview); '[A]ny minority will see it as a green light for their own particular view to be expressed....'[53] The outcome of this, for eruv objectors, would be apocalyptic – with totem poles erected on North London's Hampstead Heath. The horror of the premodern and uncivilized is fully apparent in this trope, for 'totem poles' have historically represented, for the West, a quintessential primitive symbol. Moreover, the repeated elision with Hampstead Heath – a large, prestigious area of heath and parkland – is also not coincidental. For local residents (in Barnet as well as beyond) saw the Heath as intensely urbane – indeed one might say *sacred–modern* – space.

The Heath's character as a place for 'all' to enjoy highlights a second concern: public expression of difference contravenes the majority's right not to confront cultural otherness. According to eruv opponents, public localities should be places in which everyone, regardless of their private practices, conforms to prevailing cultural norms. While eruv opponents acknowledged that difference from such norms can be pleasurable and enriching, it must be governed by individual consent, and thus function at the level of private interaction. One woman I interviewed, while hostile to what she saw as distasteful large public menorahs and Chanukah candles on her neighbourhood streets, spoke happily about her neighbour bringing around pastries cooked to celebrate an Islamic festival.

Third, for opponents the public expression of difference jeopardized the reproduction of a common national citizenship. Differences needed to be privatized in order for them to be safely expressed without Britain fragmenting into a series of disparate peoples or nations. 'Ghettos', by representing a restructuring[54] or refusal to privatize difference, were seen, in contrast, as threatening a common citizenship. A postmodern interpretation that marks them as interesting places of intense cultural expression and diversity is, I was told, dangerously naive. Ghettos represent troubled symbols of cultural ill-health and disequilibrium. Several interviewees, citing the United States, argued that, there, the capacity of cultural minorities to form local majorities enabled them to remain outside of, and thereby undermine, universal(izing) citizenship identities.[55]

Finally, opponents declared that the public expression of difference would cause the minorities themselves to suffer, including those members who had attempted to assimilate. For secular Jews, the eruv proposal publicly identified, and produced, them as alien in ways that jeopardized their place within the cultural hierarchy: 'A minority of the community having staked out and identified its precise territory leaves the whole Jewish community open to attack, abuse and vandalism.'[56] Another objector stated: 'Anglicised Jews felt [the eruv] broke the rules of the game. They saw it as unBritish.... The eruv fulfils the Jewish stereotype of pushy and aggressive' (interview); 'People now feel the extended hand of friendship has been cut off' (interview). While the eruv proposal was seen as destructive enough, Jewish safety, opponents claimed, would be further jeopardized by actual installation. Violent anti-Semites would come – (always) from 'elsewhere' – generating anti-Jewish feeling amongst local residents who had 'never previously had an anti-Semitic thought' (objector interview). In other words, anti-Semitism would come to constitute the rational response of an alienated *majority*.

In response, proponents dismissed, in interviews and in media reports, the likelihood of violence, querying the extent to which objectors really believed it would occur. Vandalism and anti-Semitism, they suggested, were simply rhetorical arguments with which to attack the proposal. Yet, while some opponents may have intentionally exaggerated their anxieties, we can hear in their concerns echoes of wider fears about religious and ethnic violence. In this respect, the eruv represented to opponents symbolic provocation, or, at best, careless indifference to the worldwide hatred and strife generated by ethnic communal claims.

Christian Hegemony and Religious Justification

> For the last 30 years, my wife and I have every Christmas put a very large tree in the front bay window of our house. This has, I venture to suggest, given a great deal of pleasure to the community....[57] The eruv will, I think, create exactly the reverse effect.[58]

I have talked so far about opponents' advocacy of a universal, modernist citizenship transcending private, 'tribal' identities. However, as feminists, in particular, have demonstrated, the public expression of citizenship is never neutral.[59] Modernist paradigms of citizenship either explicitly advocate the reproduction of existing majoritarian and historically dominant identities or, in their erasure of particularism, have the effect of leaving a residual dominant identity in place.[60] In this conflict, the abstract citizen did not have to be scratched too hard to find its Christian traces.[61] Indeed, opponents I interviewed, generally did not even try to obscure Christianity's status. Almost all identified Britain as being – at least nominally – Christian; most, including Jewish opponents, found this unproblematic, and some even thought it was beneficial, since it recognized and perpetuated Britain's historic identity.[62] According to one objector, 'Christianity is fundamental to our culture and 95 per cent of the population' (interview).

The special place of Christianity needs to be kept in mind in considering its assumed antithesis: secularism. One of modernism's key attributes,[63] secularism is usually taken to mean religion's location within the private rather than public sphere. It also signifies the rejection of religion as a foundation for institutional policy-making or political decision.[64] Yet, within Britain, the impact of secularism on different religions is uneven.[65] Not only is the universal British citizen inherently and officially Christian,[66] but Christianity is also less disadvantaged by the political subordination of religious bases for action than other faiths.[67] This is partly because Christianity is more readily *accepted* within political discourse as a justification or reason for action. More significantly, Christianity is embedded in the organization of time, political power, law, and education amongst others. Thus, it can have 'an air of neutrality…the epitome of rational abstraction… [because it] has already been the focus of past processes whose traces are not always evident in the landscape'.[68]

When eruv opponents objected to religion functioning as a criterion for action, their target was largely non-Christian faiths. One woman I interviewed proffered an analogy:

> Suppose you have a wonderful bush at the end of your garden, but the person living behind you, who shares the bush, believes it represents evil; do you have to remove the bush just to comply with their religious beliefs?

While this raises generally interesting ethical questions regarding religion's status as a basis for action, equally significant was the specific illustrative context she chose: a person from the Caribbean who 'believes in voodoo'. Thus, at the heart of her analogy lies a criticism of action to accommodate seemingly 'irrational', *non-establishment* belief systems. At the same time, there is fear. If 'irrational' beliefs can legitimately demand action simply on the ground of being a belief, does any basis for distinction remain?

Understanding Jewish Law

Construction of a justificatory pyramid in which religion is explicitly subordinated, while implicitly differentiated, parallels another modernist gesture – a hierarchy of sovereignty. In the final section of this chapter, I discuss the eruv's threat to nation-state governance. However, before turning to that issue, I want to raise the question of sovereignty in relation to law. Modernist Western discourse tends to perceive state authority as singular and hierarchical, with legality functioning similarly.[69] Within this hierarchy, religious law is clearly subordinate to state law.[70] As one interviewee put it: 'Religious law doesn't have a right to make claims on the majority. It can make claims on the minority, but it's secondary to secular law' (objector, interview).

Yet, in their opposition to the eruv, opponents did not simply treat Halakah – religious law – as subordinate law.[71] Rather, they dismissed its very legal status.[72] Jewish law was perceived as voluntary and indeterminate, lacking legitimate authority and credibility. According to one leading eruv proponent interviewed, opponents proved so unwilling and unable to comprehend Halakah that they gave up trying to explain.

> Jewish law is very complicated, we were aware of trying to explain it to people who hadn't a clue…. It's hard to find ways of expressing the idea of the eruv…. Eventually we said we can't explain it or you'll never believe it…. To explain why we need it is our business. We just want you to respect the fact we understand it. (Proponent, interview)

Opponents' conceptualization of Jewish law produced two main responses to the eruv. First, their reduction of Halakah to a set of voluntary beliefs led opponents to claim that Jews must either believe in the singular, underlying purpose they identified – not carrying on the Sabbath – (and comply) or if they did not believe in the prohibition to go ahead and carry anyway.[73] One of the most repeated accusations thrown at the eruv was hypocrisy: 'It allows people of a certain persuasion to break the law' (objector, interview). This accusation demonstrates either a complete failure to understand the complex character of legal compliance and legitimacy, or a failure to apply this understanding to religious law.

Opponents' criticism of the eruv as a legal device was further reinforced by pointing to sections of the ultra-Orthodox community who had publicly repudiated the eruv proposal.[74] Asserting the Halakah's interpretive closure

– that only one legal response to the Sabbath prohibition on carrying in public was possible – opponents claimed that if the ultra-Orthodox – those who seemed to follow religious law most closely – did not accept the eruv, then this must be the best reading (interviews by author). Thus, they rejected the possibility of equally valid competing interpretations.

At the same time, objectors' perception of Jewish law as technically obscure and contested (as well as being voluntary and simplistic) meant eruv requirements were deemed entirely plastic. In other words, an eruv could be constructed according to any measurement that suited both users and the wider community. For instance, several interviewees suggested an eruv might be more acceptable if it embraced the entire British mainland. When I replied that an eruv could only be of a limited size, enclosing a limited population, I was met with a shrug and rejoinder that since the whole thing was ridiculous, it was pointless to look for 'rational' rules.

Contested Nation-state/Governance

In this final section, I want to draw together my above analysis to locate opponents' critique within the context of modernist norms of governance and the nation-state. My comments focus first on the relationship between state and civil governance and, second, on the role of boundaries within ongoing 'nation-work'.

In the main, opponents adopted a liberal normative and analytical framework of governance, oriented around the limited state. Not only was state activity constrained within this paradigm, civil governance was also seen to have a limited role. Bodies such as Church, family or workplace might be desirable, but their authority rests on consent. In addition, civil governance should not, within the modern liberal polity, undermine individuals' direct relationship with the state.

Opponents attacked the eruv as a governance structure on two grounds. First, it embraced within its territory people who had not consented, thereby symbolically functioning as a form of *compulsory* governance. As one objector put it: '[W]ithin those physical boundaries around 80,000 people will be enclosed, the vast majority of whom have no desire at all to live within a private Jewish domain.'[75] Second, the spatial and governance function of the eruv was seen to broker and mediate the relationship of community to the state, thereby replaying the role of premodern Jewish bodies.[76]

Yet if it had not required boundaries nor asserted an ethnically particularistic community, the eruv might simply have been seen as an overactive apparatus of civil governance. It was these two features which, by racializing, or territorializing, space in counter-hegemonic ways, converted civil governance into an alternative national project. Clearly, it is important not to overstate this. Neither the inspector nor Secretary of State, for instance, saw the nation-state as in any way threatened;[77] the minister did, after all, grant planning permission. Yet, the territorial danger opponents named is important, not because it identifies a 'real' threat nor principally because it reveals 'real' fears (since to some extent the argument was a rhetorical one). Rather, the attack on the eruv, as a territorial appropriation, provides interesting insights into one aspect of nationhood – the dependency of national identity on *spatial* expressions of belonging. Some aspects of this – namely citizenship and the public–private divide – have already been discussed. Here, I want to consider briefly the construction and fortification of boundaries.

Modernist conceptions of nation require boundaries at both a physical level and at the level of the imaginary.[78] According to Balibar, the external frontiers of the state have to be constantly imagined as a 'projection...of an internal collective personality, which...enables us to inhabit the space of the state as a place where we have always been – and always will be – "at home"'.[79] The eruv, with its demarcation of new borders, disturbs this imaginary or 'map'[80] – it is a Berlin Wall separating insider from outsider on the basis of religious demography. But the eruv also troubles because its construction *centres* the perimeter. This is partly due to the effect of planning law which examines structures, thereby often ignoring an interior space but is due also to the eruv itself which begins with its exterior 'walls'.[81]

The absolute, definitional requirement for perimeter integrity, without which the eruv is nothing, renders the eruv a fragile structure – one that is easily disrupted. Nevertheless, the brittleness of the perimeter, and hence the consequent need for monitoring and surveillance, engendered, in the Barnet conflict, anxiety over intensifying fortification. Disturbing images of militarized, impenetrable borders were further fuelled when the local newspaper, *The Hampstead and Highgate Express*, claimed that it had received confidential minutes from a group of Jewish zealots who planned to patrol the perimeter.[82] Although this claim was dismissed by the Jewish Board of Deputies as a hoax,[83] the story highlighted the extent to which the eruv proposal raised fears of 'home rule'. As one councillor put it during an interview, 'The eruv is an extreme act... of a handful of fanatics'.

Yet, as well as representing excessive, unaccountable governance, this trope of border, irrationality and violence also represents a space 'out of control'. Successful nation-building often requires the maintenance of borders *against* excess – 'fortress Europe' providing an interesting, albeit supranational, example. While the eruv might seem helpful in its 'walling in' of excessive religious expression, this is undermined in two ways. First, the eruv is in danger of producing disorder[84] out of what once was a community successfully engaged in hegemonic 'nation-building'. Second, the eruv boundary may prove less one of containment or separateness than a frontier constantly threatening to split, contaminating the surrounding locale with its 'premodern' norms.

Conclusion

This chapter suggests one answer to the question of why Barnet's proposed eruv so enraged local residents. For on the surface it does seem hard to fathom why a few poles joined by a thin, high wire should have engendered such panic, hatred and fear. My argument rests on two points: first, the intense commitment of eruv opponents to modernist beliefs; second, the eruv's demonization within this framework.

However, modernist discourse and the eruv are not inherently antithetical. As the planning appeal demonstrated, the eruv could successfully 'prove' itself on utilitarian grounds. Moreover, eruv proponents also argued their case within a modernist discourse of cultural pluralism and minority rights. Modernist discourse embraces a range of different elements. Thus, I have focused on the particular selection and inflection of norms by eruv opponents.

In exploring opposition to the eruv, my analytical starting point is with competing understandings of the relationship between space, symbols and sociocultural meaning. Objectors fought so intensely because, in their view, symbolic structures could not be contained within the interpretative framework of any single community. Consequently, any addition to the spatial container would affect the character and flavour of the whole. For opponents, the eruv proposal contaminated space in three ways: by privileging minorities and also religion, and by inappropriate civil governance.

The first way epitomized an inverted utilitarianism in which majority interests were intentionally subordinated to those of vociferous minorities, destabilizing neighbourhood equilibrium, universal public citizenship and existing forms of belonging. The second form of contamination concerned the eruv's threat to the 'secular' character of the public sphere. Eruv critics fundamentally opposed allowing *new* development simply on the grounds that it furthered the interests of a religious community. However, in adopting this position, Christian hegemony remained unquestioned. The privileging of religion that opponents attacked was the privileging of *other* religions, particularly where, as in the eruv's case, there was no clear Christian analogy. (The 'parish' comparison was explicitly rejected by opponents.) Finally, fears that the eruv contaminated, or undermined, constitutional chains of command and nation-based citizenship condensed in opposition to its functioning as a governance structure. Civil forms of governance were accepted and lauded so long as their reach did not extend beyond their own constituency within already privatized space. The enclosure performed by the eruv structure, in contrast, indicated a more territorial form of governance. While it seemed unlikely to challenge the authority of the British nation-state, the eruv posed the possibility (if only symbolically) of national implosion into local, subnational forms.

In this chapter, my focus on the opposition may give the impression that their arguments were the stronger, despite the eruv's final, official sanctioning. However, placing the struggle within a wider context, we can see the defence of liberal modernist norms not as the articulation of a hegemonic agenda but rather as a desperate attempt to defend cultural traditionalism in the face of increasing attack. The growing confidence of minority communities, the state's, albeit hesitant, concessions and 'political correctness' represented for opponents a reckless disregard for norms that had, for generations, sustained Britain's equilibrium – that had 'distinguished' Britain from the rest of the world. Within this context, the eruv's primary mistake was not to *threaten* modernist norms nor paradoxically to assist, through its demonized caricature, in the ongoing process of sustaining them. The eruv's mistake or failing was in its unintentional representation of public religious expression, post-rational pluralism and territorial contingency. Thus, in this way, the eruv symbolically condensed for opponents crucial and detested aspects of a momentum-gathering, cultural revolution.

Notes

1   This chapter is a slightly revised version of an earlier paper, published as D. Cooper (1996), 'Talmudic Territory? Space, Law, and Modernist Discourse', *Journal of Law and Society*, **23**, pp. 529–48, as part of an ESRC funded research project, 'Community, Democracy and the Governance of Difference: Intra-State Conflict and the Regulation of Local Power', award no. R000221591. Thanks for assistance and comments to Rex Ahdar, Wendy Ball, Michael Freeman, Didi Herman, Bernard Jackson, Carl Stychin, and Beth Widdowson.

2   Proponents' assertion, for instance, that over 10 000 people would benefit (Eruv Committee briefing), was met with the rejoinder that the total number of under 5s and disabled people linked to United Synagogue (US) was 1333; since only 10 per cent of US members were observant, the truer figure was 133 (Inspector's Report, 10 January 1994, para. 3.29). This low figure ignores Orthodox Jews who are members of synagogues not affiliated to US.

3   Approximately 15 interviews were conducted. These were semi-structured, qualitative discussions of approximately one hour each involving participants on both sides, a few observers, and leading council members.

4   See also S. Harding (1991), 'Representing Fundamentalism: The Problem of the Repugnant Cultural Other', *Social Research*, **58**, p. 373; S. Bruce (ed.) (1992), *Religion*

and *Modernization. Sociologists and Historians Debate the Secularization Thesis*, (Oxford: Clarendon Press).

5 See generally A. Eisen (1994), 'Rethinking Jewish Modernity', *Jewish Social Studies*, **1**, p. 1. Opponents' stance contrasted with that of eruv users and supporters. Despite some suggestion by opponents, eruv advocates did not locate the eruv within postmodern or premodern beliefs. Rather, they adopted a utilitarian calculus involving 'late modernist' ideas of cultural pluralism, equality of opportunity and public minority rights.

6 Most of the opponents I interviewed identified themselves as Jewish. One woman refused to disclose her identity, and two identified themselves as non-Jewish. Many non-Jews opposed the eruv, including high-profile figures such as Lord McGregor and Lord Soper; however, some non-Jews expressed ambivalence about becoming publicly active in the campaign, in case they appeared anti-Semitic. According to one leading Barnet councillor, 'Jewish objectors were needed by non-Jews, so it would be legitimate to criticize' (interview).

7 See also M. Bunting (1993), *The Guardian*, 14 December.

8 See for instance, P. Birnbaum and I. Katznelson (eds) (1995), *Paths of Emancipation*, (Princeton, NJ: Princeton University Press).

9 Z. Bauman (1988–89), 'Strangers: The social construction of universality and particularity', *Telos*, **78**, p. 7.

10 See (1971) *Encyclopaedia Judaica*, **6**, pp. 849–850.

11 In Jewish law or Halakah, the public domain bears a particularly narrow, restrictive interpretation. The prohibition on carrying or pushing was thus extended by rabbinic law to a carmelit, a domain that is neither public nor private. Most public areas outside of central London are probably carmelits. However, since they were identified as 'public' within the Barnet eruv debate, I will do likewise, although strictly speaking within Jewish law they are not public; indeed, if they were it is doubtful whether they could become part of a private domain by means of an eruv. See Babylonian Talmud, *Eruvin* 17b, discussed in J. Metzger (1989), 'The Eruv: Can Government Constitutionally Permit Jews to Build a Fictional Wall without Breaking the Wall between Church and State?', *National Jewish Law Review*, **4**, p. 67 at p. 68.

12 This only applies to articles that can already be carried within the home. It does not, for instance, allow cars to be driven.

13 See discussion in S. Sharot (1991), 'Judaism and the Secularization Debate', *Sociological Analysis*, **52**, p. 255.

14 There is a growing literature on the changing and often contradictory approach of Jewish orthodoxy to women; see, for instance, L. Davidman (1990), 'Accommodation and Resistance to Modernity: A Comparison of Two Contemporary Orthodox Groups', *Sociological Analysis*, **51**, p. 35 at p. 43.

15 Town Planning and Research Committee, 24 February 1993, item 3, para. 8.3.1.

16 Ibid., para. 8.3.2.

17 *Inspector's Report*, 10 January 1994, para. 3.16. See also Barnet LBC *and* United Synagogue Eruv Committee, 10 PAD209 (1995).

18 See Town Planning and Research Committee, 27 October 1993, *Report*, para. 3.2.

19 Barnet LBC *and* United Synagogue Eruv Committee, 10 P.A.D 209 (1995), paras 1.3–1.4.

20 Ibid., para. 4.1.

21 Ibid., paras 4.51, 4.53–4.54.

22 Ibid., para. 4.57.

23 Ibid., paras 4.56–4.57. Here the inspector adopted a 'subjective' approach to need while maintaining a stricter 'objective' approach to the question of other material

considerations. However, recognition of 'subjective' need was based on accepting religion as a legitimate manufacturer of needs: para. 4.54. For a general discussion on the subjective, see E. Weinrib (1980), 'Utilitarianism, Economics, and Legal Theory', *University of Toronto Law Journal*, 3, p. 307.

24   Secretary of State's letter, 20 September 1994, para. 11. Barnet LBC *and* United Synagogue Eruv Committee, *op. cit.*, (1995) paras 5.5, 5.7. Cf. Planning Application Appeal against Hertsmere Borough Council, regarding change of use of Bhaktivedanta Manor Letchmore Heath to a theological college and religious community to be used, *inter alia*, for large public festivals of worship: [1996] JPL, p. 683 at p. 691. In this case, the secretary of state placed considerable weight on the religious and spiritual needs of the Hindu community and on the Manor's special role in fulfilling them.

25   Barnet LBC *and* United Synagogue Committee, *op. cit.*, para. 5.8

26   Development control can also be structured according to non-utilitarian criteria – for instance, by giving weighting to government policy or through a pro-development bias.

27   Metzger (1989), 'The Eruv', *op. cit.*, p. 67.

28   Objectors' written statement, nd.

29   See *Inspector's Report, op. cit.*, paras 2.23–2.26.

30   Criticism for this was attached to the planning inquiry rather than planning law. See generally on planning inquiries, T. Blackman (1991), 'Planning Inquiries: A Socio-legal Study', *Sociology*, 25, p. 311, and on relations with (environmental) protestors, R. Grove-White (1991), 'Land-use Law and the Environment', *Journal of Law and Society*, 18, p. 32.

31   See for instance E. Soja (1989), *Postmodern Geographies*, (London: Verso); N. Blomley and J. Bakan (1992), 'Spacing Out: Towards a Critical Geography of Law', *Osgoode Hall Law Journal*, 30, p. 661.

32   For an interesting analogy, see the conflict between Polish Catholics and Jews over the siting of a Carmelite convent in Auschwitz. See I. Wollaston (1994), 'Sharing Sacred Space? The Carmelite Controversy and the Politics of Commemoration', *Patterns of Prejudice*, 28, p. 19.

33   Outline of Mr Lush and Ms Popper argument (objectors), quoted from *Inspector's Report, op. cit.*, para. 4.41.

34   For an interesting judicial discussion of this point in relation to the display of swastikas on an outer wall of a house, see *Zdrahal* v. *Wellington City Council* [1995] 1 NZLR 700.

35   Letter of objection to Eruv Planning Application (11 November 1992), included in *Eruv Report to Town Planning and Research Committee*, 24 February 1993, p. 105.

36   See Y. Shilhav (1984), 'Spatial Strategies of the "Haredi" Population of Jerusalem', *Socio-Economic Planning Science*, 18, p. 411 at p. 413.

37   Thanks to Lisa Herman for this illustration.

38   See generally, B. Gennochio (1995), 'Discourse, Discontinuity, Difference: The Question of "Other" Spaces', in S. Watson and K. Gibson (eds), *Postmodern Cities and Spaces*, (Oxford: Blackwell).

39   The reference to Golders Green, an area seen as possessing a strongly Jewish identity, suggests that one objection to the Barnet eruv was over the fact that its boundary line would bring non-Jewish neighbourhoods within a 'Jewish' perimeter.

40   See the outline of Mr Max's objections in *Inspector's Report, op. cit.*, para. 4.52.

41   Their anxiety also had class implications since ultra-Orthodox Jews are associated with less middle-class neighbourhoods. However, there is a tension in this image, since in fact the Chassidic community did not support the eruv's establishment, as I discuss below.

42 For studies of comparable attempts to construct hegemonic, spatial meanings, see M. Swyngedouw (1995), 'The "Threatening Immigrant" in Flanders 1930–1980: Redrawing the Social Space', *New Community*, **21**, p. 325; C. Graves (1989), 'Social Space in the English Medieval Parish Church', *Economy and Society*, **18**, p. 297.

43 See D. Ley (1993), 'Co-operative Housing as a Moral Landscape', *Place, Culture and Representation*, ed. J. Duncan and D. Ley, (London: Routledge). For a discussion of negative aspects of modernist planning within the Israeli context, see O. Yiftachel (1995), 'The Dark Side of Modernism: Planning as Control of an Ethnic Minority', in Watson and Gibson, *Postmodern Cities and Spaces, op. cit.*

44 Outline of Mr Thomas's argument in *Inspector's Report, op. cit.*, para. 4.67.

45 See E. Howard (1945), *Garden Cities of Tomorrow*, (London: Faber & Faber); M. Miller and A. Gray (1992), *Hampstead Garden Suburb*, (Chichester: Phillimore).

46 There is an irony here in that non-religious opponents had a more sacralized image of their space than eruv advocates and users for whom location was entirely contingent (cf. J. Entrikin (1991), *The Between of Place: Towards a Geography of Modernity*, (Baltimore: John Hopkins University Press), pp. 62–63).

47 External religious governance also threatened opponents' *self-perception* as intelligent, middle-class professionals.

48 For discussion of HGS debate over the eruv, see interviews by author; also *The Independent Magazine*, 16 January 1993.

49 M. Walzer (1984), 'Liberalism and the Art of Separation', *Political Theory*, **12**, p. 315. See also M. Shapiro and D. Neubauer (1989), 'Spatiality and Policy Discourse: Reading the Global City', *Alternatives*, **14**, p. 301 at p. 307.

50 A similar argument is made by the Barnet Eruv Objectors Group, *Inspector's Report, op. cit.*, para. 4.12, regarding parishioners who had to pass under the eruv wires to attend church.

51 See ibid., para. 5.36. For judicial rejection of the argument that an eruv imposes religious beliefs on non-participants within it, see *ACLU* v. *City of Long Branch*, 670 F. Supp. 1293 (DNJ 1987).

52 See A. Giddens (1991), *Modernity and Self-Identity*, (Cambridge: Polity Press), p. 190.

53 Collective letter sent to councillors, 2 October 1992.

54 Thanks to Carl Stychin for this point. Areas defined as lesbian and gay ghettos provide a parallel example; here too the division between the public and private expression of homosexuality is redrawn rather than rejected.

55 See also *The Independent Magazine*, 16 January 1993. While opponents' references to American ghettoes did not seem to be concerned with areas of high Jewish concentration, some of their more general concerns can be seen in relation to communities, such as the Orthodox Jewish area of Kiryas Joel, in New York State. In this case, a legal dispute arose over the NY State Legislature's decision to carve out a special school district that gave almost total control to the Satmar Hasidic sect. This case, and the questions it raises about how far governments should go in accommodating minority religious interests has generated a considerable number of articles and comments: see, for instance, S. Levinson (1997), 'On Political Boundary Lines, Multiculturalism, and the Liberal State', *Indiana Law Journal*, **72**, p. 403.

56 Cllr Frank Davis (1992), Letter, *Hampstead and Highgate Express*, 4 December 1992.

57 Formally, the tree is in the private sphere of the home; however, its public visibility highlights some of the limitations of a simple public–private divide. Do passers-by who find the sight of the tree offensive have any right or legitimate basis for complaint? Cf. *Zdrahal* v. *Wellington City Council* [1995] 1 NZLR 700.

58 D. White (1992), Letter, *Hampstead and Highgate Express*, 16 October 1992.

59   I discuss this further in D. Cooper (1993), 'The Citizen's Charter and Radical Democracy: Empowerment and Exclusion within Citizenship Discourse', *Social and Legal Studies*, **2**, p. 149.

60   See, generally, C. Pateman (1989), *The Disorder of Women*, (Cambridge: Polity Press).

61   Although non-Anglican forms of Christianity have confronted discrimination in the UK, and are still structurally and culturally disadvantaged, from the perspective of non-Christian faiths, Christianity as a general faith category appears hegemonic.

62   For instance, concentrated clusters of Christian populations were not considered to constitute undesirable ghettos.

63   For discussion of the relationship between secularization, modernity and (theistic) faith, see for example, D. Hervieu-Leger (1990), 'Religion and Modernity in the French Context: For a New Approach to Secularization', *Sociological Analysis*, **51**, p. 515; S. Sharot, 'Judaism and the Secularization Debate', *op. cit.*, note 13 above.

64   See R. Audi (1989), 'The Separation of Church and State and the Obligations of Citizenship', *Philosophy and Public Affairs*, **18**, p. 259. This opposition, paradoxically, enables religion to retain its importance as a rationalization for *opposing* religious-based, political developments.

65   See A. Bradney (1993), *Religions, Rights and Laws*, (Leicester: Leicester University Press).

66   I discuss the relationship between Christianity, national identity and government policy further in D. Cooper (1998) *Governing out of Order: Space, Law and the Politics of Belonging*, (London: Rivers Oram), ch. 3.

67   Bradney, *Religions, Rights and Laws*, *op. cit.* For a lively critique of Christian hegemony in relation to the United States, see S. Feldman (1997), *Please Don't Wish Me a Merry Christmas*, (New York: New York University Press).

68   H. Lefebvre (1976), 'Reflections on the Politics of Space', *Antipode*, **8**, p. 30.

69   See B. Jackson (1989), 'Jewish Law or Jewish Laws', *The Jewish Annual Review*, **8**, p. 327; and for a critical discussion of a 'centralist' legal model, see J. Griffiths (1986), 'What is Legal Pluralism', *Journal of Legal Pluralism and Unofficial Law*, **24**, p. 1. See also S. Merry (1988), 'Legal Pluralism', *Law and Society Review*, **22**, p. 869; and for a critique of the pluralist legal model, B. Tamanaha (1993), 'The Folly of the "Social Scientific" Concept of Legal Pluralism', *Journal of Law and Society*, **20**, p. 192.

70   For criticism of this see J. Sachs (1992), *Crisis and Covenant: Jewish Thought after the Holocaust*, (Manchester: Manchester University Press), p. 163.

71   This is not to suggest that Jewish law and British state law *should* be analogized; rather I am interested in the implications of defining Jewish law as Other. For a discussion of the relationship between Jewish law and Western legal systems see L. Pfeffer and A. Pfeffer (1989), 'The Agunah in American Secular Law', *Journal of Church and State*, **31**, p. 487; S. Stone (1993), 'In Pursuit of the Counter-text: The Turn to the Jewish Legal Model in Contemporary American Legal Theory' *Harvard Law Review*, **106**, p. 813; D. Ashburn (1994), 'Appealing to a Higher Authority' *Detroit Mercy Law Review*, **71**, p. 295.

72   For critique of this approach, see Sachs, *Crisis and Covenant, op. cit.*

73   An alternative approach would be that refusing to carry or push prams is no longer necessary to fulfil the underlying injunction to rest/not work on the Sabbath. Thanks to Bernard Jackson for this suggestion.

74   See *Hampstead and Highgate Express*, 5 February 1993.

75   Jacobs, Witness Statement, p. 2.

76   See generally Sachs, *Crisis and Covenant, op. cit.*, pp. 117–18. H. Diner (1994), 'Jewish Self-governance, American Style', *American Jewish History*, **81**, p. 277; G.

Alderman (1995), 'English Jews or Jews of the English Persuasion', in Birnbaum and Katznelson, *Paths of Emancipation, op. cit.*, p. 131.

77   Arguably, identification of threat is linked to the scale of one's gaze, see generally B. de Sousa Santos (1987), 'Law: A Map of Misreading. Toward a Postmodern Conception of Law', *Journal of Law and Society*, **14**, p. 279.

78   Cf. the medieval world: see M. Billig (1995), *Banal Nationalism*, (London: Sage), pp. 20–21.

79   E. Balibar (1991), *Race, Nation, Class*, (London: Verso), p. 95; see also M. Billig (1995), *Banal Nationalism*, (London: Sage), p. 74.

80   de Sousa Santos, 'Law', *op. cit.*, p. 285.

81   The eruv boundary is, of course, only a symbolic wall. For a useful discussion of different types of symbolic city wall, see P. Marcuse (1995), 'Not Chaos, but Walls: Postmodernism and the Partitioned City', in Watson and Gibson, *Postmodern Cities and Spaces, op. cit.* The eruv wall could be considered a 'barricade', which Marcuse uses to refer to walls of protection and cohesion constructed through the language of street signs and architecture.

82   'Jewish Zealots: We'll Patrol Eruv', *Hampstead and Highgate Express*, 15 January 1993.

83   See letters in the *Hampstead and Highgate Express*, 22 January 1993.

84   See 'The Eruv: Hoax Claims Rebutted', *Hampstead and Highgate Express*, 22 January 1993.

Select Bibliography

Adams, Arlin M. and Charles J. Emmerich (eds), *A Nation Dedicated to Religious Liberty: The Constitutional Heritage of the Religion Clauses*, Philadelphia: University of Pennsylvania Press, 1990

Beaumont, Paul R. (ed), *Christian Perspectives on Human Rights and Legal Philosophy*, Carlisle: Paternoster Press, 1998

Berg, Thomas C., 'Religion Clause Anti-Theories', *Notre Dame Law Review*, **72** (1997) pp. 693–751

Berman, Harold J., 'Religious Freedom and the Challenge of the Modern State', *Emory Law Journal*, **39** (1990) pp. 149–164

Berman, Harold J., *Faith and Order: The Reconciliation of Law and Religion*, Atlanta: Scholars Press, 1993

Berman, Harold J., *The Interaction of Law and Religion*, Nashville: Abingdon Press, 1974

Bradney, Anthony, *Religions, Rights and Laws*, Leicester, Leicester University Press, 1993

Carmichael, Calum, *The Origins of Biblical Law*, Ithaca: Cornell University Press, 1992

Carmichael, Calum, *The Spirit of Biblical Law*, Athens: University of Georgia Press, 1996

Carter, Stephen L., *The Culture of Disbelief: How American Law and Politics Trivialize Religious Devotion*, New York: Basic Books, 1993

Daube, David, *Studies in Biblical Law*, Cambridge: Cambridge University Press, 1947

Denning, Rt. Hon. Lord, *The Influence of Religion on Law*, Lawyers' Christian Fellowship 1989

Dickson, Brice, 'The United Nations and Freedom of Religion', *International and Comparative Law Quarterly*, **44** (1995) pp. 327–357

Esbeck, Carl H., 'A Restatement of the Supreme Court's Law of Religious Freedom: Coherence, Conflict, or Chaos?', *Notre Dame Law Review* **70** (1995) pp. 581–650

Ellul, Jacques, *The Theological Foundation of Law* (trans by M. Wieser), 1st Brit. ed., London: SCM Press, 1961

Evans, Malcolm D., *Religious Liberty and International Law in Europe*, Cambridge: Cambridge University Press, 1997

Firmage, Edwin B., Weiss, Bernard G. and John W. Welch (eds), *Religion and Law: Biblical-Judaic and Islamic Perspectives*, Winona Lake: Eisenbrauns, 1990

Fish, Stanley, 'Mission Impossible: Settling the Just Bounds Between Church and State', *Columbia Law Review*, **97** (1997) pp. 2255–2333

Fort, Timothy L., *Law and Religion*, Jefferson, North Carolina: McFarland & Co., 1987

Freckleton, Ian, '"Cults", Calamities and Psychological Consequences', *Psychiatry, Psychology and Law*, **5** (1998) pp. 1–46

Hamilton, Carolyn, *Family, Law and Religion*, London: Sweet and Maxwell, 1995

Kaye, Bruce and Gordon Wenham (eds), *Law, Morality and the Bible*, Leicester: Inter-Varsity Press, 1978

King, Michael (ed), *God's Law versus State Law: The Construction of an Islamic Identity in Western Europe*, London: Grey Seal, 1995

McConnell, Michael W., 'The Origins and Historical Understanding of Free Exercise of Religion', *Harvard Law Review*, **103** (1990) pp. 1409–1517

Monsma, Stephen V. and J. Christopher Soper (eds), *Equal Treatment of Religion in a Pluralist Society*, Grand Rapids: Eerdmans, 1998

O'Connor, Justice Sandra Day, 'Religious Freedom: America's Quest for Principles', *Northern Ireland Law Quarterly*, **48** (1997) pp. 1–9

Richardson, James T., 'Minority Religions ("Cults") and the Law: Comparisons of the United States, Europe, and Australia', *University of Queensland Law Journal*, **18** (1995) pp. 181–207

Robilliard, St John A., *Religion and the Law*, Manchester: Manchester University Press, 1984

Smith, Steven D., *Foreordained Failure: The Quest for a Constitutional Principle of Religious Freedom*, New York: Oxford University Press, 1995

Tahzib, Bahiyyih G., *Freedom of Religion or Belief: Ensuring Effective International Protection*, The Hague: Martinus Nijhoff, 1996

Unsworth, Clive, 'Blasphemy, Cultural Divergence and Legal Relativism', *Modern Law Review*, **58** (1995) pp. 658–677

van Bijsterveld, Sophie C, *Godsdienstvrijheid in Europees Perspectief*, Deventer: W.E., J. Tjeenk Willink, 1998

Witte, John and Frank S. Alexander (eds), *The Weightier Matters of The Law: Essays on Law and Religion – A Tribute to Harold J. Berman*, Atlanta: Scholars Press, 1988

Witte, John and Johan van der Vyver (eds), *Religious Human Rights in*

Global Perspective: Legal Perspectives, The Hague: Martinus Nijhoff, 1996

Witte, John and Johan van der Vyver (eds), *Religious Human Rights in Global Perspective: Religious Perspectives*, The Hague: Martinus Nijhoff, 1996

Index